Mental and Physical
Health Practices
of Older People

Elaine M. Brody, M.S.W., is Director of the Department of Human Services and Associate Director of Research at the Philadelphia Geriatric Center, where her career spans 30 years. She is a past President of The Gerontological Society of America and a Fellow of that organization. Among the awards Mrs. Brody has received are the following: the 1983 Donald P. Kent Award of The Gerontological Society of America, the 1982 Distinguished Alumni Award of the University of Pittsburgh School of Social Work, the 1982 Distinguished Service Award of the Pennsylvania Association of Nonprofit Homes for the Aging, the Fourth Annual Seltzer Award Lecture, and the Haak-Lilliefors Memorial Lectureship. She has served on the editorial boards of several professional journals and on Peer Review Committees at the National Institute of Mental Health, the Administration on Aging, and a number of foundations. Mrs. Brody's publications include three books, numerous book chapters, and approximately 100 papers. She has directed many federally financed research studies on subjects such as *Individualized Treatment of Mentally Impaired Aged; Intermediate Housing for the Elderly; Mental and Physical Health Practices of Older People; The Dependent Elderly and Women's Changing Roles; Women, Work, and Care of the Aged;* and *Parent Care, Sibling Relationships, and Mental Health.*

Morton H. Kleban, Ph.D., received his master's degree (psychology) from the State University of Iowa and his doctorate (psychology) from the University of North Dakota. Presently he is a Senior Research Psychologist at the Philadelphia Geriatric Center and a Medical Research Scientist at Norristown State Hospital. In addition to serving on the editorial boards of the *Journal of Gerontology, Experimental Aging Research*, and other journals, Dr. Kleban has directed or codirected more than a dozen federally financed gerontological research studies and has been a prolific contributor to the scientific literature on aging.

William E. Oriol was staff director of the U.S. Senate Special Committee on Aging from 1967–1979. During the 1950s as a reporter for the *Bergen Evening Record,* Mr. Oriol won several journalism awards. In addition, he has been the recipient of the following honors: the Donald P. Kent Award from The Gerontological Society of America, the Alice Brophy Award of the Urban Elderly Coalition, and the Western Gerontological Society Award. Mr. Oriol's recent publications include: *Aging in All Nations: A Special Report on the 1982 World Assembly on Aging; Redefining the New Federalism: Impact on Low-Income and Other Older Americans;* and *Getting the Story on Aging: A Sourcebook on Aging for Journalists.*

Mental and Physical Health Practices of Older People

A Guide for Health Professionals

Elaine M. Brody, M.S.W.

with the assistance of
Morton H. Kleban, Ph.D., and William E. Oriol

Foreword by Barry D. Lebowitz, Ph.D.

Springer Publishing Company
New York

Springer Publishing Company, Inc.
200 Park Avenue South
New York, New York   10003

85 86 87 88 89 / 10 9 8 7 6 5 4 3 2 1

Library of Congress Cataloging in Publication Data
Brody, Elaine M.
    Mental and physical health practices of older people.
    Bibliography: p. Includes index.
    1. Aged—Care and hygiene. 2. Aged—Mental health. 3. Aged—Diseases. I. Kleban,
Morton H.   II. Oriol, William E.   III. Title.   [DNLM: 1. Aged. 2. Geriatrics. 3. Health
Services for the Aged—United States.   4. Health Surveys—United States.   5. Mental
Health—in old age.   WT 30 B864m]
RA564.8.B76   1985   613'.0438   84-22154
ISBN 0-8261-4870-0

Printed in the United States of America

Listening not to oneself but to what others may be trying to say is an essential part of social diagnosis as well as medical diagnosis. . . . It has also a value in itself . . . in implying and expressing respect in a world which values speed, busyness, efficiency and activity. The dominance of these values should lead us to ask: who is listening in society for the sounds and symptoms of need for help?

—Richard M. Titmuss, *Helping the Aged*

Contents

Foreword

Those of us involved in research, education, practice, and policy in the field of aging look with justifiable pride on the many advances and accomplishments that have been achieved in gerontology and geriatrics. We have shown that age does not equal disability, that treatments can be effective when applied appropriately, that management of chronic disabling conditions can be so structured as to maintain function at optimal levels, and that preventative interventions can indeed reduce risk. Further, we have shown the importance of the tripartite partnership of older persons, their families, and multidisciplinary practice. We have shown that older people do not face the crisis of disability alone, but that in partnership with their families, they actively engage the supplementary support of community-based and institution-based services. Finally, we have shown that comprehensive assessment and active management of relevant services can indeed produce optimal results in terms of appropriateness of care, cost containment, social, mental, and physical functioning, and quality of life.

The base of knowledge available to us is rich and varied, and as the science develops, the interest and sophistication of the questions increases and the linkages into application in policy and practice become more direct. This progression is nowhere better illustrated than in the gerontological research on the family. Here, contrary to the myth that older people are abandoned and isolated from their families, research has shown that the overwhelming majority of older persons are well integrated into multigenerational family groups where strong bonds of support, affection, and mutual aid characterize the linkages between the generations. Older people are active contributors to these relationships and are not merely the passive recipients of support. In those situations where the older person is disabled, most aid is provided by the family—though that usually means a spouse or an adult daughter, and we know that this situation has both positive and negative impacts. In positive terms, providing assistance is a fulfilling and rewarding experience, while in negative terms care can become a burden that results in stress and difficulty for all. We are beginning to identify dimensions of the stress and to develop interventions with the family to prevent or forestall negative consequences. When the resources of the family—physical, emotional, and financial—are exhausted, the family reluctantly turns to the care system of relief.

For much of the best of this work, my colleagues and I have come to look to Elaine Brody and her associates at the Philadelphia Geriatric Center. Her work has always combined the best of bio/psycho/social science with sensitivity to issues of practice and application to policy formation and development. A very special aspect of Mrs. Brody's work has been her instinct for identifying problems that are critical but overlooked or ignored because of false information, mistake, or bias.

In this book, as in her other work, Mrs. Brody has once again identified such an issue. For as Mrs. Brody has clearly pointed out, although the knowledge base in the field of aging has been substantially enriched, sensitivity to that knowledge and use of it scarcely extends beyond gerontologists to older people and to those who care about them and for them. Page after page in the book contains reports of misinformation, failure, and silence. Problems are not identified, efficacious treatments are not selected, appropriate service is not requested, and outreach efforts are not consistently made. The situation would be interesting or even curious if its consequences were not so tragic. For this research has begun to point out the hopelessness, the concerns, and the pain that unfortunately remain a part of old age in our society, and the tragedy is that it need not be so. The knowledge that can be used to make improvements in the situation is available on many issues and areas. Information will continue to accumulate, though, and will do so at an accelerated pace; further research is certainly needed in all the areas Mrs. Brody identifies.

Yet we would all be remiss if we let the need for further study stand in the way of action where the direction for such action is clearly identifiable. In this case, part of the issue is clear. That is, we have a situation where the information from research in the field is not making its way to many of those who provide service and to many of those who seek or could benefit from service. Clearly, a solution would require a comprehensive approach to public and professional information dissemination, service system reorganization, professional education, and, always, further research and study. Though strategies and efforts in all these areas have been developed, a blueprint for effective action and program development has not emerged. This book underscores the need to continue moving in this area—to learn, to listen, and to act so that the great gains we have made in research in aging can be matched by equally impressive improvements in our society and in our lives. Elaine Brody's research is an impressive and provocative contribution to these developments, and my colleagues and I are delighted at having been able to play a part in it.

Barry D. Lebowitz, Ph. D.
Chief, Center for Studies of the
Mental Health of the Aging;
National Institute of Mental Health

Introduction

Health professionals are spending more and more of their time with older people—a trend that will continue. Indeed, some experts estimate that professionals now entering the health field will be spending more than half of their time with patients who are 65 years of age or older. In 1900, one of every 25 Americans was 65 years of age or older. In 1980, every ninth American or 25 million people had reached that age. By the year 2000, there will be 35 million older people (almost every seventh American), and by 2025, the number will have grown to 58.6 million (almost every fifth American).

Because the phenomenon of a large aging population is new to this century, there is still a great deal to be learned about the "normal" processes of aging, about age-related diseases and declines, and about preventive and therapeutic methods of dealing with the mental and physical health problems of older people.

The goal of this book is to begin to fill in one of the major gaps in knowledge by providing health professionals with new and needed information about the day-to-day mental and physical health experiences and practices of the elderly.

The usual sources of information available to professionals are their traditional contacts with elderly patients—office or clinic visits, phone calls, and periods of hospitalization. Between such contacts, however, the lives and health problems (mental and physical) of the older people continue. They experience symptoms which may or may not be reported to professionals. They comply or fail to comply with professional recommendations. They discuss their health problems with family members or friends and may be given (as well as take) advice about what to do. And they may engage in practices designed to maintain their health that are based on misinformation. Much of that world of health experiences is usually invisible to professionals and, in the main, has not been explored.

The consequences of misinformation and inappropriate health behavior, however, often are brought to our attention in dramatic ways. One example is the current flood of reports about drug misuse by older people which too frequently has severe repercussions.

In order to enable the Philadelphia Geriatric Center (PGC) to conduct a beginning investigation of what goes on in the day-to-day mental and physical lives of older people, the National Institute of Mental Health awarded a research grant to us in 1977 (Grant #MH27361). The PGC is a nonprofit multiservice agency that serves over 1,100 older people who live on its campus in a variety of facilities (nursing facilities, high-rise service-supported apartment buildings, small-scale community housing, and a fully accredited geriatric acute care hospital). It also serves elderly community residents and their families by means of a varied spectrum of services: a consultation and diagnostic center, a rehabilitation day center, a hospice/home care program, in-home services, a satellite medical clinic, and a respite program for families caring for people with Alzheimer's disease and related disorders.

The PGC's proposal for the exploratory research had been stimulated by years of experience at the Center with thousands of older people who had requested admission to our facilities. Our staff members who were involved in the evaluation, assessment, and treatment of those elderly individuals— physicians, psychiatrists, social workers, psychologists, and nurses—often were appalled by the neglect of significant (even life-threatening) illnesses, by the multiple interacting drugs being taken (some from long outdated prescriptions, some purchased over-the-counter, and some of unknown origin), and by various kinds of prolonged, severe discomfort that was being endured but that was amenable to treatment. Sometimes confusion or other mental symptoms diminished or disappeared with the withdrawal of some drugs when the older person was admitted to our care. And sometimes dramatic improvements occurred with careful diagnosis and appropriate treatment.

Why was this happening?

It would be all too easy to place the entire responsibility on the health professionals under whose care the older people had been. It was apparent to us, however, that many of the older people themselves had not always sought health care when they should have done so and had not always told health professionals about various symptoms or about what they did about them. They evidenced a lack of knowledge about their health. They often used medicines incorrectly and had not always reported adverse medication effects. They had not always followed the doctor's advice in carrying out prescribed health regimens, relying for advice on friends or relatives instead.

In short, something seemed to be missing in the connection between patient and professional. If the older people lacked knowledge, so did the professionals; the latter often were unaware of many of the day-to-day symptoms their patients experienced and were equally unaware of the day-to-day health practices of those patients.

If the situation was to be remedied, it seemed to us that it would be important to find out what was happening, not in the doctor's office or clinic or in the hospital, but in the home where practical implementation of professional advice takes place or is ignored. Unless professionals are aware of the translation of their diagnoses and prescriptions for treatment into action (appropriate or not) or inaction, and unless they become aware of some of the things they often are not told about, the most sophisticated mental and/or physical health care can be sabotaged.

The project therefore undertook, as one small step toward remedying the situation, to gather detailed information about the day-to-day symptoms of a small sample of older people (132 individuals) and about the actions they took in attempting to deal with those symptoms. The sample included people with three types of mental functioning: those with normal mental status; those with a history of a functional mental disorder; and those with senile dementia. Based on the information assembled, we wanted to provide health professionals with a glimpse of the world of their patients' health experiences to which they usually do not have access and which would offer some guidelines for them in caring for this population. Hence, this volume reports what we found out.

We wish to emphasize that this is the first but by no means the last word about what is largely uncharted territory. The study had limitations—it was small, for example, and relied on self-reports (rather than professional evaluation) in order to obtain the perceptions of the older people themselves. Much more should be done to investigate this and related matters.

Part I of the book (Chapters 1 and 2) places the study in its context by presenting an overview of the health situation and needs of older people in the United States. It describes the demographic developments which will lead to the need for vastly increased attention to the mental and physical health of this population in the future (Chapter 1). The present health and mental health care systems are then described as they now respond, or fail to respond, to those needs (Chapter 2).

Part II focuses on the research study itself. Chapter 3 presents an overview of the project—its rationale, approach, and the research plan. This chapter includes a description of the 132 people studied and some basic information about their health, functional capacities, use of health services, and attitudes about health care. In Chapter 4, the main findings of the study concerning the day-to-day mental and physical health symptoms experienced by the older people are presented. These findings are derived from the four 24-hour logs for each older person in the study that were completed in the course of "yesterday" interviews. The report includes what the mental and physical symptoms reported were, the frequency with which they occurred, the degrees of discomfort they caused, and the activities with which they interfered. Chapter 5 looks at the findings about what actions the older people took in attempting to relieve the discomfort caused by their symptoms. Chapter 6 presents an analysis of how many of a predetermined checklist of 20 potentially serious symptoms the older people had experienced in a four-week period and whom they told about those symptoms. The checklist findings are compared with the data from the logs. Chapter 7 discusses a brief lifestyle report in three parts. First, there is a description of measures the older people took to prevent illness or promote health as a matter of routine (rather than in response to specific symptoms). Second, there is a special report on the older people in the study whose severely impaired cognitive functioning prevented them from responding to interview questions. Third, there is a special report on enjoyable activities in which the older people reported they participated.

Chapter 8 describes the findings from a substudy which examined in depth the ways in which a small sample of older people used "lay consultation" (advice from nonprofessionals) in managing their health problems. This substudy was done by Anne Linda Furstenberg as her doctoral dissertation.

Part III contains three chapters. Chapters 9, 10, and 11 present case studies of the three groups of older people who participated in the research. These illustrate some of the main findings of the research as the different sets of data converged in different ways in different people. They transform the statistics into people by describing their symptoms and remedies as they happen in the older people's day-to-day lives—in the context of their socioeconomic and physical environments and in their interpersonal relationships. The case studies also illustrate the effects of caregiving on the significant others or collaterals of the older people.

Part IV of the book contains three chapters (Chapters 12, 13, and 14). Chapter 12 addresses the health education of older people. During the same time that the study was under way, a related effort was being carried out at the PGC on the development of training materials for the health education of older people themselves. The development of those materials, called Aids, was stimulated by the same experiences that prompted the health practices research. The Aids project was made possible by a grant from the Administration on Aging (Grant #90–A–1229). The project and its findings are described in the chapter, and the Aids themselves are appended.

Chapter 13 summarizes the implications of the study for the ways in which professionals should work with older people and their families. This chapter, though suggested by the study findings, was also influenced by our contacts with the older people in the study and their caregivers and by clinical experience over the years with thousands of other older people.

Finally, Chapter 14 is a comment on the material in the book from the perspective of the researchers. It is addressed to mental health and physical health professionals and to policymakers.

Many people contributed their time and effort to the research described and to the production of this book. The help of Dr. Morton H. Kleban and Mr. William Oriol was invaluable. Dr. Kleban was my associate in the research throughout the entire study. Mr. Oriol participated in the organization and preparation of the text.

We are indebted to the Center on Aging at the National Institute of Mental Health (directed first by Dr. Gene Cohen and currently directed by Dr. Barry Lebowitz) which financed the project. Encouragement and skilled monitoring and consultation was provided by Dr. Lebowitz, who was our Project Officer. Mr. Bernard Liebowitz, Executive Vice President of the Philadelphia Geriatric Center, creates an atmosphere at that agency that is hospitable to research; without his support in facilitating studies, nothing could happen. As always, we owe much to Dr. M. Powell Lawton, who is always in the research picture at the PGC, for sharing his expertise by means of generous consultation.

Dr. Stanley Brody of the University of Pennsylvania reviewed parts of the manuscript. Mr. Herman Brotman, in the role familiar to gerontologists everywhere, responded readily to requests for the latest demographic data.

A special word of thanks is due to Mrs. Rhona Cooper, who was the nurse on the staffs of both projects and who continued to give us the benefit of her consultation after the study was officially ended. Others who participated in the collection and analysis of the data are Mary Attig; Linda Davis; Leo Freeman, M.D.; Elizabeth Moles; Knight Steel, M.D.; Sandra Tannenbaum; and Patricia Turner-Massey. And Mrs. Anita Roffman, as usual, was a Super-Secretary, carrying out her responsibilities with intelligence, initiative, and exceptional skill.

Finally, any research investigation of this type ultimately relies on the participation of other organizations and on the people being studied. A list of the 34 agencies that helped us to identify suitable older people for the study and to whom we are indebted is appended. To the 132 elderly Philadelphians and to their relatives, friends, and neighbors who participated in the research, we express our deep appreciation for the patience, tolerance, humor, and generosity with which they shared their lives with us.

Elaine M. Brody, M.S.W.

The Context

1 The Mental and Physical Health of Older People in the United States

The phenomenon of a large aging population is one of the most dramatic and influential developments of the twentieth century. This demographic situation, unique to our time, has profound significance for all mental and physical health professionals and for the planning and delivery of health and social services.

The urgency of the situation is such that many experts have proclaimed a "geriatric imperative"—that is, the placing of a high priority on policies that will anticipate the health and social needs of older persons and will meet them more effectively than is now the case.

The Demographic Imperative

Population projections indicate that the numerical and proportionate increase of people 65 years of age and older is a trend that will continue. The most common projection is that today's (1983) 26.8 million persons 65 and over in the United States will be 35 million by the year 2000 and about 58.6 million by the year 2025 (Brotman, 1982a).

For the purpose of estimating future health care needs, however, the sheer increase in the number of people who reach their 65th birthday is only a gross indicator. Because disabling chronic illnesses—mental and physical—are more likely to occur in advanced old age, the growth in the number of persons who will reach age 75 and over is even more important. It is highly significant, therefore, that the population group of people 75 and over is the fastest growing age group in the United States: it increased from one million individuals in 1900 to 9.5 million in 1980. By 1990 there will be more than 13 million who are 75 and over; by 2000, there will be more than 17 million; and by 2025 there will be more than 25 million. The 85 and over population, which was about 2.3 million in 1980, will almost triple by the year 2025, reaching more than 7 million (Brotman, 1982b).

The causes of the demographic explosion of older people are illustrated by the chart (Table 1–1) of the chronology of personal, demographic, social, and health events during the lifetime of a real woman who is now 75-years-old.

3

When she was born in 1908, there were fewer than four million people 65 or over in the United States, and her own life expectancy was less than 50 years. By the time she was 25-years-old (in 1933), five of her family members had died of diseases that are now under control: an eight-year-old brother had died of pneumonia; her maternal grandmother had died of tuberculosis (TB) at age 58; her father and paternal grandfather had died of Spanish flu in the great epidemic of 1918 at ages 43 and 70 respectively; and her five-year-old daughter had died of poliomyelitis in 1933.

The chart shows biomedical advances such as the development of antibiotics and vaccines which (together with advances in public health) resulted in a dramatic drop in the proportion of deaths due to such illnesses. Between 1900 and 1980, the percentages of deaths due to infectious diseases had dropped from 40% to 6%, and life expectancy had risen to about 75 years.

Among the forseeable epidemiological consequences of the rise in the number and proportion of very old people are increases in the incidence and prevalence of age-related disorders such as senile dementia, diabetes, rheumatoid arthritis, osteoporosis, cardiovascular and cerebrovascular diseases, and others (Butler, 1976). Gruenberg calls this phenomenon the "Failures of Success" (1977), pointing out that the postponement of death has resulted in increases in the duration of many chronic conditions.

As a result, utilization of health services of all types is expected to increase within the next two decades. The annual number of hospital days for people 65 and over, for example, may increase 80%, to 171 million by the year 2000; for those 85 years of age and over, it may increase 3.3 times to 44 million days (U.S. National Center for Health Statistics, 1982). These undoubtedly will be paralleled by increased needs for supportive social/health services such as in-home nursing and personal care, household maintenance, transportation, day care, respite services for caregivers, and others. Any scientific breakthroughs that result in further prolongation of life may increase the number of years during which older people suffer from chronic ailments which require their dependence on such social/health supports.

Though social/health supports are by no means fully developed, much more activity has been occurring than in the early part of the century. The chart on our 75-year-old woman makes it apparent that much legislation affecting older people has been enacted in the past several decades, beginning with the Social Security Act of 1935. By the time this older woman developed chronic health problems (arthritis and congestive heart failure), Medicare was available to help with the costs of medical care and hospitalization. The day hospital program she now attends is governmentally funded—a program that was nonexistent when her mother needed care.

The chart also illustrates the major role of the family as the provider of health/social services. (That role will be discussed in detail in Chapter 13.)

Our 75-year-old woman had moved in and out of the job market as her family responsibilities and economic situation indicated. Ironically, she became a grandmother the same year in which she quit her job to take care of her mother (who then had become a great-grandmother). She took her mother into her home when the older woman suffered a stroke. In turn, thirty years later (in 1980) her own daughter quit her job to take care of her.

Much depends, of course, on the state of health experienced by future cohorts of older people. Considerable emphasis, therefore, is being placed on efforts to prevent illness and to promote or enhance health in the earlier years of life as a deterrent to premature illness in the later years. The hope is that the resultant avoidance or postponement of illness will have a significant effect in reducing the demand for health care resources. In placing a high priority upon preventive health care, the U.S. Department of Health and Human Services (Schweiker, 1982) acknowledges that many of the chronic diseases that characterize the aged can only be successfully avoided or delayed if preventive practices and lifestyle modifications are followed over the long term (Schweiker, 1982).

In the meantime, the mental and physical health care needs of today's older people are great, and all possible avenues leading to improved health should be explored. One such avenue is the close scrutiny of the day-to-day mental and physical health practices of the elderly that were the focus of the research that will be described in this book. Since the study to be described should be seen in the larger context of the health of the elderly in the United States, this chapter will provide some general knowledge about the physical and mental health of the aged. Though the physical and mental aspects of health are interlocked, available data most often are developed separately for each and therefore will be presented in that way.

Chronicity and Physical/Mental Interactions

Among the best-documented facts in gerontology are that the incidence of mental and physical health problems increases with advancing age, that mental and physical ailments are highly correlated and interact strongly, and that the symptoms of one ailment often mask and exacerbate others (Goldfarb, 1962; Lowenthal, 1964; Schuckit, 1974). Moreover, both mental and physical ailments are, in the main, characterized by chronicity. In contrast with acute illnesses, therefore, they cannot be "cured" and require sustained supportive health/social services as well as ongoing medical and medically related treatment.

These chronic ailments of older people have major effects on social functioning. A host of studies have regularly found a correlation between health and morale, health and social behavior, and health and leisure activity

Table 1–1. A Chronology of Events during the Life of a Woman Now 75 Years Old

Year	Age	Personal History	Demographic and Social Climate	Health Advances	Social and Health Legislation and Landmark Reports
1900			3 million people 65+ (4% of population). Life expectancy at birth: 47 years. (40% of deaths due to infectious diseases.)		
1908	0	Born (4th child).		Test for susceptibility to diptheria devised. Pasteurization of milk made mandatory in New York City.	
1909	1	Brother (age 8) dies of pneumonia.		Typhus vaccine developed.	
1910	2		4 million people 65+ (4.3% of population). Life expectancy at birth: 50 years.		Flexner Report
1911	3				
1912	4	Maternal grandmother (age 58) dies of TB.	President: Wilson. Titanic sinks.	X-ray crystallography developing. Concept of "vitamins" introduced.	
1913	5			Vitamin A discovered. Van Slyke devises tests to measure acid-base balance, urea clearance, blood sugar (1913–24).	
1914	6	Starts school.	Panama Canal opens. World War I.		Harrison Narcotic Act.
1915	7		Federal Reserve Bank Act.		National Birth Registration Area established. National Board of Medical Examiners.

Source: Developed by Stanley J. Brody and Elaine M. Brody.

Year	Age				
1916	8		Income Tax Amendment.		
1917	9	Oldest brother drafted.	U.S. enters World War I.		
1918	10	Father (age 43) and paternal grandfather (age 68) die of Spanish Flu.	Spanish Flu: 500,000 die in U.S. Compulsory education in all states.		
1919	11		Versailles Peace Conference. League of Nations created.		
1920	12		5 million people 65+ (4.7% of population). Life expectancy at birth: 54.2 yrs. President: Harding. "Return to normalcy." Prohibition. Women vote.		Vocational Rehabilitation Act (P.L. 66–236).
1921	13			Herrick described clinical picture of reduced coronary blood flow, thrombosis. Isolation of Insulin.	Shepperd–Towner Act—federal aid for maternal/child health.
1922	14	Drops out of school to work in factory.			
1923	15		President: Coolidge. Radio available.	Tetanus toxoid developed.	
1924	16				
1925	17				
1926	18		Motion pictures with sound.		
1927	19	Married.	T.V. invented.	Iron Lung machine invented.	
1928	20	First child born (female).		Penicillin discovered.	Shepperd–Towner Act not reenacted.

Continued on next page

Table 1–1. *(continued)*

Year	Age	Personal History	Demographic and Social Climate	Health Advances	Social and Health legislation and Landmark Reports
1929	21	Second child born (female).	President: Hoover. Stock market crash. Depression.		Baylor University Hospital initiates hospital insurance.
1930	22	Husband loses job. She has miscarriage.	6.6 million people 65+ (5.4% of population). Life expectancy at birth: 60 yrs. Bank failures.	(1930s on) Tomography developed with studies of lungs.	
1931	23	Third child born (male).		Discovery of blood groups.	Public housing.
1932	24	Votes in presidential election.			Committee on Cost of Medical Care report.
1933	25	First child (age 5) dies of polio.	President: Roosevelt. "New Deal." 25% unemployed.		Federal Emergency Relief Administration (emergency medical care for needy).
1934	26	Family receives Emergency Relief.			
1935	27	Husband returns to work.		Hearing aid invented. Sulfanilamide discovered.	National Health Survey. Social Security Act (Public Assistance, Old Age Insurance, Maternal-Child Health, Public Health). Pre-pay Health Groups; Blue Cross.
1936	28	Fourth child born (male).		Cortisone discovered.	

Year	Age	Personal	Social/Population	Science/Medicine	Legislation/Programs
1937	29	She and husband buy house.			Beginning of federal appropriations for cancer, TB, VD, mental health, heart disease, etc. (1937–47).
1938	30				Food, Drug, and Cosmetic Act.
1939	31	Returns to work at a hospital	Blue Cross concept. World War II begins.		Wagner National Health Bill introduced.
1940	32		9 million people 65+ (6.8% of population). Life expectancy at birth: 63 yrs.		
1941	33		U.S. enters World War II.	Fluoride developed for prevention of dental caries. Commercial production of Penicillin.	Lanham Act (Construction of Community Hospitals & Facilities).
1942	34			Kidney dialysis developed.	American Geriatrics Society organized. Beveridge Report (England).
1943	35		LSD discovered.	Pap smear developed.	Emergency Maternal and Infant Care Program. Wagner-Murray-Dingell Act introduced (Health Insurance under SSA) (1943-47).

Continued on next page

Table 1-1. *(continued)*

Year	Age	Personal History	Demographic and Social Climate	Health Advances	Social and Health Legislation and Landmark Reports
1944	36			Streptomycin isolated.	Public Health Service Act (78-410).
1945	37		President: Truman. Dropping of Atomic Bomb. World War II ends. United Nations. GI Bill of Rights. Truman endorses National Health program. Beginning ascendancy of medical specialization. Blue Shield established.		The Gerontological Society of America organized.
1946	38	Learns to drive a car; changes jobs.	"Fair Deal."		Hill-Burton Hospital Survey and Construction Act.
1947	39	Second child finishes school, begins work as secretary	First supersonic flight.	Folic acid antagonists developed for cancer treatment.	National Retired Teachers Association organized.
1948	40	Second child marries. Third child begins college.		Radioactive cobalt introduced.	World Health Organization created.
1949	41		Television introduced.	Framingham Heart Study initiated.	
1950	42	Mother suffers stroke and moves into household.	12.3 million people 65+ (8% of population). Life expectancy at birth: 68 yrs. Korean War starts. "McCarthyism."	Structure of DNA discovered.	National Conference on Aging. Medical vendor payments for welfare recipients. Health Insurance for SSA beneficiaries proposed.

Year	Age				
1951	43	Becomes a grandmother. Quits job to care for mother.			Murray-Humphrey-Dingell Bill (Health Insurance for SSA beneficiaries).
1952	44	Third child drops out of college due to family finances.	President: Eisenhower.	Birth Control pill developed.	Department of HEW established with Cabinet status.
1953	45			Relationship of smoking to lung cancer identified.	
1954	46	Fourth child finishes high school; starts factory job.			
1955	47			Salk Vaccine for Polio developed.	Social Security Amendments—Disability Insurance added. CHAMPUS enacted.
1956	48				
1957	49	Cervical cancer discovered; hysterectomy successful.			Forand Bill introduced.
1958	50	Mother (age 80) dies.	Alaska becomes a state. Hawaii becomes a state.		American Association of Retired Persons organized.
1959	51	Third child marries, moves to California.			U.S. Subcommittee on Aging created.
1960	52	Returns to work.	16.5 million people 65+ (9.2% of population). Life expectancy at birth: 70 yrs. President: Kennedy. "We will place man on moon."	Development of heart pacemaker.	National Council on Aging organized. Kerr-Mills Act (Medical Assistance).

Continued on next page

Table 1–1. *(continued)*

Year	Age	Personal History	Demographic and Social Climate	Health Advances	Social and Health Legislation and Landmark Reports
1961	53	Fourth child begins night school.			First White House Conference on Aging.
1962	54	Seeks medical care for rheumatoid arthritis.		Sabin Vaccine (for polio).	
1963	55		Kennedy assassinated. President: Johnson.		
1964	56	Fourth child marries.	"Great Society."	Surgeon General's report on smoking.	Food Stamp Act. Economic Opportunity Act of 1964 (P.L. 88–452). Civil Rights Act of 1964 (P.L. 88-352).
1965	57		Vietnam involvement. "Guns and Butter."		Soc. Sec. Amendment—Medicare Legislation; Medicaid (P.L. 89-97). Older Americans Act (P.L. 89-73).
1966	58	House mortgage paid off.			Comprehensive Health Planning and Public Service Amendments (P.L. 89–73). Administration on Aging established. WHO war on smallpox.

12

Year	Age				
1967	59	Husband (age 62) dies from myocardial infarction.		First heart transplant.	
1968	60	Receives psychiatric care for depression. Grandson becomes hippie.	Martin Luther King assassinated. President: Nixon.		
1969	61	Returns to work part-time.	U.S. man walks on moon.		
1970	62	Grandson drafted (Vietnam).	20 million people 65+ (9.8% of population). Life expectancy at birth: 71 yrs.	Automated laboratory testing developed (1970s on).	Occupational Safety and Health Act of 1970 (P.L. 91-956). Second White House Conference on Aging.
1971	63				Rehabilitation Act (P.L. 93-112). Health Maintenance Organization Act (P.L. 93-222).
1972	64				
1973	65	Retirement begins.	Watergate hearings.	CAT-Scan techniques reported.	
1974	66		Debates about National Health Insurance programs. Nixon resigns. President: Ford. Inflation.	CABG surgery becoming more common.	Social Security Amendments (COLA added), SSI. National Health Planning and Resources Development Act (93-641). U.S. House of Representatives Select Committee on Aging established. Section 202

Continued on next page

Table 1–1. *(continued)*

Year	Age	Personal History	Demographic and Social Climate	Health Advances	Social and Health Legislation and Landmark Reports
1974 (cont.)					(housing loans for elderly and disabled). Employee Retirement Income Security Act of 1974 (ERISA).
1975	67		22.4 million people 65+ (10.3% of population).		Title XX of SSA (Social Services).
1976	68				National Institute on Aging created, NIMH Center on Aging created.
1977	69	Increasing debilitation due to arthritis and heart condition.	Life expectancy at birth: 73.3 yrs. President: Carter.		
1978	70	Moves in with daughter.			
1979	71	Hospitalization for congestive heart failure.			
1980	72	Daughter quits her job to care for her mother.	25.5 million people 65+ (11.3% of population). Life expectancy at birth: 75 yrs. 6% of deaths attributable to infectious diseases. 68% of deaths due to heart disease and cancer. President: Reagan.		
1981	73				3rd White House Conference on Aging.
1982	74		26.6 million people 65+.		Block Grants for Social Services.
1983	75	Enters day hospital program.		Artificial heart implantation.	

14

(Lawton & Cohen, 1974). Emotional factors and stress can precipitate physical illness. Conversely, physical illness can trigger negative psychological and emotional reactions. Chronic physical disability, for example, is strongly implicated in the etiology of depression (Gurland, 1976). The cumulative effect of the multiple mental and physical assaults experienced by the aged is a lowering of the self-esteem so central to the integrity of the human personality. All of this knowledge underlines the interlocking of physical and mental health and therefore the importance of evaluating problems in both spheres simultaneously.

Two other general aspects of the health of the elderly are emphasized by geriatricians and gerontologists. First, "normal" age-related changes should not be confused with disease processes, but there is still much to learn in order to sort out the two processes from one another. The nature and causes of the processes of aging are to a great extent still undetermined, and no sharp line can be drawn to differentiate between decline resulting from normal aging or senescence and disease processes. Although senescence is thought to be genetically determined, it may be accelerated or interrupted by physical and social environmental stresses.

Second, there is wide variability among the many groups and subgroups called "the elderly." Though many persons in the later years of life have in common certain losses, or what have been called the insults of aging, generalizations and stereotypes should yield to highly individualized judgments. A widely accepted negative image of old people depicts them as dramatically and universally sick, isolated, and deprived, but the vast majority do not fit that stereotype and age successfully (that is, they maintain good functional capacity intellectually, physically, and socially). It has been shown that older people can continue to learn, to demonstrate growth and change in personality, and to show widely varied modes of adaptation and competence in coping with stress.

Aging as a Developmental Stage

The literature on personality theory reiterates the variability, individuality, and diversity of patterns of aging and of adaptation to that phase of life. Each style of adaptation has potential for success and must be evaluated in the framework of the individual's previous life history.

There is as yet no generally accepted theory of the psychosocial problems of adjustment and adaptation intrinsic to the aging process (as distinct from social problems associated with old age). Psychodynamic theories, formulated prior to the existence of a large aging population, conceptualized aging as a gradual decline from the peak of maturity that ends in death.

The concept of aging as a normal developmental stage of life is now widely accepted. That is, the aging phase of life is seen as having its own tasks that can be successfully mastered as were tasks of earlier phases of life. (For complete discussion and reviews of the literature, see Neugarten, 1964, 1968, 1973; Riegel, 1959; Pincus, 1967.) This concept helps offset generally negative and pessimistic attitudes toward working with the elderly, provides positive goals within a theoretical framework, and recognizes a variety of lifestyles and the unique potentials of the aged for psychological well-being.

In the words of Bernice Neugarten,

> Human behavior is malleable. Infants learn; old people learn. We all learn best what we are motivated to learn. We all see ways of exercising our competencies as long as we live. Aging (or development) is social as well as biological destiny (1982).

The best known theoretical framework is that of Erik Erikson, who conceptualized eight stages of ego development from early infancy to old age. His stages take note of the effects of maturation, experience, and social institutions and each represents a choice or a crisis (1963).

Erikson's seventh stage is middle adulthood or the development of generativity versus ego stagnation: "generativity" includes productivity, creativity, and "the concern in establishing and guiding the next generation." The eighth and final stage—late adulthood—is the development of a sense of ego integrity versus despair (fear of death) which involves acceptance of one's one and only life cycle; it comes only to one who "in some way has taken care of things and people" and continues to be involved (that is, in working on life problems). Further, "the lack or loss of this accrued ego integration is signi-fied by fear of death. . . . Despair expresses the feeling that the time is now short . . . for the attempt to start another life and to try out alternative roads to integrity."

Robert Peck (1968) elaborated on Erikson's eighth stage and divided it into middle age and old age, each with its own set of stages. An important contribution made by Peck is his emphasis on the use of developmental criteria rather than age criteria in looking at the later stages of life. He also points out that the study of later life is different from the study of earlier life in many respects. First, there is far greater variability in the chronological age at which a given psychic crisis arises. That is, older persons who reach similar stages may vary widely in their ages. For example, the ages of various parents when their children leave home vary widely. Similarly, the stage of retire-ment may occur for one person at 55, another at 65, and still another at age 85.

Second, children at the same stage almost all work on the same total set of developmental tasks. With adults, however, the patterns can vary widely. A 40-year-old and a 60-year-old may share the stage of one's children being grown. The 40-year-old, however, may not have yet experienced menopause or the male climacteric and may still be working "uphill" to master the vocational role. The 60-year-old may be nearing retirement and may have experienced age-related deaths among family members and peers.

The literature also emphasizes the persistence of personality traits throughout later years of life even while individuality and heterogeneity in later life are recognized. Not only do older people carry their own unique personalities into the aging phase of life, but they also have had longer lives and more varied experiences that produce a higher degree of differentiation. The ways in which aging individuals deal with the events and new situations related to old age—widowhood, retirement, grandparenthood, illness, the process of dying—are a function of personality and reflect long-standing lifestyles.

There is no sharp discontinuity of personality with age but instead an increasing consistency. Personality is continuous over time; central character-istics become even more clearly delineated; and cherished values become even more salient. That is, barring severe pathology, old age itself does not transform personality, but personality patterns may stand out in bolder relief.

The "Insults" of Aging

Older persons are not universally ill, feeble, isolated, or impoverished de-spite widespread assumptions to the contrary. Indeed, the majority age successfully. As stated above, old age is not equivalent to illness, and older people are often remarkably resilient in adapting to age-related changes. Nevertheless, it is undeniable that as a group, older people are subject to a multiplicity of personal and environmental stresses that may occur concur-rently and that have been characterized as the "insults" of aging.

Beginning with birth, human beings experience developmental phases that include what have been termed the "normal" life crises: puberty, leaving school, falling in love, disappointments in love, marriage, bearing or fathering a child, disappointments in vocational or financial life, loss of a loved person, and the involutional period (English & Pearson, 1937). These developmental crises occur, of course, in the context of socioeconomic events (such as wars and economic depressions) that themselves constitute crises for many people.

The "normal life crises" usually occur in a somewhat orderly and gradual progression and are transitional, with the well-integrated individual master-ing each crisis and moving on. Extraordinary crises such as major illnesses and interpersonal losses generally take place one at a time. In contrast, the aging phase of life in our society is often characterized by the relative abruptness, clustering, and dynamic interaction of age-related stresses. These assaults, which occur with increasing frequency as the individual moves toward ad-vanced old age, include decrements in physical and mental capacities; chronic and/or catastrophic illnesses; interpersonal losses such as death or severe illness of spouse, other relatives, peers, and even adult children; diminished income; the cessation of productive working experience; and the loss of social roles and status.

Generally speaking, such insults begin to have a cumulative impact at around age 75. It is this pronounced tendency that led Bernice Neugarten to characterize older persons as the "young old" and the "old old" (1975). The U.S. Federal Council on the Aging (1978) has applied the term "frail elderly" to the same age group (that is, those 75 or over), nevertheless making the point that there are many exceptions to this categorization.

The difficulties of determining the point at which very old age begins are intensified by the interlocking and interweaving of physical health, mental health, and social, economic, and environmental factors. Living arrangements, for example, may be determined by physical condition, income, and family structure as well as by preferences. Mental and physical problems are highly correlated. Maintenance of one's valued independence, or the ability to function at an acceptable level of health and well-being, may depend upon the availability of social supports—both informal (family and friends) and formal supports (government and agencies)—which in turn reflect broad social policies and legislative enactments.

Normal Physiological Aging Versus Disease

In Shock's words, "Aging represents the progressive, irreversible changes which occur in a cell, an organ, or the total organism with the passage of time" (1977, p. 148). Based on the available evidence, he states that

> ". . . aging in the total animal may be more than the summation of changes that take place at the cellular, tissue, or organ level. Life of the total animal requires the integrated activity of all of the organ systems of the body to meet the stresses of living."

How does a health care professional sort out disease-related changes from changes that are a normal accompaniment to aging? That challenge is posed by biological researchers who frankly acknowledge that the answer is elusive. Leonard Hayflick, for example, has said that if all pathological disease in old age were to be eliminated, there would still be intrinsic declines caused by fundamental biological changes that are part of the aging process. Normal aging does not occur suddenly; related changes take place over a period of years (Hayflick, 1974).

The fact that the processes of aging vary widely among individuals and the different organ systems are affected differently suggests that aging results from a number of processes that progress at differing rates. Moreover, not all physiological functions show significant decrements. Characteristics of the blood, for example, remain stable even into advanced old age. Gradual rather than abrupt decline in functions occur in cardiac output, kidney and pulmonary function, muscle strength, and the capacity for physical work.

Much research must yet be done before clear distinctions can be made, but the gerontological literature is fairly consistent in designating some changes as "normal." Rockstein and Sussman, in their review of biological changes related to aging (1979), observe that an older person is usually some-one whose skin is wrinkled, whose hair is gray, and who may be stooped and move slowly. They also describe less conspicuous, internal functional changes typically involving a "more or less linear decrement in performance for most of the organ systems of the body." Among the decrements they noted are

- failing motor ability, involving reduced speed and diminished vigor of muscle contraction;
- deterioration of the nervous system, which is manifested gradually by slowing of reflex responses, poorer muscular coordination, and failing vision;
- a lessening in the ability of the body to maintain its normal core temperature;
- changes in the cardiovascular system which include (1) diminishing capability of the heart rate to compensate in response to stress, (2) decreasing efficiency of the heart as a pump, (3) hardening of the arteries (arteriosclerosis), (4) reduction in the elasticity of blood vessel walls, (5) increasing peripheral vascular resistance, and (6) increased blood pressure;
- "irreversible changes" in the respiratory system such as reduced vital capacity caused by alterations in the structures of the rib cage and of the small air passageways and air sacs of the lungs;
- lowered immunity to infection, as well as chronic bronchitis of unknown etiology, which makes older people especially susceptible to viral and bacterial respiratory infection, particularly pneumonia.

Rockstein and Sussman emphasize that the norms of aging are, at best, statistically defined; total physiological capacity may vary widely among older persons as does the pace at which changes take place. In addition, "Age does not necessarily have the same effect on the different organ systems within one individual nor on the same organ in different persons. Thus, a 75-year-old person may have the cardiac output of an average 60-year-old, whereas renal function may be that of an average person of the same age or older" (1979).

Such complexities in human aging make it impossible to provide clearcut rules to be followed by the health professional who deals with a large number of people aging at different rates in varying ways. From the stand-point of treatment, the practical consequences of mistaking disease and normal aging for each other are obvious. The difficulties of doing so were underscored by findings from a recent survey of physicians throughout the United States. When asked to classify 15 conditions observed into either category, numerous errors were made in classifying disease-related condi-tions as normal and the reverse (Dye & Sassenrath, 1979).

Available knowledge does, however, provide some guidelines for profes-sionals For example, an alert physician will be on the watch for signs of withdrawal and other adverse psychological effects that often accompany hearing loss (Oyer, Kapur, & Deal, 1976). A nurse attending to an institu-tionalized person can do her job better if she knows that a woman in her late seventies usually needs three times as much light to read as her teenage granddaughter (University of Michigan, 1975). And a busy pharmacist will avoid the mistake of assuming that the elderly person can read the physician's directions on a prescription or has kin or friends who can do so.

Psychological Aging

As with other areas of study of older people, a major difficulty is to sort out the psychological changes that are intrinsic to aging from those that are age-related but due to other factors.

In the past, many studies simply compared groups of older people to groups of younger people with regard to cognitive and personality function-ing. However, it now is generally recognized that such studies did not sufficiently take into account factors that were responsible for many differ-ences that appeared. For example, declines with age in intelligence testing were later shown to be largely due not to the fact that one becomes less intelligent with age but to the fact that older people of today have significantly less education than younger people. When longitudinal studies were carried out (that is studying the same individuals over time), age decrements in intelligence did not appear. Such factors as the different periods of history through which the groups being compared had lived, social deprivation, cultural differences, value structures, the level of anxiety, physical health, and organic mental impairments such as senile dementia must also be taken into account when comparing differences between young and old.

In general, it is agreed that the old adage "old dogs cannot learn new tricks" is incorrect. However, aptitude test studies have found that the speed of response tends to decline with age, as does performance of tasks dependent on perceptual discrimination and spatial visualization. Motor skills decline but not to the extent that had generally been supposed. Slowing is evidenced in psychomotor speed, learning, and decision making, and there are in-creased difficulties in problem solving. Existing difficulties are often exacerbated by the older person's anxiety and fear of making mistakes, which in turn may lead to reluctance to take risks and overcautiousness. Physiological decrements such as visual and hearing decrements may interact with psychological factors (such as, worry about not hearing or seeing correctly) to further confound the picture.

In short, though some decrements may occur with age, many of them have been shown to be due to influences other than age per se. Individuals within the age category called "old" vary much more from each other than do the average differences among those in the same age levels.

Chronic Physical Health Conditions

The most common chronic conditions that afflict older persons at much higher rates than younger people are arthritis (443 per thousand people 65 and over versus 253 per thousand people aged 45–64), hypertension (385 per thousand versus 214 per thousand), heart disease (274 per thousand versus 128), visual impairments (118 versus 58), and diabetes (80 versus 58) (U.S. National Center for Health Statistics, 1981b, p. 35). When translated into the actual number of men and women 65 and over who are affected by major chronic conditions, the rates become less abstract. For example, 10.3 million older people suffer from arthritis.

Persons 65 and over also rank somewhat higher than younger age groups in rates of chronic bronchitis, emphysema, frequent constipation, ulcer of the stomach and duodenum, functional and symptomatic upper gastrointestinal disorder, diverticula of intestine, and chronic enteritis and colitis (U.S. NCHS, 1981b).

Functional Disability and the Need for Help

A most important consequence of the chronic illnesses of the aged is that they tend to lead to impairments and in turn to disability (that is, to limitations on mobility and daily activities). For some, the disability is such that they become dependent on others.

To put the matter in perspective, it again is emphasized that the stereotype of old age as inevitably associated with disability is incorrect. At any one time, approximately 55% of all older Americans have no activity limitations due to chronic conditions. Many of those with health problems are able to perform essential tasks, sometimes with help from families and significant others among their friends and acquaintances. However, as people move through the aging phase of life their chances of needing help increase; very few people reach advanced old age without some need for assistance.

The National Center for Health Statistics (NCHS) has provided the most recent (1981a) information about chronicity and the extent of disability. Its National Health Interview produced these findings:

1. Approximately 10.7 million persons 65 and over (about 46%) have some limitation of activity because of chronic conditions. The proportion is more than twice that for the 45–64 age group and four times that of the 17–44 age group.
2. The number of those 65 or over with any limitation in their major activity is 9.1 million or about 39% of the age group, as compared with 18.8% of the 45–64 group and 5.5% of those 16–44. (NCHS defines major activity as the ability to work, keep house, or engage in school or preschool activities.)

Various surveys have been concerned with the activity limitations of older people and estimates of their need for help from others. Those estimates cluster around the 30% mark for people who are not institutionalized. Shanas, for example, estimates that one-fourth of older people require home care services, including those who are bedfast or housebound (8%) or able to go out but with difficulty (6–7%) (1974). Depending on the nature of services included, others estimate the proportion at one-third (Brody, S., 1973), 41% (Pfeiffer, 1973), 27% (Gottesman et al., 1975) and 30% (Gurland, 1976).

Among older people who need some help are some who need considerable help. About 10% of the noninstitutionalized elderly (more than 2.5 million individuals), for example, are as severely disabled as the 5% who live in nursing homes and other institutions.

The NCHS found that 2.1% of noninstitutionalized persons aged 65 and older were confined to bed; 2.6% needed help with bathing; 2.6% needed help with dressing; 1.4% needed help with using the toilet; and .08% with eating. While percentages are helpful, it should be remembered that they are being applied to a population of about 26.8 million persons 65 or over in the United States. One percent of that total therefore represents 268,000 individuals. If, therefore, 2% of the noninstitutionalized elderly are confined to bed, they number somewhere about 536,000.

In Shanas's 1979 survey (Shanas, 1982), about 2.8 million older persons were found to be either bedfast, housebound, or able to go outdoors only with some difficulty. Over a third of those who are among the most incapacitated are over 80; nine out of every ten are women; and six out of ten are married. Four out of every ten persons 65 or over reported difficulty in cutting their own toenails. One percent reported that they had fallen during the prior week because of a dizzy spell.

There is a greatly increased risk of physical disability with advancing age. Age 75 is a rough marker for significant increases in the need for help in personal care activities, such as grooming, bathing, dressing, and ambulation (Jette & Branch, 1981), and in instrumental activities such as housekeeping chores, shopping, and transportation.

Functional Assessment

The above information about the capacities (and incapacities) of older people is of vital importance not only because the extent of disability determines how they function in their daily lives but also because it determines the need for the provision of health and social services by the family and society. It is for those reasons that gerontologists insist on functional criteria of health and functional assessment rather than medical diagnosis alone (Lawton, 1972; World Health Organization, 1974). The importance of individual assessment cannot be overstated since it is pivotal in the decision-making process to determine the kind of treatment, support, and care required and in the implementation of the plan of care.

Functional assessment has been defined as any systematic attempt to measure objectively the level at which an individual is functioning in any of a variety of areas (Lawton, 1971). Thus, assessment of self-care functioning includes such activities as eating, dressing, toileting, ambulating, and bathing. Assessment of the capacity for carrying out instrumental tasks includes such activities as shopping and household tasks. Though early efforts at developing assessment tools focused primarily on physical function, it is now accepted that social functioning should be assessed as well—that is, the capacity of the individual to enact social roles and to meet the human needs for recreation and creativity (Lawton, 1972). Lawton and colleagues have developed a complete battery of assessment instruments called the MAI (Multi-level Assessment Instrument) (Lawton et al., 1982).

A reminder is in order that assessment of the individual older person, no matter how complete and objective, should not be confused with the decision-making process of which it is a part. When used by health practitioners, it should be accompanied by assessment of the older person's potential and by the setting of realistic goals which in turn may qualify the choice of plan. Moreover, it should be complemented by a parallel process of assessment of the social/health resources and supports available to meet the individual's need and of the physical environment as it operates to facilitate or bar maximum functioning. Older people with identical diagnoses and functional assessments may require different plans. Indicators of a feasible plan include the socioeconomic situation, physical environment, eligibility for various benefits and entitlements, and availability of needed services (including those that can be provided by families). Finally, the preferences of the older person and family must be taken into consideration. People with identical assessments may want very different plans, depending on such factors as personality, lifestyle, and ethnic background.

Mental Health

Comprehensive epidemiological data and community surveys of the mental health status of older people are badly needed. Though the true prevalence of the need of the aged for mental health care has not been fully established (Butler & Lewis, 1973; Schuckit, 1974), the evidence that has been accumulating indicates that between 18% and 25% of older people have significant mental health symptoms. Again, those who are 75 years of age or older are at highest risk. As is true of physically disabled older people, larger numbers of the mentally disturbed reside in the community than in institutions.

Dr. Gene Cohen, the head of the Center on Aging of the National Institute of Mental Health, emphasizes the following facts (1980):

- Mental illness is more prevalent among the elderly than among younger adults; 18–25% of older persons have significant mental symptoms.
- Psychosis increases significantly after age 65 and is more than twice as common in the over-75-year-age group than in 25–35 year olds.
- Senile dementia is thought to be the fourth leading cause of death.
- Suicide occurs more frequently among the elderly than in any other age group.
- The vast majority of older people have chronic physical ailments, with at least 15% of the aged having serious problems. Many result in significant negative psychological reactions.

Among other experiences common to many older people that contribute to and intensify their mental health problems are their reduced opportunities for social interaction, their high incidence of reduced income and poverty, losses of roles, and the multiple personal losses they suffer such as death of a spouse, other relatives, and peers.

Neurotic disorders and symptoms experienced as psychological disturbance do not increase by age. However, the elderly show a sharp increase in psychosis (organic and functional) and in symptoms experienced as physical illness.

One of the reasons for the sharp rise in rates of mental impairment with advancing age is the entry into the ranks of the mentally ill of those with chronic organic mental disorders associated with the later phase of life—that is, the forms of senile dementia now often referred to as Alzheimer's and related disorders. The dementias are characterized by relatively permanent deficit in the capacity of intellectual functioning with symptoms such as confusion, impairment of orientation, memory and perception, knowledge, and judgment. Old people with such disorders (and to some extent those with functional mental problems) are likely to have various forms of physical illness.

No preventive or curative measures have yet been discovered for senile dementia. Again, there is a lack of definitive data, but some good surveys estimate that about 7% of older people in the community have a significant degree of such impairment and an equal proportion are mildly impaired (see Kay & Bergmann, 1980, for complete summary of such estimates). The incidence of senile dementia rises with advancing age so that about 22% of those 80 or over are afflicted.

Old people with such diagnoses are overrepresented in institutions, undoubtedly because the symptoms make such heavy demands on caregivers that it has been called one of the most socially disruptive of all ailments (Brody, 1967). About 60% of the 1.2 million older people in nursing homes and old age homes at any given time have that diagnosis, and an additional 16,000 reside in psychiatric facilities. The elderly represent about one-fifth of all first admissions to psychiatric hospitals and occupy almost one-fourth of those beds. The vast majority of these patients have senile dementia or functional psychoses. (For reviews, see Schuckit, 1976; Butler & Lewis, 1973; Kramer et al., 1973.) Overall, a minimum of about 675,000 older people with senile dementia are in institutions of various types (see Brody, 1981, for review).

It is particularly difficult to estimate the proportion of older people who suffer from depression. Estimates of the proportion of elderly community residents who have depressive disorders range from 10% to 25%. It is clear, however, that rates are higher than among younger people.

Suicide rates rise dramatically among older people, particularly among men. About one out of every four suicides is committed by a person 60 years of age or over (U.S. DHEW Secretary's Committee, 1980). At ages 70–74, the rate for men is twice that for men of all ages (Butler, 1979).

Institutionalized Older People

In addition to the older people whose ailments and disabilities are described above, a segment of the elderly population that is particularly disabled (mentally and physically) lives in institutions. About 5% of older people (about 1.2 million individuals) are in institutions at any one time. The risk of admission rises with advancing age; rates rise from 2.1% of those between the ages of 65 and 74 to 19.3% of those 85 and over (Institute of Medicine, 1977).

By comparison with the noninstitutionalized, this group has a much larger number of physical and mental diagnoses (about 60% have some degree of senile dementia). Their poor health is reflected in severe functional disabilities. Majorities need help in all activities of daily living and personal care, and about half are incontinent. Most are in advanced old age, with an average age of almost 82 or about a decade higher than the average age of the total elderly population.

The Perceptions of the Aged about Their Health

Just as there are wide variations among older people in the processes of aging, there are also wide variations in the ways in which older people perceive their own health. In addition to individual differences, those perceptions are also related to ethnic group membership, economic situations, and age (among other factors).

A U.S. National Center for Health Statistics survey (1981b) found that 69% of persons 65 and over (as compared to 89% of those under 65) reported that their health was good or excellent in relation to the health of others in their age group. The self-assessment rate of "good to excellent" was somewhat lower, however, among blacks and Hispanics. Higher income was associated with more favorable self-appraisal (White House Conference, 1981). Similar tendencies were noted in another survey (Harris, 1981) in which a majority of the elderly (56%) were positive about their health status. But 63% of elderly blacks reported poor health, as did 62% of elderly Hispanics and 62% of those in the under–$5,000 income group.

The self-image of the elderly also varies by age. Shanas found that

> The most likely of all older people to describe their health as good and the least likely to say their health is poor are those aged 65 and 66. Fewer persons age 67 to 69 say their health is good. After the decline in reports of good health at ages 67 to 69, the proportions reporting good health remain relatively stable in each successive age cohort. Even at the ages of 80 and over, half of the elderly population report their health as good (1978).

Elaborating on the fact that elderly persons tend to judge their health status on the basis of comparisons with their peers, Shanas makes the following points:

- The aged who report that their health was poor appear to be the most alienated persons among the elderly. Their low opinion of their condition is associated with reports of loneliness, of time passing slowly for them, and complaints about neighbors keeping to themselves.
- Those who think they are in poor health are sure their health is worse than that of other people.
- Those who believe they are in good health are sure their health is better than the health of other people.

Causes of Mortality

The accuracy of death certificates has been questioned with respect to how they reflect the actual cause(s) of death of older people. However, data from NCHS indicate that in 1978 three-fourths of all deaths of people 65 or over were caused by heart disease, cancer, and stroke (U.S. NCHS, 1982). Heart disease caused about 31% of deaths in the 45–54 age range, 41% in 65–74, 44% in 75–84, and 48.2% among those 85 and over. Cancer accounted for 31% of deaths among those 54–64 but slipped to 18% among those 75–84. Stroke was reported to account for 15.5% of deaths among those 85 and over and 12.7% for those between 75–84.

Cancer (malignant neoplasms) is the only major cause of death for which rates among the elderly have continued to rise since 1900. The NCHS identifies lung cancer mortality as the source of most of the increase and associates the rise with cigarette smoking.

Overall, however, mortality rates are going down, even though more older persons die simply because there are more older persons. The increase in life expectancy at age 65 has been gradual. In 1940, a 65-year-old man could expect to live on the average 12.1 more years, and in 1978 it was 14 years; for women, the 1940 expectancy was 13.6 and 18.4 in 1978 (U.S. NCHS, 1982).

In summary, it again is emphasized that age 65 does not signal automatic breakdown of mental or physical health; rather, aging is a significant period of life during which change and growth are possible. Not only are older people extremely heterogeneous as to age levels and with respect to their health status, but those with similar deficits may react, behave, and function differently. Most older persons remain competent and able to function independently. It is undeniable, however, that older people are at high risk of chronic mental and physical health problems which require special responses from the systems of care; those risks increase with advancing age. Many have functional physical limitations and mental/emotional problems requiring supportive social/health services as well as medical care. The next chapter will discuss the health/mental health systems as they meet (or fail to meet) the needs of the elderly in the United States.

2 The Elderly and the Formal Health and Mental Health Systems

Health, in the sense that was enunciated by the late Rene Dubos, reflected the ability of the individual to adapt—that is, to function well physically and mentally and to express the range of one's potentialities (Dubos, 1968). Since health includes both physical and mental health, it follows that "health care" and "mental health care," which aim to support adaptation and function, include but are not limited to medical, psychiatric, and related services. Rather, health care also includes preventive, supportive, and therapeutic services provided by other professionals (such as psychologists, social workers, dentists, podiatrists) and nonprofessionals (such as the patients themselves, family members, or friends). Among those services are advice or emotional support, giving medication, diagnostic procedures such as taking temperature, personal care (such as help in dressing and bathing), transportation to the sources of formal health care, and many others.

When the phrase "health care system" is used, it generally calls to mind what has come to be known as the formal system—that is, the services and programs provided by professionals, agencies, and government. Recently, there has been growing recognition of the major role played by the "informal" system of family, friends, and neighbors. In fact, the amount of service provided by the informal system to chronically ill older adults dwarfs that which is provided by formal means.

Most of this chapter will be concerned with the formal system. However, the activities of the informal system cannot be overemphasized. Health professionals of all types should be constantly aware that the myth that families do not take care of their aged the way they did in the good old days is just that: a myth. There has been a steady stream of research that has produced consistent findings:

- Ties between the generations are strong and viable.
- Most older people (84%) who have children live close to at least one of them and see them (and their grandchildren) frequently (Shanas, 1980).
- Family members (not professionals) give 80% of medically related care to the impaired elderly such as bandage-changing, injections, and the giving of medications (U.S. DHEW, PHS, 1972).

- Ninety percent of home help services are given by family members including household maintenance and personal care (U.S. Comptroller General, 1977).
- Many families maintain impaired older people in their homes for long periods of time at immense cost to their lifestyles, freedom, and sometimes to their own health.
- Families do not "dump" their elderly into nursing homes and other institutions. Institutionalization most often is the last resort when all other alternatives have been explored and/or tried, with the family often exhausting itself mentally, physically, and financially in the process.

In short, families play a major role in the health care of the aged. Their significance is such that a large portion of Chapter 13 is devoted to the relationships of families and professionals. That chapter will provide information about family members and suggest ways in which professionals can work with them to make health care of the elderly effective.

The Formal Health Care Systems

Older Americans require a large share of the public and private dollars spent for health care. At the same time, there is growing recognition that the formal mental and physical health care systems are geared more to the treatment of acute illness than to the chronic problems that characterize the ever-increasing numbers of older persons.

This seeming paradox—high expenditures for acute medical care of older persons versus widespread concern about the appropriateness and effectiveness of such care—is important to health professionals. In carrying out their daily responsibilities, they are likely to encounter problems related to the structure, funding policies, eligibility criteria, availability, and other aspects of the systems in which they work.

Health Cost Outlays for the Elderly

Approximately $225 billion was spent in 1981 for health care, and about $83.2 billion of this was for persons 65 years or older (Brotman, 1982b). Per capita costs were $828 for people under 65 years of age and $3,140 for those 65 or older. Per capita costs for different types of services are striking when age groups are compared. For example, per capita hospital costs were $1,381 for those 65 or over compared with $392 for younger people; physicians' services cost $589 versus $189; drug costs were $192 versus $79; and nursing home care cost $732 per capita for older people compared with $23 for younger people. Of the total of $3,140 per capita for those 65 or over, $1,132 was paid from private sources, and $2,008 was paid from public sources (Brotman, 1982a).

The total cost of hospital care in 1981 was $118 billion, of which $32 billion was spent for persons 65 years or older. In other words, more than 20% of hospital costs were devoted to about 11% of the population. (Among the elderly, 9% consume 70% of Medicare expenditures.) The cost of nursing home care in that year was $24.2 billion, of which more than $19 billion was for the 65+ group (Gibson & Waldo, 1982).

Evidence is emerging that older people who are dying are the major consumers of hospital services and account for most of the hospital costs for the aged (Brody & Persily, 1983). Moreover, many professionals observe that hospitals are often used inappropriately and unofficially as a respite service to provide temporary relief to exhausted family caregivers.

The Need for Chronic Care versus a Bias toward Acute Care

Chronic illness has been described as the major health problem of this generation, with chronic care superseding acute care as the prime need for most elderly persons (Brody, S., 1973). Yet the acute care system predominates: more than 40% of health resources for people of all ages are consumed by hospital care. For the elderly alone, approximately $30 billion is spent for medical services while $1 billion is spent for health/social services, a ratio that has been called the 30-to-one paradox of health needs and medical responses (Brody, 1979).

One reason for the imbalance in the funding patterns is that the United States has not adhered to any clearly enunciated goals for long-term care. The desirability of a health/social model of support has been underscored by three recent international conferences. These are the Long-Term Care Data Conference in Tucson, Arizona, May 1975; the Conference on Care of the Elderly, Meeting the Challenge of Dependency, cosponsored by the U.S. Institute of Medicine of the National Academy of Medicine and the Royal Society of Medicine, Washington, DC, May 1976; and the Institute de la Vie's Conference on Aging: A Challenge to Science and Society, April 1977, Vichy, France. The published report of one conference stated

> Perhaps the single most pervasive theme throughout the discussion was the deficiencies and dangers of applying a strictly medical model based on acute episodic care to long-term care. The goals of long-term health care are to improve and maintain the ability of individuals to function independently and to cope with impairments and disabilities. This is a basically different orientation from that of curing disease. (Murnaghan, 1976)

Despite such emphasis, however, the prevailing values of the health systems and patients alike continue to express faith in dramatic high technology rather than the less glamorous but more appropriate supportive health/social services.

Much thought has been devoted to identifying the components needed to comprise a system that would provide the kinds of support actually needed by growing numbers of the elderly. The Health Resources Administration, for example, has developed a definition which clearly recognizes that long-term care is not limited to institutional or medical treatment, and defines it as follows:

> . . . those services designed to provide diagnostic, preventive, therapeutic, rehabilitative, supportive and maintenance services for individuals . . . who have chronic physical and/or mental impairments in a variety of institutional and noninstitutional health care settings, including the home, with the goal of promoting the optimum level of physical, social and psychological functioning. (U.S. HRA, 1977)

Each of the various elements of that definition are significant.

First, the definition refers to "diagnostic, preventive, therapeutic, rehabilitative, supportive and maintenance services." It rejects the concept of simple maintenance, often characterized by the phrase "custodial care."

Second, the definition recognizes that the impairments of those in need of long-term care are chronic rather than acute. By definition, then, the services needed must be ongoing, rather than applied and then withdrawn as in a model of care that aims to cure.

Third, the definition states its goal as "promoting the optimum level of physical, social and psychological functioning." Thus, it speaks to the importance of all three spheres of function that are relevant to well-being and consequently to the quality of life. It therefore is consonant with the firm consensus of gerontologists that an interdisciplinary approach to the problems of the impaired aged is an absolute necessity.

Finally, the definition makes explicit the fact that there are many different settings in which long-term care can take place including nursing homes and other institutional facilities; specialized housing (personal care and domiciliary care facilities, boarding homes, congregate housing, retirement communities, and others); settings in the community (day-care settings, senior citizens centers); and one's own home (or the home of a relative or friend). There are other components of a long-term care continuum, including accurate multidisciplinary assessment (to determine appropriate treatment plans) and the acute general hospital (which is often the entry point to long-term care and to which those receiving long-term care often go for acute illnesses or exacerbations of their chronic ailments).

The current climate favoring deinstitutionalization and alternatives places nursing homes in a false position of competition with noninstitutional facilities and services. To the contrary, both types of programs are necessary to meet the varying needs of a heterogeneous population.

In applying these principles to varying configurations that a system of services could take at the community level, Stanley Brody, who designed the paradigm in Figure 2–1, is careful to describe it as a long-term support, rather than a care system (Brody, 1979), even though care components are included. The array of services is related to a counseling/assessing/monitoring function responsive to individuals coming into the system from a variety of entry points. In this view,

> The problem is to rationalize these varied planning and delivery agencies into a community system which takes into consideration the availability or unavailability of informal supports and the nature of the local ecology. . . . The role of the federal government is to provide incentives and supports to local communities in their efforts to enunciate a long term support system. A goal of the incentives is to assure that the constituent elements are related to achieve the objectives of assessment, continuity of care, monitoring and counseling. Where and how these functions are to be performed is a local concern and related to the values and resources within each community. The incentives should also be a force for balancing the participation of medical and health/social services within the provider role of planning the system. The reallocation of available federal funding between the two elements would also contribute to the objective of equalization. (Brody & Brody, 1981)

Clearly, the essential goal is to have a rational system of long-term support and care if the needs of older people are to be met. Many elements of case-finding and of services are already in place in varying quantities in most communities. But they exist in parallel and overlapping arrangements called community mental health and retardation, vocational rehabilitation, housing, area agencies on aging, health systems agencies, and veterans' services. In the main, the supply of many services is inadequate, they are unevenly distributed, and some services are virtually nonexistent.

Problems in Mental Health Care

The connection between many health and mental health problems has already been described in Chapter 1. An important point about the mental health needs of the nation's elderly, as stated in 1977 by an HEW national study committee, is that such problems continue to remain largely ignored (U.S. DHEW, 1980). Despite the compelling need for effective actions, the emotional needs of older people go largely unmet or inadequately met, and there is limited access to a full spectrum of appropriate services.

It is estimated that about one-quarter of the older population suffers from

Figure 2-1. Inventory of Recommended Available Services Appropriate to a Long-Term Care/Support System*

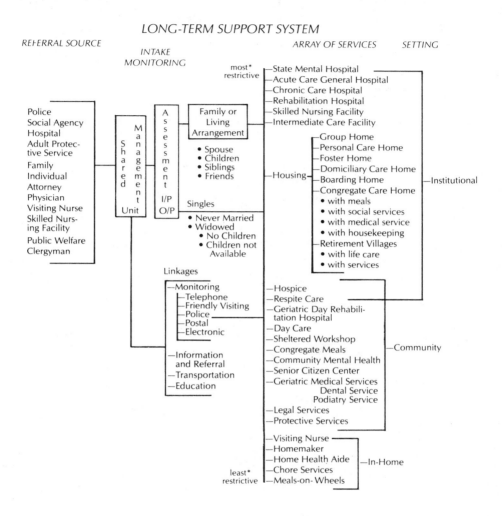

*The classification of from most to least restrictive is a general view of services and may vary within each service.

Reprinted with permission from "Data for Long Term Care Planning by Health Systems Agencies" by S. J. Brody and C. Masciocchi, in *Journal of the American Health Association,* Vol. 70, No. 11, pp. 1194–1198.

significant mental health problems but is served at less than one-fourth the rate of the 25- to 44-year age group (President's Commission on Mental Health, 1978). Moreover, they tend to have mental and emotional symptoms for long periods of time, often years, before receiving help (Eisdorfer & Lawton, 1973).

A recent critique by the U.S. Senate Committee on Aging (1982) reported that the elderly—despite their increased risk for mental disorder—have been consistently underserved by both the private and public health care sectors: only 4% of community mental health center patients are elderly, and only 2% are among those served by private practitioners and clinics. The Senate report noted that such data are "particularly disconcerting because many of the mental disorders of the elderly are treatable and reversible."

Among the barriers to mental health care cited by the Committee and by others (see, for example, Hagebak & Hagebak, 1983) are

- reimbursement structures under federal health care programs and other financial barriers (the limitations of Medicare in this respect will be discussed later in this chapter);
- the fragmented, disorganized system of health and social services available to the elderly;
- the low number of mental health professionals who are interested and trained to provide care to the elderly;
- continued ageism, or negative attitudes toward aging and the aged, on the part of mental health and health professionals;
- fear of the cost of treating the mentally ill in general;
- the limited availability of transportation services and other problems involving accessibility;
- "turf-guarding" by agencies seeking to protect their share of reduced resources.

Hagebak and Hagebak (1983) point out that elderly persons themselves may not seek mental health care because of the following:

- a lack of awareness of mental health services;
- distrust and fear based on stigmas created by attitudes toward mental health which were prevalent a generation ago;
- low levels of self-esteem resulting from loss of meaningful life roles, which may deter the older people from seeking help;
- beliefs that senile dementia and other mental conditions are part of normal aging.

The scarcity of reimbursement for mental health services is, of course, a basic problem. But the President's Commission on Mental Health emphasized that coordination of existing resources is a necessity if they are to be exploited fully (1978). That is, effective linkages and integration are needed among mental health services, health services, other human service providers, and community organizations such as churches.

Medicare and Medicaid: Accomplishments and Limitations

Two programs that are of prime importance to older persons in the United States are, of course, Medicare and Medicaid. Medicare is directed almost totally to the 65+ population while Medicaid includes elderly individuals among the low-income population it serves.

Enactment of Medicare and Medicaid in 1965 has had far-reaching consequences for the health care system and for older people. These programs have a record of many accomplishments, but they also have many shortcomings.

Medicare

The U.S. Senate Committee on Aging, at the height of the legislative struggle over Medicare two decades ago, marshalled arguments in support of its position that "beyond any possible doubt, a positive program of hospital and related benefits is absolutely essential to the maintenance of both the health and well-being of older Americans" (1963). A key point was that the elderly were found at the top of every conventional index by which hospital utilization is measured, but that the high costs of such care were rapidly outdistancing the capacity of older persons to pay for them. Private health insurance was deemed to be excessively expensive for the elderly and often provided only partial protection, and many older people were unable to find such insurance at any price.

The Senate Committee pointed to other health care needs as well. For example, it declared that "the dental health of the large majority of older citizens is appalling." But its major focus, and that of other advocates of Medicare, was on the need to provide protection to those older persons who might otherwise experience economic disaster because of high hospital bills. That emphasis was reflected in the law that brought Medicare into being.

Provisions of Medicare

All citizens 65 and older who are eligible to receive Old Age and Survivors Disability Insurance (OASDI) benefits are also eligible for Medicare benefits. For those few (3%) who are not eligible for automatic inclusion in Medicare, Hospital Insurance (HI) under Part A of Medicare can be purchased.

From the beginning, Medicare hospital patients were expected to pay part of the cost of hospitalization; in 1982 this charge was $304 for any part of the first 60 days in the hospital, after which daily charges were to be paid. Other items covered under HI include laboratory and X-ray services at the hospital, regular hospital nursing services, medications and blood (up to the third pint) provided during the hospital stay, surgery-related costs, and some rehabilitation services. Skilled nursing care is provided when related to recuperation from the hospital stay; a home treatment plan may be established by the physician within 14 days of discharge from a hospital or skilled nursing facility, but this service has been narrowly defined to apply to "medically necessary" care.

Part B of Medicare is called Supplementary Medical Insurance (SMI). Nearly everyone covered by hospital insurance enrolls for SMI coverage, which is contingent upon payment of a monthly premium ($12.20 in 1982, as compared to $9.90 in 1980). For the most part, this premium is deducted from Social Security checks. SMI pays for physicians' services as well as physician-ordered services and supplies. It also covers outpatient services, rural health clinic visits, and home health visits. However, there are several health care services that the aged generally use on a continuing basis—such as drugs, dental care, routine eye examinations, and preventive services—that are not covered by Medicare. Long-term institutional services are not covered either.

Under SMI, payment of bills does not begin until after the elderly participant has paid $75 in a calendar year. In addition, beneficiaries must pay 20% of what Medicare establishes as reasonable costs for allowed services in their area. This is true, however, for physician's services only if the physician chooses to "take assignment," that is, to accept as full payment the amount Medicare allows for the service. One of the major problems in SMI, in fact, is that many physicians are highly selective in accepting assignment.

Provisions of Medicaid

Unlike Medicare, which is administered through the federal government (although private intermediaries manage the actual payments of claims), Medicaid is a federal-state partnership to pay for a wide variety of health care services to low-income persons and to those who are eligible for public assistance.

States have leeway on the total range of services to be provided once they have offered certain basic services, including inpatient hospital services, outpatient hospital services, laboratory and X-ray services, skilled nursing facility services for individuals 21 years of age and older, home health care services for individuals eligible for skilled nursing services, physicians' services, rural health clinic services, and early and periodic screening. If states choose to do so, they may include a number of other services including prescription drugs, eyeglasses, private duty nursing, intermediate care facility services, inpatient psychiatric care for the aged, physical therapy, and dental care. Thus, an older person with an income slightly or considerably above Medicaid eligibility levels may not be poor enough to receive certain of the services they most need and want and which are not covered under Medicare.

Medicaid payments are made directly to providers of service, who must accept the Medicaid reimbursement level as payment in full. Federal contributions to the states range from 50% to 77.5% of program expenditures.

The important differences between Medicare and Medicaid are reflected in the ways in which the bulk of their expenditures are targeted. The U.S. Health Care Financing Administration (HCFA) sums up the situation as follows:

> Medicare's orientation toward acute care services [is] consistent with its statute. Inpatient hospital care accounts for 67.8% of total Medicare reimbursements (HI and SMI combined). Only 1.3% of Medicare reimbursements go to nursing homes, with coverage limited to short-term, post-hospital care. In contrast, while inpatient hospital services absorb only 31.4% of total Medicaid payments, payments for long-term care in nursing homes, both intermediate care facilities and skilled nursing facilities, make up 42.3% of total Medicaid payments. (1982a)

Accomplishments of Medicare and Medicaid

Medicare and Medicaid have been major forces for an historic change in the way health care costs of the elderly are paid. In 1966, government funds paid for about 30% of all health care costs for persons 65 and over. In 1978, that share had risen to nearly two-thirds, with an especially dramatic increase in public payment of hospital costs, from one-half in 1965 to 90% in 1978 (U.S. White House Conference, 1981).

In 1981, when the total health care cost for all age groups came to $287 billion, outlays for Medicare and Medicaid benefits totaled $73 billion, including $42 billion for hospital care. The two programs combined paid for 28.6% of all personal health care in the nation (U.S. HCFA, 1982b). In 1979, the average reimbursement for a Medicare recipient was $1,663; the average Medicaid payment per recipient was $950.

Robert Ball, former Social Security Commissioner and a prominent member of the National Commission on Social Security Reform in 1982–1983, is a respected advocate for the Social Security system of which Medicare is part. His view of the achievements of Medicare notes the shift from private to public payment of health care expenses for the elderly, but he identifies other positive results as well:

> Not only were people financially protected, but they had received care they otherwise might not have had. Health and safety standards in smaller hospitals and approved skilled nursing homes were considerably improved at Medicare's

insistence. Medicare is largely responsible, too, for the desegregation of inpatient hospital facilities in the South and some other areas of the country where
segregation of blacks was still a common practice in 1965. Although probably
contributing to the increasing cost of hospital care—and this is hardly a plus—the
willingness of Medicare to pay the full cost of its beneficiaries permitted institutions to keep up with the rapid technological advances of the last 15 years and to
raise the salaries and wages of underpaid hospital staffs, improve working conditions, and reduce turnover. Without Medicare, hospitals today would be in a very
precarious financial condition. The program is well administered and administra-
tive costs are reasonable. (1981)

The net effect of Medicare, considering the subscription costs and con-
tributory requirements, is to protect the elderly from the catastrophic costs of
acute care.

Medicaid, in terms of national response to health needs of the poor and
near-poor, has taken the United States to new levels of responsibility for such
care. The federal-state working relationship has gradually extended to all
states, including those that had resisted earlier programs to extend medical
assistance to low-income persons. The special importance of Medicaid to its
elderly participants is underscored by the observation that the

. . . aged are the only group for which there has been any substantial increase in
real services in the last few years. The tendency to place large numbers of elderly
persons in nursing homes—where average Medicaid expenditures were $2,500
in fiscal year 1973—accounts for a major proportion of Medicaid costs. Three out
of five Medicaid dollars pay for services provided to aged or disabled adults.
(Davis, 1981)

The high dollar proportion of Medicaid expenditures devoted to the 65+
population is further documented by the fact that the aged comprise 15.6% of
Medicaid recipients (about 3.7 million individuals) but receive services total-
ling 37.4% of Medicaid payments. It is also significant that 38.3% of the
elderly Medicaid recipients were on medical assistance only; that is, they
were not receiving cash assistance through the Supplemental Security Income (SSI) program. Thus, nearly two-fifths of elderly Medicaid recipients
had incomes somewhat higher than bedrock SSI levels but nevertheless were
eligible for medical assistance.

The fact that under the Medicaid program individual states have options
has both positive and negative aspects. A strength of the program is that states
can cover services essential to the "medically indigent," or those who have
enough income to pay for their basic living expenses but not enough income to
pay for their medical care. At the same time, however, giving states options
that affect the services available to Medicaid recipients means that protection
varies markedly from state to state.

Shortcomings of Medicare and Medicaid

One of the most frequent complaints made about Medicare is that it leaves large gaps in the protection it affords to the elderly, particularly in the day-to-day care of chronic ailments. The U.S. Senate Committee on Aging, in a recent (1982) assessment of the value of Medicare to its participants, noted the following shortcomings:

1. Persons aged 65 and over paid 36.8% of their health care costs through private payments in 1978;
2. Medicare does not cover many items and services widely used by the elderly (such as hearing aids, eyeglasses, dental care, and most outpatient prescription drugs) and has narrow coverage for home health and nursing home care;
3. the charges paid by Medicare participants keep going up;
4. private health insurance policies which supplement Medicare coverage have increased, or plan to increase, their rates as well.

The refusal of some physicians to accept assignment under Part B of Medicare was also of concern to the Senate Committee. Only a little over 50% of services paid by Medicare in 1980 were assigned, with the physician agreement agreeing to send the bill directly to Medicare at the agreed-upon rate of 80% of reasonable charges. When assignment is refused, the elderly Medicare beneficiary must tend to the paperwork and is likely to pay substantially more than the charges set by Medicare, thus adding to the older people's uncertainties and tensions about the amount of income that must be set aside for health care costs.

It should be noted that the availability of Medicare did not result in a substantial rise in the number of doctor visits reported by older people, even though it was instrumental in increasing hospital utilization (Shanas, 1982; Maddox, 1976). One comparison of health care practices among the elderly in 1962 and in 1975 showed that about the same proportion of older persons— three out of every ten—reported that they saw a physician the month before they were interviewed (Shanas, 1978). (There was a shift from clinic care to private care, however.) On the other hand, fewer persons in 1975 than in 1962 were likely to report that they had not seen a doctor during the past year or even longer. The same study reported that about 4% of all older people in 1975, roughly three-quarters of a million persons, said that they put off needed medical treatment because of lack of money; about 7%, or 1.4 million, said they put off dental care for that reason.

Though Robert Ball is emphatic in his praise of Medicare's achievements, he nevertheless states that important changes are needed. Among those he has suggested (1978) are the following: (1) full protection against hospital costs without cost sharing (except for an initial deductible as under present law); (2) physician participation under Medicare should be on an all-or-nothing basis (that is, doctors would not have the option of accepting or refusing assignment); (3) there should be an annual limit on the total amount that anyone should have to pay in deductibles and co-insurance under SMI; (4) combining HI and SMI and eliminating the SMI monthly premium for retirees; and (5) coverage of prescription drugs for chronic illness.

Ball and others are troubled by the fact that less than half of the health costs of elderly people are reimbursed by Medicare. Another major problem is the runaway costs of these programs. The elderly already spend almost two and a half times more out of pocket for health care than do younger adults (Fisher, 1980). There is widespread concern, therefore, about the potential negative effect on older people of the administration's proposals to limit Medicare and to increase patient contributions.

Medicaid has drawn criticism almost since its founding because of the state-by-state variations in covered services mentioned above. The advisability of relying on a state-administered, means-tested program (such as Medicaid) for the bulk of long-term care provided to the elderly has been called into question. As with Medicare, the cost of the program is a source of concern; it was $31.3 billion in fiscal year 1981 in combined federal and state funds (U.S. HCFA, 1982a). It is important to recognize, however, that the increases in program costs do not mean that proportionately more people are being served. The U.S. HCFA (1982a) attributes the increase in Medicaid expenditures during 1974–1975 to the following: 58% to higher costs; 35.5% to higher prices; 35.5% to changes in health practice such as increased technology and intensification of service; and only 6% to an increase in the number of recipients.

Medicaid has not fully solved the problems of older people who need nursing home care but cannot pay for it. The number of older people in nursing homes does not reflect the number who need care in such facilities. When reimbursement rates are low, many cannot obtain that service because of the scarcity of beds made available to Medicaid recipients or because of discrimination against hard-to-care-for patients who require a lot of attention from staff.

Another criticism of Medicaid concerns the "spend-down effect" often triggered when an older person needs care but does not meet the income standards. Vladeck (1980) describes the problems as follows:

> The drafters of Medicaid specifically sought to insulate middle-aged children from the prospect of financial catastrophe engendered by the need to institutionalize aged parents. Through the concept of "medical indigency," they also began to move in the direction of eligibility on the basis of need, rather than complete impoverishment. But generous definitions of medical indigency contributed to unexpectedly rapid increases in program costs and were soon barred by Congress, while the states, which retained substantial discretion over eligi-

bility standards, rarely broke the old welfare molds. Thus the "spend-down" grew up. Middle-aged children are not forced to exhaust all their own resources in order to provide nursing home care for their parents, but they are forced to witness the destruction of their inheritances, for which their parents may have scrimped for a lifetime. Or else they break the laws for the first time in their lives to effect covert transfers of their parents' assets. That is hardly as bad a dilemma as that which prevailed before Medicaid, but it remains demeaning, humiliating, and often tragic. Which is to say that it remains in keeping with the culture of welfare policy.

In 1960 and again in 1980, Alvin Schorr's classic monographs documented the destructive effects of compelling adult children to provide economic support to elderly parents, let alone requiring them to pay for the high costs of their health care. It therefore is of serious concern that in February 1983, the U.S. Department of Health and Human Services informed the states (through a Medicaid transmittal) that HCFA would no longer prohibit states from requiring adult children to pay for nursing home care of parents who are Medicaid recipients.

In the early 1980s, cutbacks have been increasing health care costs to older people and restricting coverage. Budget reductions at the federal level have been extensive, but since Medicaid is a federal-state program, the situation is also affected by uneven service cutbacks and other actions taken by states. Twenty states, for example, have restricted the number of covered hospital days or set limits according to diagnosis, and at least nine states took indirect steps to restrict the use of nursing home service (Luehrs, 1982). No early easing of the fiscal constraints was foreseen.

The Special Problems of Mental Health Care

A persistent complaint about Medicare and Medicaid is that they come close to bypassing any real help in the area of mental health. The U.S. Senate Committee on Aging has asserted, for example, that "Medicare discriminates against provision of mental health services for older Americans. Medicaid fails to live up to a legislative mandate that it provide such services" (1971). In 1982, the Committee reported that

> Medicare Part A limits lifetime inpatient psychiatric coverage to 190 days. Part B limits annual outpatient coverage to $250 a year (50% co-payment of $500). Medicaid coverage is generally as low or lower and varies from state to state. Yet studies have shown the potential cost effectiveness of mental health services.

Individual criticisms and other evaluations of Medicare and Medicaid are far more numerous than suggested by this brief account. Historians for both programs say in one way or another that a certain amount of imperfection was embraced at the outset by advocates for these two programs because they anticipated that they would be interim in nature, until a fully fleshed-out national health insurance program for all age groups could be made acceptable to the general public and to Congress. But the high costs entailed have reinforced legislators' determination *not* to take steps toward broader coverage, particularly for long-term care. The formidable political and economic problems standing in the way of far-ranging structural change in the health care systems are likely to persist for some time to come, despite growing concern about the increasing numbers of older persons who need such care. Meanwhile, it is important that health professionals and the elderly individuals they serve make maximum positive use of what is now available.

Negative Attitudes and Information Gaps

Complicating other problems involved in providing help and care to older persons are attitudinal and communication problems between the older people and health professionals. For one thing, large numbers of older persons do not seek the care they need. This is documented by studies that go back for two decades or more and report a "reservoir of illness" in the aged that was not reported to health professionals (Williamson et al., 1964). Recent information, including findings from the research which will be described in Part II of this book, suggest the persistence of that situation. The elderly tend not to see a doctor unless they consider the illness to be serious. This was noted by Shanas in a study before Medicare began (1961) and again in a later one conducted almost ten years after Medicare had been enacted (Shanas, 1978).

The frequent inaccuracy of information or opinions on which older persons often base their health care decisions is confirmed by Litman's study (1971) of the family and health care in three-generation families. Litman reported: "Although the overall level of knowledge and information about matters of health care for the study population as a whole left much to be desired . . . the ill preparedness and lack of sophistication exhibited by the senior generation was especially disconcerting." He described what he called "folk-fatalism" (that is, the ready acceptance of the idea that ailments among the elderly were to be borne rather than dealt with) and urged better and more extensive health education.

The fact that the problems of the elderly often do not receive professional attention makes it difficult, of course, to identify the nature of their day-to-day symptoms and experiences. Thus, important signals of serious illness and suffering that might be ameliorated by appropriate intervention are lost.

A frustration frequently mentioned by health professionals (and families as well) is the unwillingness or inability of older people to use certain in-home services even when they are badly needed. Many impaired or convalescing elderly individuals, for example, are reported to be difficult in their relationships with home health aides or homemakers. Among their complaints are that such personnel "don't do things the way I am used to," refuse to do heavy household maintenance tasks, or intrude on privacy. Lack of experience and sophistication on the part of the older people about the functions of such health personnel undoubtedly play a role as does the individual's personality. Increased attention should be paid in personnel training programs to understanding and dealing with such problems.

Attitudes of Professionals

Negative professional attitudes are frequently cited as significant barriers to the appropriate utilization of health care services for chronic conditions. These apply to those who deal with mental as well as physical health problems. One expert has referred to a pervasive "therapeutic nihilism" (Eisdorfer, 1977) that interferes with objective appraisal of the mental health problems of older persons.

Aspects of this problem have been identified as differential treatment based on negative stereotyping (Mock, 1977; Kosberg & Harris, 1976; Ford & Sbordone, 1980), poor prognosis and perceived futility of treatment (Ford & Sbordone, 1980), and difficulties experienced by the professionals with their own parental figures (Cohen, 1977).

The reluctance of professionals is probably compounded by negative feelings among older persons about seeking help for mental problems. Kahn (1975) speaks of "a reciprocal aversiveness between the mental health establishment and older persons, based on the interaction of such factors as mental health ideology, social characteristics, and consideration of age appropriateness."

Pessimism about long-term outcomes, or even overt hostility on the part of professionals to older patients, serves to reinforce the elderly patient's own internalized stereotypes regarding aging, chronic illness, and the futility of treatment. Even perceived lack of warmth has intimidated older persons against seeking medical help or has resulted in their noncompliance with prescribed regimens (Francis et al., 1969; Haug, 1979).

Professional Training and the Need for Personnel

Part of the problem may be traced back to professional training. For example, Dr. Robert Butler, former director of the National Institute on Aging, was critical of shortcomings at schools of medicine. He stated that accurate diagnosis, sensitive care, and effective treatment for older people are not likely unless more geriatric content is introduced into the curricula of the nation's 114 medical schools, into intern and residency training, and into programs of continuing education.

The question is, how can we expose every physician to the procedures of primary care which are necessary to deal with older patients just as we have exposed other primary care physicians—pediatricians, family and general practitioners, internists, and gynecologists. The body of knowledge required to care for older people is not just disease-categorical; it is broad in perspective and in keeping with the complex character of human experience—including the multiple physical, personal, and social processes that occur with age. (1976)

Though the situation is improving, similar comments could be made about programs that train health professionals of all types.

It is also clear that more attention must be paid to the present and future shortages of trained health professionals who have adequate knowledge of gerontology and geriatrics. Some measure of the distance yet to go in dealing with today's problems—not to mention those of the future—is provided by several recent studies of the needs for health personnel that are likely to be intensified by the projected increase in the number of old and very-old persons.

One study, conducted by the Institute of Medicine (IOM) of the National Academy of Sciences (Institute of Medicine, 1978) dealt primarily with physician education, although it noted that improvement in services for the elderly requires changes in many sectors of health and medical care. One of the conclusions of the IOM was that substantial improvement in teaching about the process of aging and the problems of the aged is required at all levels of medical education. It also stated that some reorientation of current educational programs and the provision of additional resources will be needed to achieve the improvements.

Among the study's recommendations were that

1. Medical schools should include appropriate content on aging in basic and clinical science courses and should establish a complementary required course that integrates knowledge about aging and the problems of the elderly.
2. Preparation for the care of the aged should be included in clinical clerkships and in training programs for house staff, as well as in examinations for certification and licensure.
3. Nursing homes and other long-term care facilities should be included in clinical rotations for medical students and house staff. Experience with home health programs and other noninstitutional care was also regarded as desirable.
4. Teaching about aging should receive increased emphasis in continuing medical education (CME).
5. Medical schools should develop a cadre of faculty to teach gerontology and geriatrics to medical students and house staff.

Another study (Kane et al., 1980) focused on the difficulties involved in training a sufficient number of geriatricians to serve as faculty for training primary care providers who will be likely to continue to offer most of the care to the aged in this country and the training of those primary care providers themselves. The study estimated a need for at least 900 academic geriatricians just to staff existing training programs in internal medicine and family practice, as well as to provide a core group of geriatricians in each medical school. For the actual delivery of services, the United States will require between 7,000 and 10,300 geriatricians by 1990, the best intermediate estimate being about 8,000. The variation in the estimates is based upon differing rates of anticipated delegation of responsibility by the physician to nurse practitioners, physicians' assistants, and social workers. The authors of the study assume that at least some delegation of care will be feasible and desirable.

The 1981 Final Report of the White House Conference on Aging also addressed the need for trained health personnel, emphasizing the needs of long-term care facilities. It recommended the establishment of teaching nursing homes that are affiliated with established medical centers. The report cautioned that there should be avoidance of a narrow concentration on the medical model to the exclusion of a broader sociomedical model that also incorporates in-home and community services (p. 113, Vol. 1).

The magnitude of the challenge to education and training is suggested by the finding that only about 600 physicians in the United States describe themselves as having particular expertise in geriatrics (U.S. Senate Committee on Aging, 1982). The 1977 national sample survey of registered nurses indicated that qualified geriatric nurses are in short supply and that many other allied health professionals are also needed to meet the health needs of older Americans. Among such needed personnel are social workers, physical therapists, dentists, pharmacists, and health educators—all of whom have a substantial amount of contact with the elderly. Among the signs of progress were that schools of medicine have begun to respond to the need for better education and training of physicians. A 1981 study of 126 medical schools, for example, showed that 92 schools offered training in geriatrics at the undergraduate, graduate, and faculty levels. Few of the schools, however, made such training a requirement (U.S. Senate Special Committee on Aging, 1982).

The Aged in the Future

Finally, future increases in the aged population, in its utilization of health services, and in the need for health personnel will be accompanied by changes in the nature of the elderly population. As Brotman (1982b) points out, every day approximately 5,200 Americans become age 65 and about 3,600 die; the net increase is about 600,000 older people per year. The older population, then, is not static but changes constantly.

A glance at the chart of our 75-year-old woman (Table 1–1) will show how very different her personal life history and the times in which she has lived are from the history of a person born, for example, in 1945. Future cohorts of the elderly will include more native-born Americans who will be better educated, who will have had access to better health care, and who will have experienced a higher standard of living. Those differences undoubtedly will be reflected in more sophistication about health matters and in higher expectations of health care and health personnel.

Formidable as future needs may appear to be, present realities must be acknowledged and understood if efforts are to be made to provide quality health care to older people. Among those realities are the mental and physical health experiences and practices of today's older people. Those practices may operate so as to prevent maximum maintenance of health and functioning and thus contribute to declines. The next section of this book, which reports in detail the findings of the study of older people in the Philadelphia area, will cast some light on that matter.

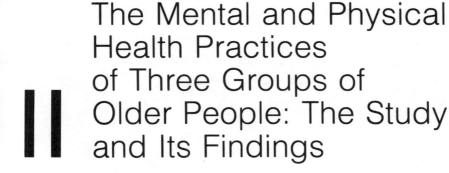

The Mental and Physical Health Practices of Three Groups of Older People: The Study and Its Findings

3 The Research Project and the People Studied: An Overview

Older adults, like people of all ages, are the best sources of information about how they regard their own mental and physical health, what symptoms and bothers they experience, and what they do to relieve discomfort, to prevent illness, and to promote health. But it often is difficult for health professionals to obtain a complete picture of such matters because of several complicating factors that have been well documented:

- Older people often are pessimistic and fatalistic about their health complaints. Their acceptance of their ills as inevitable in old age reduces the likelihood that they will report their problems and, therefore, that they will receive appropriate treatment.
- Many health care professionals tend to have a similarly pessimistic viewpoint and may dismiss complaints with comments such as, "After all, this is to be expected at your age."
- Many older people are seriously lacking in knowledge or are misinformed about health and health care.
- Some older people are reluctant to report their complaints because they feel that nobody really cares or they do not want to bother others with their problems.
- Many older people have multiple physical and mental ailments which interact with and exacerbate each other, but care may be fragmented among a number of professionals rather than coordinated in such a way as to put it all together.

In addition to such factors, professionals are not always aware of the impact of health problems on the lifestyles of older people and rarely have the opportunity to know what goes on in the day-to-day health lives of the elderly—the myriad of symptoms and bothers that occur between phone calls, office or clinic visits to professionals, and periods of hospitalizations. Even when such contacts do take place, they often fail to reveal many of the actions the older people take to relieve their discomfort, to prevent illness, or to promote health. Moreover, because of the chronicity of the ailments of older people, self-care and compliance issues are of critical importance. During

49

acute illnesses, professional prescriptions are for relatively short periods of time and are more under professional control. Chronic care often goes on for years and is much more subject to the judgment of the individual concerned.

Information about these matters should be available if health professionals are to do their work well so that older people receive the health care they need. The gaps in knowledge about the health experiences and practices of the elderly should be filled in: professionals should know what questions to ask, and older people should know what information to provide.

The research study which will be described in this part of the book was a first step in that direction in that it took us into the homes and daily lives of a sample of older people. It allowed us a glimpse of their day-to-day, even minute-to-minute mental and physical symptoms. It permitted us to see how health professionals' diagnoses and prescriptions for treatment were transformed into action or inaction, and what the older people actually did about their health that was not based on professional advice.

The Purpose and Limitations of the Study

The basic purpose of the study, then, was to collect and analyze detailed information about the day-to-day mental and physical health concerns and symptoms of older people and the actions they took in response to those bothers. The aim was to produce data that would help professionals in their work and provide guidelines for the kinds of information health professionals need about older people.

The project undertook to study three different groups of people with differing mental statuses. The assumption was that mental status could be a determinant of health experiences and practices. It was not intended to match the three groups for age, race, physical health, or other variables. Nor were the three groups expected to be representative of the total elderly population or even of people with similar mental statuses. Rather, the purpose was to obtain maximum contrast among groups with specific mental characteristics.

The exploratory study was planned to be small and in depth rather than a survey of large numbers of people. The preliminary information developed would offer clues as to what further research might be necessary. Since mental and physical health is so closely interrelated (as indicated in Chapter 1), we felt it essential to study mental/emotional and physical problems simultaneously.

Certain limitations of the study should be kept in mind. First, it is reiterated that the people studied were not intended to be typical of all older people and the findings, therefore, cannot be generalized to the total elderly population. The members of two of the three groups had serious mental impairments. And they had relatively low socioeconomic status.

Second, by design the research asked questions about the negative experiences—that is, the mental and physical symptoms and bothers of the older people. The findings, therefore, do not present a rounded picture of their lives and must be seen in that perspective.

Third, again by design, the information collected represents the perceptions of the elderly people themselves about their experiences and actions.

The Three Mental Status Groups

The selection criteria for the three mental status groups studied were as follows:

1. *Normals:* The people in this group had normal mental functioning. That is, they were free of a history of a functional mental disorder and did not have senile dementia.
2. *Functionals:* The people in this group had a recorded history of a diagnosed functional mental disturbance.
3. *Senile Dementia Group:* People included in this group had been diagnosed as suffering from senile dementia and were assessed by the referring agency as being chronically confused and disoriented. In addition, they were required to have a score on the Kahn–Goldfarb Mental Status Questionnaire (administered by the project interviewer) that indicated moderate to severe impairment.

One hundred and thirty-two older people living in the Philadelphia area were studied in the project. All of them were over the age of 60 and all lived in the community, alone or with a relative or another person; none was in a nursing home or other institution. None was acutely ill during the study, though virtually all of them had one or more chronic ailments. The few who became acutely ill and/or were hospitalized before the series of interviews was completed were dropped from the study.

We knew at the outset of the project that the older people afflicted with senile dementia, because of the very nature of that ailment, would be unable to provide complete or reliable information, and some would be unable to provide any information at all. Despite these limitations in their capacities to respond appropriately, we decided to include them in the research for two reasons. First, not all people with that diagnosis have the same amount of cognitive deficit; they could be expected to vary in their capacities to report their experiences. Second, virtually nothing is known about the perceptions of this uniquely deprived group about their mental and physical bothers; anything that could be learned would be worth the effort. As matters worked out, both assumptions proved correct. Some of these older people were able to tell us many things about their experiences; others were not. But we did learn something—even about those who were completely unresponsive.

Thirty-four social, health, and mental health agencies cooperated with the research by referring older people to us. (A listing of those organizations appears as Appendix A.) We gained access to the normal subjects mainly through churches, synagogues, senior centers, and apartment complexes. The functional subjects and those with senile dementia were reached through public welfare departments, community mental health centers, multiservice centers, drop-in centers, meals-on-wheels programs, and family agencies. The older people in the study were assigned to the three mental status groups on a random basis from the pools of the three types of participants referred.

How the Information Was Collected

The original plan had been to ask the older people participating in the study to keep structured diaries about their mental and physical complaints and the actions they took to alleviate them. That approach was abandoned very quickly when we pretested the procedures. We had known that some of the participants (notably those with senile dementia) would not be able to keep diaries at all and had hoped their collaterals could do so. The diaries of the collaterals were not satisfactory, partly because it was necessary for them to make judgments about what the older person was experiencing. Moreover, in the pretest, it was found that the information recorded on the diaries by the older people in the other two groups was sketchy and incomplete.

It was therefore decided that a different approach would be used—the "yesterday" interview. Interviewers trained by the project staff were sent to each participant's home four times, with the interviews spaced at weekly intervals. During each visit, the interviewer reviewed the previous 24 hours—yesterday—with the older person, taking him or her step-by-step through the health experiences of the night and day and noting the responses on an instrument developed by the project staff for that purpose. That instrument was called the "log."

The log was simply a form designed to organize the information provided by the older people about their physical and mental health complaints. Each of the four logs filled out for each participant had several pages. The previous 24-hour day which was the subject of the interview was divided into four periods: morning (from arising until noon), afternoon (from noon to 5 p.m.), evening (from 5 p.m. until retiring), and night (from retiring until arising).

"Tell Me Everything. . . ."

The older people were asked to provide the details—"tell me everything"—of every mental, physical, and emotional experience that had bothered them. That is, the log did not ask about any predetermined symptoms or bothers. Rather, the participants were encouraged to describe their experiences in their own words. As each bother was mentioned, the interviewer asked additional questions about it:

- How often does this happen? The older people rated how often on a four-point scale: never before, occasionally, often, or very often.
- How much did it bother you? Again, the ratings were on a four-point scale: not at all, a little, a medium amount, or a lot.
- Did it interfere with any of your activities (or sleep)? If so, with what activity did it interfere?
- What did you do about it (the symptom or bother)?

At the end of each interview, when all the log information had been noted, the older person was asked a number of open-ended questions such as:

- What enjoyable things did you do today?
- Would you tell me everything you ate or drank today?
- Are there some things you do to prevent yourself from getting sick or to keep yourself healthy?

In short, every effort was made to make the log thorough, in that it invited the older people to mention all bothers whether or not they regarded them as significant, and nontechnical, in that it asked for information in terms that one might use in describing experiences to an interested relative or friend. The answers were recorded in the language used by the older people.

Baseline Questionnaire

Other information was collected in addition to the log data. Each time the interviewer visited an older person, part of a questionnaire was completed to obtain baseline information. The questionnaire asked about such matters as their demographic characteristics, mental and physical health history, functional capacities, patterns of health utilization, and attitudes toward professional health providers.

An important part of the baseline interview was a twenty-symptom checklist. We knew that the four yesterday interviews might have missed any number of symptoms that had not occurred on those particular days. Therefore, after the last interview, the older people were asked if they had experienced any of a prepared list of 20 potential symptoms during the past month. If they had, they were asked if they had told anyone about it and who that person was.

The Characteristics of the People Studied

The social and demographic characteristics of the 132 older people studied are summarized in Table 3–1. Those in the senile dementia (SD) group were the oldest, with an average age of 84, as compared with average ages of 71 and 69 for the normal and functional groups respectively. This is not unexpected, since the incidence of senile dementia is age-linked, rising with advancing age. Other characteristics of the SDs were also consistent with their age and diagnosis; fewer of them were currently married, for example, and many more of them lived with family members (other than spouse). A higher proportion of the normals than of the other two groups lived alone. Widowed older people in all three groups followed the usual pattern in that when they lived with an adult child, they were more likely to live with a daughter than a son. Black and Jewish people were overrepresented in the senile dementia and functional groups as were Jews in all three groups. Twenty-five percent of the normals and 31% of the SDs were foreign born.

The home settings in which these older people were living varied considerably. Some were in low-income areas and others in more comfortable parts of the city. Private homes and apartments were about equally numerous.

Some older people were reluctant to provide information about their incomes, though almost four-fifths did so. Of those about whom information is available about one-third had annual incomes of less than $3,000 if single or $4,000 if married. Another third were above that level but had less than $6,000 if single or $8,400 if married. About one-fourth of the participants received between $6,000 and $10,000 if single or between $8,400 and $14,300 if married. A minority (about 10%) had incomes above those levels.

The normal subjects tended to have more income than the older people in the other two groups. This was reflected in the responses of the participants to a question eliciting their perceptions of the adequacy of their incomes. More than half of the normals, but only 15% of the functional group and 25% of the SDs, replied that they were "comfortable." Sixty-one percent of the functionals, 37% of the normals, and 31% of the SDs felt that they had just enough money to get along. (The replies of those in the SD group who could reply are included although, as is the case with other of their replies, their reliability is questionable.)

Health and Functional Capacities

As part of the baseline interview, the older people also were asked questions about their health and functional capacities, other aspects of their health, their information about health, their utilization of health services, and their attitudes with respect to the health care they were receiving. Only the responses of the normals and functionals are reported here because, as so often was the case, few of those with SD were able to answer the questions appropriately.

Virtually all of the older people had one or more chronic conditions, with an average of six diagnoses. Their most frequent preexisting health conditions and functional incapacities appear on Table 3–2. Like the total population of older people, large proportions of our research participants reported having arthritis, hypertension and circulatory problems, vision and hearing deficits, and other age-related ailments.

The people in the normal group were, in the main, independent in self-care and instrumental activities. Those in the functional group were somewhat more dependent; significant minorities needed help with instrumental activities such as transportation, food shopping, housekeeping, and laundry. The subjects suffering from SD were the most dependent; large proportions needed help with various personal care activities (such as toileting, dressing, grooming, eating, bathing, home mobility), and almost all needed assistance with instrumental activities.

Three out of four subjects felt that they usually or always ate what they should for good health. Those who did not attributed their lack of an adequate diet to financial reasons, difficulties in acquiring or preparing food, poor appetite, lethargy, or overeating.

Sources of Health Care

Most medical care was received from private physicians or clinics. More of the normals (75%) than of the functionals (43%) or SDs (60%) used private physicians. Forty-six percent of the functionals, 32% of the SDs, but only 19% of the normals used clinics as their usual source of medical care. The normals averaged 6.2 physician visits per year, the functionals 8.3 visits, and the SDs 7.6 visits. The notion that older people constantly badger their doctors with phone calls was not supported; about half of them stated they called physicians less than once a year, and only 12% claimed to call as often as once a month. More of the functionals (35%) than of the normals (16%) reported difficulties in visiting their physicians. Among those in both groups who had such difficulties, transportation was the main problem.

Table 3–1. Selected Demographic and Social Characteristics: Percentages by Group

Characteristics	Normal cognitive function N = 51	Functional mental disorders N = 46	Senile dementia N = 35
Age distribution (range 62-98)	mean = 71	mean = 69	mean = 84
62–69	45	52	09
70–79	49	33	20
80+	06	15	66
Sex			
Male	39	20	17
Female	61	80	83
Race			
Black	08	22	34
White	92	78	66
Religion			
Catholic	27	24	06
Jewish	49	33	37
Protestant	22	35	26
Other/none	02	09	06

Marital status			
Married	49	24	11
Separated/divorced	06	06	00
Widowed	41	63	71
Single	04	07	06
Place of birth			
United States	75	98	49
Foreign	25	02	31
Living arrangement			
Alone	37	48	29
With spouse	51	22	11
With daughter	06	13	34
With son	06	04	03
With other relative	00	00	09
With non-relative	00	13	14
Adult child within one hour distance	70	63	68
In touch with at least one child	86	69	74

Source: Reprinted from "Day-to-Day Mental and Physical Health Symptoms of Older People: Report on Health Logs" by Elaine M. Brody and Morton H. Kleban, in The Gerontologist, Vol. 23, No. 1, 1983, p. 77.

Table 3–2. Most Frequent Pre-Existing Health Conditions and Functional Dependencies: Percentages by Groups

Pre-existing health conditions	Normal	Functional	Senile dementia
Arthritis	66	63	56
Foot trouble	45	35	35
Visual impairment	33	56	56
High blood pressure	33	41	53
Circulation problems	31	26	62
Hearing impairment	27	43	26
Diabetes	25	09	24
Elimination problems	22	52	59
Digestive problems	14	33	38
Nervous breakdown	00	40	00

Dependent in	Normal	Functional	Senile dementia
Toileting	00	00	35
Feeding	00	00	26
Dressing	02	05	50
Grooming	00	07	47
Home mobility	00	02	29
Bathing	02	16	79
Cutting toenails	16	44	91
Telephoning	00	02	62
Shopping (food)	16	35	97
Food preparation	02	09	79
Housekeeping	10	23	88
Laundry	08	26	94
Transportation	08	30	82
Taking medications	02	05	82
Handling finances	04	14	97

Note: Data for normal and functional groups obtained from subjects: data about dependencies of SD group obtained from collaterals.
Source: Reprinted from "Day-to-Day Mental and Physical Health Symptoms of Older People: Report on Health Logs" by Elaine M. Brody and Morton H. Kleban, in *The Gerontologist*, Vol. 23, No. 1, 1983, p. 78.

Attitudes toward Health Care

The majority of the people studied were completely satisfied with their medical care (63% of the normals and 70% of the functionals). Of those who were not (34% of the total), the normals most often cited the patient/doctor relationship as the cause of their dissatisfaction, offering such reasons as the doctors' impersonal attitudes, coldness, abruptness, and not paying attention. Other reasons offered by people in both groups for their dissatisfaction were the futility of treatment (no cure, ailments due to age, or "nothing can be done"), convenience factors, and economic costs.

About one-third of the older people were of the opinion that doctors do not take an interest in what happens to their patients, and an equal proportion attributed the same lack of interest to hospital staff. One-quarter felt that doctors tend to give better treatment to younger patients. And more than half questioned physicians' honesty in telling their patients the truth about their health. Despite these attitudes, the overwhelming majority (85%) of these older people felt that a person should always follow the doctor's advice!

In summary, the information from the baseline interviews with the older people begins to illustrate the interlocking of social and health factors—for example, the importance of transportation in providing access to medical care and the relationships among income, services, and nutrition.

How the Study Findings Will Be Reported

The above information, of course, was gleaned from the older people's responses to attitude questions of a survey type. The chapters that follow will move to what was actually happening in their mental and physical health lives—that is, their actual experiences and behaviors.

Chapters 4 and 5 will report the findings from the logs, moving sequentially through its columns: What the symptoms were (including their frequency, degrees of bother, and interference with activities), and what the older people did in response to the symptoms in attempting to relieve their discomfort.

Chapter 6 reports the analysis of the information from the 20-symptom checklist—whether those symptoms had been experienced, and whom (if anyone) the older people had told about them. Since the findings from the log and the 20-symptom checklist complement and supplement each other, this chapter discusses that relationship.

Chapter 7 reports three lifestyle segments of the study. First, there is a description of the measures the older people took routinely to promote health or prevent illness. Second, since a number of the old people in the senile dementia group were totally unresponsive, a special questionnaire was developed for the collaterals who cared for them. The information gleaned from that questionnaire provides a glimpse of the lives of those afflicted older people and their caregivers. Third, the responses of all the participants to the question "What enjoyable things did you do today?" are described.

The final chapter in this part of the book (Chapter 13) is a report on a special qualitative substudy carried out as the main research effort was proceeding. It is an in-depth exploration of how some older persons use lay consultation about their health problems—that is, advice or exchange of information with family members, neighbors, or friends.

4

Information from the Logs: The Day-to-Day Mental and Physical Symptoms

The findings from the four 24-hour logs assembled for each participating older person constitute the main body of information collected by the project. This chapter reports the older people's responses to the log questions about the mental and physical symptoms they experienced, how frequently those symptoms occurred and how distressing they were, and whether or not the symptoms interfered with any of the older people's activities or sleep.

The pervasive themes that emerged regarding the day-to-day health experiences of the people studied were pain, symptoms of emotional/mental distress, and fatigue/weakness/unsteadiness on feet. The extent of discomfort is such that professionals need to ask themselves whether they are fully aware of the day-to-day difficulties experienced by many of the older persons with whom they work.

As stated in Chapter 3, the participants in the study were taken step-by-step through each of four yesterdays, with encouragement to mention in their own words everything that had bothered them mentally, physically, or emotionally during that time. Each bother mentioned triggered an additional series of questions. The analyses of the log will be described sequentially as follows:

- Health incidents: The types of symptoms experienced by the older people (grouped in categories) and the number of times they were reported in the course of the four periods of the four sampled days and nights. (It was possible, therefore, for any given symptom not to be reported at all or to be reported as many as 16 times if, for example, it was experienced four times in each 24-hour period.)
- Frequency of incidents: The respondents' ratings of each symptom they mentioned on a 4-point scale (never before to very often).
- Degrees of bother: The older persons' ratings on a 4-point scale (not at all to a lot) of how much each symptom bothered them.

Much of the material in this chapter first appeared in Brody, E. M. and Kleban, M. H., "Day-to-Day Mental and Physical Health Symptoms of Older People: A Report on Health Logs," *The Gerontologist*, 1983, 23:75–85.

- Interference with activities or sleep: Identification of the activity (or sleep) affected when such interference was present.

In addition, the periods of the day or night during which various symptoms occurred were analyzed.

Before describing the findings, we wish to emphasize the framework within which the information should be viewed.

First, it cannot be assumed that all symptoms reported necessarily required professional attention.

Second, no judgments can be made regarding the comparative significance of the various kinds of symptoms. Rather, they are described to inform health professionals about what goes on in the day-to-day lives of elderly persons as they themselves report their experiences.

Third, the data may not necessarily present a completely accurate picture of all symptoms experienced during the four sampled days and nights. Though some overreporting may have occurred, we think it is more likely that more symptoms were experienced than were captured on the logs. Mental and emotional symptoms may have been underreported, for example, since current cohorts of older people generally are not sophisticated about psychological problems and may be guarded about revealing them. And there undoubtedly was underreporting of all types of symptoms by those with senile dementia.

Despite such qualifications, the descriptive data that follow do provide an initial account of the prevalence and frequency of various types of symptoms among these elderly people, the degrees of discomfort caused, the time of day (or night) at which they are likely to occur, and the extent to which there is interference with activities or sleep. The well-known complex and delicate relationships among different kinds of symptoms and between psyche and soma are illustrated. The often artificial division of physical and mental symptoms again is underlined, since older people are more likely than younger people to experience mental symptoms as physical illness.

The Types of Mental and Physical Health Symptoms: "Tell me everything . . ."

Those 120 older people who could report about their symptoms (12 people with SD could not tell of their own experiences) catalogued a collective grand total of 1,893 mental/physical health symptoms or bothers for the four 24-hour periods during which each person was studied. That is, they averaged 3.9 symptoms for each individual for each reported day. The functionals reported the highest number of symptoms, averaging five per day; the averages for the normals and SDs were 3.1 and 3.5 respectively.

The 1,893 symptoms or bothers reported in the older people's own words were grouped and categorized by the professional staff of the project, which included a master's level R.N., a psychologist, and a social worker, all with long experience in gerontology.

Table 4–1 displays for each of the three groups, and for the three groups together, the types of complaints reported spontaneously, the number of incidents in each category, and the number and proportion of persons who experienced each type of symptom. The responses of the 23 out of 35 people with SD who could respond to some extent are included in the table. (The mean score on the Kahn-Goldfarb MSQ was 3.6 correct answers for the 23 people with SD who made some responses and 1.2 for the 12 who did not respond at all.) It should be kept in mind, however, that the older people in that group varied in the degree of their cognitive impairment and capacity to respond. The information they provided cannot be considered to be complete and reliable.

Many categories of symptoms are self-explanatory, since the category labels generally reflect the actual words used by the people in describing their health experiences. In reporting on pain or aches, they identified the site of the discomfort and often volunteered the information that pain in the extremities and back was due to arthritis or rheumatism. The fatigue/weakness/unsteady-on-feet category includes such complaints as "felt bone weary," "very tired," "physically exhausted," "awoke feeling washed out," "no strength in body," "weak and tired," and "weak all over." The digestive discomfort category is comprised mainly of complaints of indigestion, upset stomach, or gas. When the participant reported getting up at night to urinate, the interviewer asked how many times this had occurred during that particular night; after consultation with a urologist and geriatrician, only those who rose three or more times a night were counted as having nocturia.

As shown on the table, the symptoms grouped as mental health complaints include depression, nervousness/anxiety/tension, loneliness, boredom, restlessness, and other negative emotions and subjective experiences. An expression of a wish to cry or to die was considered to be depression. Complaints such as "nervous like my head would burst," "nervous like I'm coming apart," "overwrought," and "felt like I'd explode" were assigned to the nervousness/anxiety/tension category. The loneliness category includes complaints in which that word was actually used and linked to an absence of other people, such as "cut off from others," "alone and demoralized," or "no one around." Other negative emotions expressed were "felt sad" or "felt afraid," and, in the case of the SDs, statements such as "I felt crazy," "I don't know

Table 4-1. Types and Number of Symptoms Reported by Number and Percentages of Subjects Reporting Them

Types of symptoms	Normal (N = 51)			Functional (N = 46)			Senile dementia (N = 23)			Total (N = 120)		
	No. of reports	No. of subjects	Percentage of subjects	No. of reports	No. of subjects	Percentage of subjects	No. of reports	No. of subjects	Percentage of subjects	No. of reports	No. of subjects	Percentage of subjects
Pain (all types combined)	256	32	63*	372	38	83*	125	17	74	753	87	73
Extremities, hip, neck, back, feet	164	24	47	195	31	67	66	14	61	425	69	58
Head	28	8	16	64	18	39	18	10	44	110	36	30
Chest	19	9	18	36	14	30	16	8	35	71	31	26
Eyes and ears	19	7	14	30	10	22	6	4	17	55	21	18
Overall aches and pains	7	4	08	21	9	20	18	4	17	46	17	14
Mouth and throat	6	1	02	9	6	13	—	—	—	15	7	06
Rectum	3	2	04	13	2	04	1	1	04	17	5	04
Skin	9	1	02	—	—	—	—	—	—	9	1	001
Teeth	1	1	02	4	3	07	—	—	—	5	4	03
Fatigue/weakness/unsteady on feet	93	33	65	116	32	70	62	15	65	271	80	67
Mental health symptoms	38	20	39**	156	35	76*,**	45	11	48**	239	66	55
Depression	4	2	04	48	18	39	10	5	22	62	25	21
Boredom and restlessness	3	3	06	7	6	13	2	2	09	12	11	09
Loneliness	—	—	—	19	11	24	8	4	17	27	15	13
Nervousness/anxiety/tension	4	3	06	31	14	30	3	3	13	38	20	17
Negative emotions (sadness, fear, etc.)	6	5	10	9	6	13	12	7	30	27	18	15
Sleep problems (wakefulness, nightmares)	21	14	28	42	23	50	10	5	22	73	42	35

Worries (all types combined)	78	28	55	86	25	54	37	9	39	201	62	52
About self (physical health, cognitive decline, ADL decline)	30	15	30	28	14	30	17	5	22	75	34	28
About other people (family & friends)	23	14	28	37	16	35	16	6	26	76	36	30
Physical environment (household & neighborhood)	15	10	20	12	5	11	3	2	09	30	17	14
Money	10	7	14	9	5	11	1	1	04	20	13	11
Upsets (reactions to events or conditions)	47	22	43	50	22	48	19	8	35	116	52	43
Digestive discomfort	36	12	24	34	11	24	10	3	13	80	26	22
Fever/colds	23	12	24	28	14	30	9	6	26	60	32	27
Nocturia (3 or more times during each night)	23	12	24	28	16	35	7	4	17	58	32	27
Other symptoms	42	19	37*	60	28	61*	13	11	48	115	58	48
Dry mouth, hangover, thirst	6	6	12	21	14	30	4	3	13	31	23	19
Numbness & tingling in extremities	9	5	10	18	8	17	5	4	17	32	17	14
Elimination problems (constipation, diarrhea)	4	2	04	12	8	17	2	2	09	18	12	10
Swellings (feet, legs, etc.)	17	5	10	7	3	07	2	1	04	26	9	08
Skin (bruises or rash)	2	2	04	2	2	04	—	—	—	4	4	03
Stiffness	4	3	06	—	—	—	—	—	—	4	3	03
Total	636 (M 3.1 subject day)			930 (M 5 subject day)			327 (M 3.5 subject day)			1893 (M 3.94 subject day)		

Note: t-test for independent proportions employed for data analysis.

*Functional > Normal, $p \leq .05$

**Functional > SD, $p \leq .05$

Source: Reprinted from "Day-to Day Mental and Physical Health Symptoms of Older People: Report on Health Logs" by Elaine M. Brody and Morton H. Kleban, in *The Gerontologist,* Vol. 23, No. 1, 1983, p. 79.

what I do half the time," "My mind is confused," "I feel in a fog," "I'm afraid to go to bed (or sit on the toilet or of thunder or of going out)."

"Worries" and "upsets" each were categorized separately from the other mental/emotional health complaints because (by contrast with complaints labelled "mental health symptoms"), those actual words were used and linked to a specific source of the worry or upset.

Prevalence of Various Complaints

Pain was the most frequent and prevalent complaint reported, with mental health symptoms and fatigue/weakness following closely.

Pain was reported at least once by three-fourths of the older people, and fatigue/weakness was reported at least once by two-thirds of them. Mental health symptoms, worries, and upsets were reported respectively by 55%, 52%, and 43% of the respondents. Other symptoms bothering 20% to 30% of the older people were nocturia, digestive difficulties, and fever and colds.

The proportion of people who experienced a given symptom at least once, however, does not indicate the frequency with which it was reported on the logs. Pain of various types was the most frequently reported symptom; the 753 reports of pain accounted for 38% of all bothers: pain in the extremities, hip, neck, and back predominated, accounting for more than half of all pain reports. Ten percent of the complaints in this category were of foot problems such as callouses, corns, and bunions.

All emotional/mental bothers together—that is, mental health symptoms, worries, and upsets—accounted for about 28% of all symptoms reported. Within this combined category were 239 reports (12% of all reports) of mental health symptoms (such as depression and anxiety); 201 reports (10% of the total) of worries about various matters (their own declining health and functional capacities, health and problems of family and friends, the household and neighborhood, environment, and money); and 116 upsets (6% of the total).

Next in order of the frequency with which it occurred (271 incidents or 13.6% of the total) was the group of symptoms including fatigue, weakness, and unsteadiness on feet. These usually were reported in terms of the difficulties encountered in carrying out various activities of daily living ("I felt so weak that I couldn't go out").

Group Similarities and Differences in Symptom Reports

Some symptoms were relatively even-handed in bothering large proportions of the people in each of the three groups. These symptoms were fatigue/weakness, worries (primarily about their own declining health and about relatives and friends), and upsets.

There were, however, some significant differences among the three groups. For example, the functionals surpassed the normals in reporting more pain and more mental health symptoms (nervousness/tension, depression, loneliness, sleep problems). The higher frequency of some symptoms among people in that group should not obscure the fact that noteworthy proportions of the other two groups also reported them. Thus, three-quarters of the SD group and two-thirds of the normals as well as 83% of the functionals reported pain. Forty-seven percent of the normals reported pain in the extremities and back as did 67% of the functionals and 61% of the SDs. Sleep problems were reported by 28% of the normals and 22% of the SD group as well as by half of the functionals.

Frequency of Symptoms: "How Often Does This Happen?"

Pain, fatigue/weakness, and mental/emotional distress were rated by the older people as occurring very often.

Table 4–2 summarizes for the most commonly reported symptoms the percentages of people responding on a four-point scale to the question "How often does this happen?" The chronicity of certain major types of symptoms is apparent, since 62% of the people reporting pain stated that they experienced pain symptoms very often and high percentages made that response when they experienced fatigue/weakness (59%), mental health symptoms (54%), worries (40%), and nocturia (86%). Chest pain, digestive problems, and upsets were exceptions to this pattern, being more evenly distributed along the four points of the scale.

Degrees of Bother: "How Much Did It Bother You?"

The most bothersome symptoms were emotional or mental distress and pain.

As each symptom was reported, the older people were asked to rate the degree to which it was bothersome on a four-point scale: not at all, very little, a medium amount, or a lot. Since they reported some symptoms more than once and those symptoms sometimes bothered them in different degrees at different times, each individual's responses were classified in terms of the modal "bother" rating across all instances of a given symptom category. Table 4–3 displays the proportions of people in each group whose modal bother ratings fell into the "a lot" or "medium amount" categories for each type of symptom.

Rated as being most bothersome—that is, rated "a lot"—were worries (73%) and mental health symptoms (48%). Pain and upsets each bothered 40% of those reporting them "a lot," digestive problems 46%, fatigue/weakness 30%, fever/colds 22%, and nocturia 22%.

The functionals generally tended more than the normals to rate their symptoms as bothering them "a lot," particularly mental health symptoms

Table 4–2. Number and Percentage of Responses for Most Commonly Reported Symptoms

	Never before		Occasionally		Often		Very often		Total	
	N	%	N	%	N	%	N	%	N	%
Pain (all types combined)	19	03	121	16	140	19	463	62	743	100
Extremities	11	03	55	13	70	17	287	68	423	101
Head	3	03	29	28	21	20	52	50	105	101
Chest	2	03	19	27	26	37	23	33	70	100
Eyes and ears	2	04	8	15	7	13	37	69	54	101
Overall	—	—	6	13	12	26	28	61	46	100
Fatigue/weakness/unsteady on feet	5	02	57	22	47	18	155	59	264	101
Mental health symptoms	4	02	61	26	43	18	126	54	234	100
Worries (all types combined)	26	13	53	27	39	20	79	40	197	100
Upsets (reactions to events or conditions)	20	17	40	35	23	20	32	28	115	100
Digestive discomfort	4	05	26	35	19	25	26	35	75	100
Fever/colds	2	03	21	36	5	08	31	53	59	100
Nocturia (3 or more times during each night)	1	02	3	05	4	07	49	86	57	100

Note: Percentages sometimes do not sum to 100 due to rounding effects.
Source: Reprinted from "Day-to-Day Mental and Physical Health Symptoms of Older People: Report on Health Logs" by Elaine M. Brody and Morton H. Kleban, in *The Gerontologist*, Vol. 23, No. 1, 1983, p. 80.

Table 4-3. Percentages of Subjects Experiencing the Symptom who Were Bothered "A Lot" or "A Medium Amount"

Symptom	Group 1 (Normals) (N = 51)		Group 2 (Functionals) (N = 46)		Group 3 (SD) (N = 23)		Total (N = 120)	
	A lot	A lot or med. amt.	A lot	A lot or med. amt.	A lot	A lot or med. amt.	A lot	A lot or med. amt.
Pain (all types combined)	41	66	42	84	29	71	39	75
Fatigue/weakness/unsteady on feet	15	30*	41	78*	40	60	30	55
Mental health symptoms (depression, anxiety, etc.)	25*	35*	63*	74*	46	73	48	62
Worries (all types combined)	68	86	80	96	67	78	73	89
Upsets	36	55	46	77	38	75	40	67
Digestive discomfort	33	58	55	100	67	100	46	81
Fever/colds	08	50	36	57	17	50	22	53
Nocturia (3 or more times during each night)	33	42	19	38	—	25	22	38

Note: t-test for independent proportions employed for data analysis.

*Functional > Normal, $p \leq .05$. Group 3 was not included in statistical tests for group differences because these respondents were unable to rate how much they were bothered by many of the symptoms they reported.

Source: Reprinted from "Day-to-Day Mental and Physical Health Symptoms of Older People: Report on Health Logs" by Elaine M. Brody and Morton H. Kleban, in *The Gerontologist*, Vol. 23, No. 1, 1983, p. 81.

and fatigue. Even when differences were not statistically significant or were not tested because of small numbers, they were invariably in the same direction.

Interference with Activities or Sleep

Pain interfered with daytime activities, while mental or emotional distress disturbed sleep.

Of the 1,893 symptoms reported, 686 (or 36%) resulted in interference with some activity or sleep. Table 4–4 displays the number of activities disturbed, the proportion of all disturbances caused by the different symptoms, and the types of activities disturbed by given symptoms.

Pain, which disturbed the largest proportion of participants, also accounted for the highest proportion (40%) of activity disturbances—principally, activities involving physical movement such as walking and household activities or chores, but also affecting sleep and social and leisure activities. Fewer activities (14%) were disturbed by fatigue/weakness; the activities disturbed were similar but relatively more frequent for household chores than for walking and other types of movement.

Emotional and mental symptoms in all categories—such as mental health symptoms, worries, and upsets—accounted for 30% of all disturbances. They did not interfere greatly with the older people's daytime physical activities but disturbed their sleep considerably. Digestive problems and fever/colds account for small proportions of all disturbances, but when experienced, they disrupted sleep. Fever/colds were reported to disturb "everything" by some people. And digestive problems (expectedly) affected eating.

Time of Day: "When Did It Happen?"

Of the four segments of the day about which the participants reported, the overall pattern was that physical symptoms (pain, fatigue, digestive problems, and colds/fever) were most bothersome in the morning rather than in the afternoon or evening. Sleep generally provided some relief. (See Table 4–5.)

The night sleeping hours also provided the people with some respite from worries and upsets but not from mental health problems, which often were expressed as sleep disturbances.

Discussion of the Findings

The beginning of this chapter emphasized that the data from this exploratory study do not represent a complete account of all the health experiences of the older people, nor can it be stated that all the symptoms reported required

Table 4-4. Symptoms, Disturbances, and Activities Disturbed by Symptoms

Symptom	No. of symptom reports	No. of disturbances	Percentage of reports considered disturbing	Percentage of all disturbances	Percentages of activities disturbed by symptoms							
					Everything	Sleep	Household Activities, Chores	Eating	Social & Leisure Activities	Walking, Movement	Other	Total
Pain (all types combined)	753	272	36	40	09	19	20	03	14	30	06	101
Fatigue/weakness/unsteady on feet	271	98	36	14	11	04	41	02	15	17	09	99
Mental health symptoms (depression, anxiety, etc.)	239	107	45	16	12	65	08	02	07	02	06	102
Worries (all types combined)	201	51	25	08	12	55	08	00	10	02	14	101
Upsets	116	40	34	06	08	35	08	05	13	10	23	102
Digestive discomfort	80	37	46	05	05	32	08	49	03	00	03	100
Fever/colds	60	14	23	02	29	43	00	00	07	07	14	100
Nocturia (3 or more times during the night)	58	30	52	04	00	100	00	00	00	00	00	100
Other symptoms	115	37	32	05	03	24	08	11	11	32	11	100
Total	1893	686	36	100								

Note: Percentages sometimes do not sum to 100 due to rounding effects.

Source: Reprinted from "Day-to-Day Mental and Physical Health Symptoms of Older People: Report on Health Logs" by Elaine M. Brody and Morton H. Kleban, in *The Gerontologist,* Vol. 23, No. 1, 1983, p. 81.

Table 4-5. Period of the Day (or Night) During Which Symptoms Occurred: Percentages of Symptom Reports

Symptom	Morning	Afternoon	Evening	Night	Total
Pain (all types combined)	36	29	25	09	99
Fatigue/weakness/unsteady on feet	44	32	21	04	101
Mental health symptoms (depression, anxiety, etc.)	22	18	22	38	100
Worries (all types combined)	27	27	32	14	100
Upsets	30	33	26	11	100
Digestive discomfort	35	28	25	13	101
Fever/colds	35	30	25	10	100

Note: Percentages sometimes do not sum to 100 due to rounding effects.
Source: Reprinted from "Day-to-Day Mental and Physical Health Symptoms of Older People: Report on Health Logs" by Elaine M. Brody and Morton H. Kleban, in *The Gerontologist*, Vol. 23, No. 1, 1983, p. 82.

professional attention. The purpose was to obtain information from the perspective of the participants themselves on the mental and physical health experiences they found bothersome.

Any interpretation of the information reported must take into account the complex and delicate relationships among the different types of symptoms and between psyche and soma. Both elderly patients and health professionals may misattribute symptoms—that is, interpret physical symptoms as mental problems and vice versa (Weiss, 1981). In addition, it is generally accepted that the distinction between mental and physical symptoms is, to some extent, artificial and that older people are more likely than younger people to experience mental symptoms as physical illness. In reviewing the literature, Kart (1981) concluded that the elderly attribute too many symptoms to the aging process per se and warns that such misattributions may have tragic consequences.

Pain, which was the most frequent and prevalent complaint of the older people in this study, illustrates this clearly. Pain not only bothered more people more often than any other types of symptom, but it interfered with daily activities more than other symptoms and was reported to cause a great deal of bother. The large number of pain reports undoubtedly reflects the unrelenting nature of pain and is consistent with the large number of the older people who had reported having a diagnosis of arthritis. Davis and colleagues (1980) emphasize that "the dichotomy between organic and psychogenic pain is not only difficult to define operationally, but also not heuristically valuable." They point out that pain sensitivity is altered in some psychiatric illnesses and that the symptoms of depression and the effects (physiological, behavioral, and affective) of chronic pain are quite similar. Both are typically reported, for example, as loss of appetite and sleep disturbances.

Further complications are noted by Butler and Gastel, who report that in older people

- "there is a tendency . . . for pain to be referred from the site or origin to other parts of the body;
- some diseases may produce only behavioral changes (that is, confusion, restlessness, and fatigue);
- multiple diseases may simultaneously produce pain in the same part of the body;
- psychological and social problems (such as loneliness, boredom, fear, and depression) can contribute to pain." (1980)

Those authors therefore underline the need for careful differential diagnoses when pain is a presenting symptom in any part of the body. In addition, since the literature indicates that little is known concerning pain tolerance or the effects of pain related to pathology in older people (see

Harkins & Warner, 1980), there is a great need for systematic evaluation of the prevalence and characteristics of discomfort, clinical pain, chronic pain, and suffering in the aged.

Whatever its etiology—physiological or psychological, and recognizing that there are varying reactions deriving from personal characteristics and cultural differences—the amount of pain reported by the older people in this study is impressive.

Fatigue/weakness, which also afflicted so many of these individuals, also underlines subtle mind/body relationships. Depression, for example, often masquerades as fatigue, and fatigue is likely to be regarded by older people as a normal consequence of aging.

In view of the known underreporting of symptoms, attitudes of older people that nothing can be done, professional pessimism, and other indications of under treatment, concerted efforts to reduce these large reservoirs of pain and fatigue are indicated—including sensitivity to its existence, by appropriate diagnosis, treatment, and management, and certainly through further research.

The high reporting of mental health symptoms, worries, and upsets also merits professional attention. More of the older people with a history of functional mental disorder reported depression, anxiety, and related symptoms on many more occasions than their peers in the other two groups, a finding that is, of course, consistent with their diagnosis. Emotional distress described as worries and upsets, on the other hand, was experienced by roughly equal proportions of the three groups and with similar frequency, undoubtedly because those terms are used by all people in common parlance, as contrasted with more explicitly named mental health symptoms.

While worries and upsets are not unique to older persons, the sources to which many were attributed suggest their relationship to age. Many reports of worries, for example, were linked to the declining health and functional capacities of the older people themselves or of their family members and friends (not unexpected when spouses or friends are also in old age and adult children are so often in late middle age). Similarly, the causes of the upsets were often suggestive of age-related vulnerability—"I was upset because it rained (or snowed) so I couldn't go out," "I had to wait a long time in the doctor's office." Such events may be relatively minor, but they add up, and daily hassles have been shown to be capable of producing psychiatric symptoms (Kanner et al., 1981).

Significantly, these three types of emotional/mental symptoms (mental health symptoms, worries, and upsets), when experienced, were rated as causing "a lot" of bother more often than physical symptoms. Since so few older people are served by mental health professionals and so few are likely to seek such help on their own, health professionals have a responsibility to be alert and responsive to this aspect of their patients' lives and to make appropriate referrals when indicated.

The predominance of pain, fatigue/weakness, and various emotional-mental bothers should not obscure the importance of other symptoms reported. For example, though reported by fewer subjects, nocturia and digestive problems each affected roughly one-quarter of the subjects. Both may signal acute problems amenable to treatment and requiring prompt attention.

The differences among the three groups are, in the main, consistent with the differences in their mental status. Those with normal mental functioning are most similar to the noninstitutionalized elderly usually described as the "well aged." Yet large majorities frequently experienced pain and fatigue/weakness with significant degrees of bother and activity interference. Though the normals usually did not use words like anxiety and depression to describe mental/emotional complaints, as stated above, many reported sleep disturbances and worries that were primarily age-related.

A pattern emerged in which subjective (such as pain), mental health, and autonomic symptoms (such as dry mouth) but not symptoms of more probable somatic origin were more frequent among the people in the functional group. The functionals invariably tended to rate their symptoms as more bothersome than did the normals and, in the baseline interview, reported more preexisting health conditions than the normals. It is not known, of course, whether they actually experienced more symptoms and more discomfort than the normals or simply reported more. In any event, we do not interpret their reporting to mean that they malinger or imagine the symptoms they report. Rather, they may be more vulnerable to symptoms of any kind and/or experience more distress when they occur.

Large majorities of the normals frequently experienced pain and fatigue/weakness with significant discomfort and activity interference. They should not be dismissed as merely complainers. Some older people with troubling symptoms do not voice their complaints, while others express their distress.

Data derived from those with senile dementia are, of course, incomplete. One-third could not respond at all, and the rest varied in their capacities to respond; the same individual sometimes could respond on one interview day but not the next and to some questions but not others. Even so, they averaged more reported symptoms than those in the normal group. Unquestionably they experience many more bothers than they reported; they were considerably older than the other two groups, much more impaired functionally, and, in general, exemplified the significant correlation between senile dementia and physical disease.

Attention is called to the fact that two-thirds of the elderly people with senile dementia did indeed respond to some extent to the questions they were asked. Older people with this diagnosis often are omitted from research studies with the rationale that they are unable to communicate. It is suggested that such exclusion is not well-founded and impedes the development of knowledge about people who are among the most disabled and deprived of all the elderly and whose condition has a profound impact on family members.

Despite their limitations, those older people were able to tell us, however incompletely, about their pain, their worries, their fatigue, and other bothers. However unreliable, their reports often were roughly proportionate in nature and degree of bother to the reports of the people in the other groups.

And some of their responses allow a glimpse of their inner world and amorphous anxieties:

> "I felt crazy."
> "I don't know what I do half the time."
> "I feel in a fog."
> "I'm afraid to go to bed."
> "I'm afraid to sit on the toilet."
> "I'm afraid of thunder."
> "I'm afraid of going out."

The silence of the one-third of those with senile dementia who could not articulate their experiences at all is particularly poignant. How much of their suffering is unmarked and, therefore, unrelieved?

Overall, pain, fatigue, and emotional discomfort are major themes in the lives of this sample of older people. The intimate relationships among physical functioning and emotional well-being are underscored. Such information reinforces the critical need to sort out the highly varied problems via an interdisciplinary approach and to make special efforts to elicit information that often is unreported. Health professionals must judge for themselves the extent to which they are aware of how their older patients' diagnoses color and limit those patients' day-to-day lives. Apart from issues of prevention and cure, the important question is: What measures can be taken to alleviate the discomfort the older people experience and endure on a day-to-day basis?

5 What the Older People Did about Their Symptoms

This chapter reports what two of the groups of older people studied—the normals and those with functional mental disorders—did in response to the many mental and physical health symptoms they experienced (described in the previous chapter). The group with senile dementia is not included in this analysis because of their inability to respond to the questions asking what actions they had taken.

As we will see, some action was taken in response to four out of five of the symptoms experienced; those actions include taking many drugs—prescription drugs, over-the-counter drugs, and drugs the older people could not identify. Practically none of any of the symptoms logged were reported to health professionals. (It should be kept in mind, however, that the older people had been invited to report everything, whether or not they considered the symptom to be important or serious.) Overall, the findings from this part of the survey strongly suggest that older people need education about health matters and that health professionals need considerably more information about the actual health practices of their elderly patients.

Before the specific findings are described, it is emphasized that the factors determining how people of all ages behave in response to health problems are complex and interacting. They include the individual's health motivation; perceptions of vulnerability to illness and its potential severity; beliefs about the effectiveness of alternative actions and about the physical, economic, and psychological costs associated with those actions; and personal characteristics such as age, sex, socioeconomic status, knowledge, and general coping ability (Becker et al., 1977).

While most of the research on health behaviors concerns younger populations, many of the same factors undoubtedly are at work in the health behaviors of the elderly. There are, however, additional considerations that relate to the seeking of preventive or ameliorative care by the aged and to the ways in which they manage their ailments. As Chapter 1 indicated, older people have more health conditions than younger people. They are likely, therefore, to have many more symptoms. Moreover, the problems of older people often are different in nature from those of younger people. In the

Some of the material in this chapter was included in Brody, E. M., Johnsen, P. T., Fulcomer, M. C., & Lang, A. M., "Women's Changing Roles and Help to Elderly Parents: Attitudes of Three Generations of Women," *Journal of Gerontology*, 1983, 38:597–607.

main, the illnesses of the elderly are characterized by chronicity; mental and physical problems are highly correlated and often interact with each other; and the symptoms of one impairment in one sphere may mask those in the other(s). The chronic ailments tend to lead to disability and, in turn, to dependence on others.

There is no doubt but that the "multiplicity, chronicity, and duplicity" (Zeman, 1965) of older people's health problems and the resulting disability present special diagnostic and treatment challenges for professionals. However, they also pose special and difficult problems for older people themselves in determining when to seek care and in complying with medical advice. Moreover, the capacity of the elderly to comply may be complicated by the very conditions that are common among the aged, such as diminished vision and hearing, functional deficits, and the confusion and forgetfulness associated with cognitive impairments.

By now, the universal emphasis by geriatricians on the importance of preventive care, early detection of illness, early intervention, and ongoing monitoring needs no further elaboration. Without such care, health problems may continue unabated, go beyond the point at which they can be treated successfully, and lead to dependency. The implementation of such health surveillance relies, of course, on many factors other than the characteristics of the elderly patients and their health-related behaviors—factors such as health care systems geared to active case-finding and chronic care, and the training, attitudes, and behaviors of health professionals.

If health professionals are to give appropriate care to older people, it is necessary for them to have detailed information not only about diagnosed health conditions and compliance with medical regimens prescribed for those conditions but about the actions they take to ameliorate their day-to-day symptoms.

What the Older People Did about Their Symptoms

As indicated in Chapter 3, each time a symptom or bother was reported by the participants in the study, they were asked a series of questions including, "What did you do about it?" The answers were noted on the logs in each respondent's own words and later were categorized and grouped by the master's-level R.N. on our staff.

Only the most frequently reported categories of symptoms and the most frequently reported remedies were used for the analysis in this chapter—specifically, the main types of pain, fatigue/weakness, mental and emotional bothers, digestive problems, and nocturia. The findings on those symptoms will be reported in turn.

Again, the reader is cautioned about generalizing the findings to all older people. It also should be noted that the tables summarizing the findings are based on the number of older people who experienced each of the various types of symptoms, so that the number of people varies with each symptom category. The tables also are based on the sheer number of remedies of various types. Since some of the people reported more instances of symptoms of various types and therefore more remedies than did others, the data on the tables should be interpreted only on a descriptive level. Statistical tests for differences between the groups were not used because the various remedies were used by small numbers of people.

Remedies for Pain. Table 5–1 displays the remedies for the three most frequently reported types of pain: pain in the extremities/hip/back, chest pain, and head pain. (Because the sample was small, other types of pain—in eyes, mouth, throat, rectum, teeth, skin, and overall aches—were reported too infrequently to permit meaningful descriptive analysis of the different remedies.)

Fifty-five of the older people had reported experiencing 394 episodes of pain in the extremities/hip/back during the four days each individual was studied. The most frequent action they took to alleviate such pain was to take medicine; that action constituted 22% of all responses. Thirty-nine percent of the 87 doses taken were prescription drugs, 40% were OTC (over-the-counter) preparations, and 21% could not be identified by the subjects. Virtually all of the prescription and OTC drugs were analgesics. Applications of heat or cold constituted 15% of the remedies, and applications of ointments or other preparations (such as alcohol, vasoline, and liniments) were 12% of the remedies. The elderly participants also responded to pain by resting, sleeping, or decreasing their activity (11% of the remedies) and by positioning (12% of the remedies). Only about 1% of these pain symptoms were reported to professionals.

Sixty-one episodes of chest pain had been reported by 23 individuals, and 81 episodes of head pain had been reported by 26 people. The most frequent remedies for such pain taken by both groups were to take medication and to rest, sleep, or reduce activity. About 70% of the drug doses taken for chest pain and a similar proportion of those taken for head pain were either OTC drugs or could not be identified by the older people who took them. Of the medication doses for chest pain, the prescription drugs were cardiac medications and the OTC drugs were a mix of analgesics and antacids. Almost all of the prescription and OTC drugs taken for head pain were analgesics. Reports to professionals were rare for both types of pain.

Remedies for Fatigue/Weakness/Unsteadiness on Feet. Two hundred-twenty such symptoms were reported by 65 participants. As indicated on Table 5–2, about half of the remedies taken were to rest or sleep; others were to take medications (such as analgesics or vitamins), to increase social or leisure activity, and to take nourishment. None of these symptoms was reported to professionals.

Table 5–1. Numbers and Percentages of Remedies for Three Types of Pain by Mental Status Group

	Normal Subjects						Functionally Disturbed Subjects						All Subjects					
	Pain in Extremities, Hip, Neck, Back (n = 24)		Chest Pain (n = 9)		Head Pain (n = 8)		Pain in Extremities, Hip, Neck, Back (n = 31)		Chest Pain (n = 14)		Head Pain (n = 18)		Pain in Extremities, Hip, Neck, Back (n = 55)		Chest Pain (n = 23)		Head Pain (n = 26)	
	No.	%	No.	%	No.	%	No.	%	No.	%	No.	%	No.	%	No.	%	No.	%
Nothing	47	24	4	16	12	52	41	21	3	8	8	14	88	22	7	11	20	25
All medications	30	16	12	48	8	35	57	29	14	39	35	60	87	22	26	43	43	53
Prescription medications	15	50	4	33	1	12	19	33	4	29	12	34	34	39	8	31	13	30
Over-the-counter medications	11	37	6	50	7	88	24	42	7	50	19	54	35	40	13	50	26	61
Unidentified medications	4	13	2	17	—	—	14	25	3	21	4	11	18	21	5	19	4	9
Applied treatments (heat or cold)	31	16	—	—	—	—	29	15	—	—	—	—	60	15	—	—	—	—
Applied ointments or other preparations	23	12	—	—	—	—	24	12	—	—	—	—	47	12	—	—	—	—
Rest, sleep, decreased activity	20	10	4	16	—	—	25	13	10	28	8	14	45	11	14	23	8	10
Positioning or exercise	34	18	—	—	—	—	15	8	—	—	—	—	49	12	—	—	—	—
Increased activity (social, leisure, chores)	4	2	—	—	—	—	5	3	—	—	—	—	9	2	—	—	—	—
Contact of health professional	4	2	1	4	—	—	—	—	2	6	2	3	4	1	3	5	2	2
Other*	1	1	4	16	3	13	4	2	7	19	5	9	5	1	11	18	8	10
TOTAL	194	100	25	100	23	100	200	100	36	100	58	100	394	100	61	100	81	100

*Other remedies were those used less than a total of five times (except for contacting a health professional): thought, eating or drinking, crying or worrying, and going to bathroom.

Source: Reprinted with permission from "What Older People Do About Their Day-to-Day Mental and Physical Health Symptoms" by Elaine M. Brody, Morton H. Kleban, and Elizabeth Moles, in Journal of the American Geriatrics Society, Vol. 31, No. 8, August 1983, p. 493.

Table 5–2. Numbers and Percentages of Remedies for Fatigue and Weakness, Digestive Discomfort, and Nocturia*

| | Fatigue and Weakness | | | | | | Digestive Discomfort | | | | | | Nocturia | | | | | |
| | Normal Subjects (n = 33) | | Functionally Disturbed Subjects (n = 32) | | All Subjects (n = 65) | | Normal Subjects (n = 12) | | Functionally Disturbed Subjects (n = 11) | | All Subjects (n = 23) | | Normal Subjects (n = 12) | | Functionally Disturbed Subjects (n = 16) | | All Subjects (n = 28) | |
	No.	%	No.	%	No.	%	No.	%	No.	%	No.	%	No.	%	No.	%	No.	%
Nothing	15	13	14	13	29	13	4	10	1	3	5	6	8	29	7	23	15	25
Rest, sleep, decreased activity	49	44	56	52	105	48	7	17	6	16	13	16	8	29	7	23	15	25
All medications	10	9	14	13	24	11	18	44	19	50	37	47	—	—	—	—	—	—
Prescription medications	1	10	6	44	7	29	4	22	2	10	6	16	—	—	—	—	—	—
Over-the-counter medications	4	40	3	21	7	29	12	67	15	80	27	73	—	—	—	—	—	—
Unidentified medications	5	50	5	35	10	42	2	11	2	10	4	11	—	—	—	—	—	—
Increased activity (social, leisure, chores)	13	12	12	11	25	11	—	—	—	—	—	—	—	—	—	—	—	—
Eating, drinking	14	13	4	4	18	8	8	20	4	11	12	15	—	—	—	—	—	—
Going to bathroom	—	—	—	—	—	—	1	2	4	11	5	6	9	32	15	48	24	41
Contact of health professional	—	—	—	—	—	—	1	2	1	3	2	3	—	—	—	—	—	—
Other†	11	10	8	7	19	9	2	5	3	8	5	6	3	11	2	7	5	8
TOTAL	112	100	108	100	220	100	41	100	38	100	79	100	28	100	31	100	59	100

*After consultation with a urologist and a geriatrician, nocturia was defined arbitrarily as getting up three or more times at night to urinate.
†Other remedies were those used less than a total of five times (except for contacting a health professional): applied treatment, thought, exercise, positioning, applied preparation, and crying or worrying.

Source: Reprinted with permission from "What Older People Do About Their Day-to-Day Mental and Physical Health Symptoms" by Elaine M. Brody, Morton H. Kleban, and Elizabeth Moles, in *Journal of the American Geriatrics Society,* Vol. 31, No. 8, August 1983, p. 494.

Remedies for Digestive Problems.   Seventy-one symptoms were reported by 23 people (Table 5–2). Medicine (mainly OTC antacids) were taken in response to about half of these complaints. About 3% of these symptoms were reported to professionals.

Remedies for Nocturia.   Twenty-eight participants reported 59 episodes of nocturia. (After consultation with a urologist and a geriatrician, nocturia was defined as getting up at night three or more times in order to urinate. Virtually all of the people in the study reported getting up at least once or twice during the night for that purpose.) Going to the bathroom and going back to sleep were virtually the only responses; none of the episodes was reported to professionals.

Remedies for Mental/Emotional Bothers.   Table 5–3 displays the subjects' responses to the three types of such symptoms—that is, mental health symptoms, worries, and upsets. As indicated in Chapter 4, mental health symptoms were specific complaints such as anxiety, depression, nervousness, and irrational fears. Worries were linked primarily to the older people's own declining health and functional capacities, similar conditions in relatives and friends, and environmental hazards. Upsets were incidents occurring during the day. The remedies taken for these three types of mental/emotional bothers were primarily increasing or decreasing activity and thinking and problem solving. Only about 7% of the responses were to take medicine (most of which were prescription drugs). Only 1% of these symptoms were reported to professionals.

Discussion of the Study

It is apparent that in attempting to alleviate their discomfort, the elderly people in the study took some action in response to the vast majority of their day-to-day mental and physical health symptoms.

We make no judgments about whether or not the actions taken were appropriate. But the findings suggest that there is no one-to-one relationship between the doctor's prescription for treatment for a diagnosed condition and the elderly patient's treatment of the symptoms of that condition. In their baseline interviews, for example (see Chapter 3), three-fifths of the older people studied had reported having a diagnosis of arthritis; of those, slightly more than half reported taking medicines, four-fifths of which were prescribed by their doctors with the remainder being drugs that were selected by the older people or recommended by friends or neighbors. In the log data, a similar proportion of the older people reported symptoms of pain in the extremities, hip, neck, or back, but three-quarters of the doses of medicine they took were either OTC drugs or could not be identified by them. Similarly, in their baseline interviews, all of the older people who claimed that their physicians had diagnosed them as having heart conditions reported taking drugs prescribed by their physicians. But on the log data, 70% of the doses taken in response to chest pain were either OTC drugs or could not be identified. Similar proportions of OTC and unidentified doses were taken for head pain and fatigue/weakness and even higher percentages for digestive discomfort.

Overall, almost two-fifths of all doses of medicine taken by the elderly people for the symptoms studied were prescription drugs, two-fifths were OTC drugs, and one-fifth could not be identified by the people who took them. Other investigators have also found that OTC preparations account for at least 40% of all drugs used by the elderly and estimate that almost 70% of elderly patients regularly use such medication (as compared with about 10% of the general adult population) (see Koch-Weser, 1983, for review). When drugs were taken, the general tendency was for more prescription drugs than OTC drugs to be taken for mental health symptoms, while more OTC drugs were taken for pain and digestive difficulties. The taking of prescription rather than OTC drugs for mental health symptoms is not surprising, since tran-quilizers require a prescription.

The implication to be drawn is that there are aspects to issues about the compliance of older people other than adherence to medical recommenda-tions. While the older people in the study may have been taking their prescription drugs, they obviously were taking many other medicines as well. Though some of the OTC drugs may have been recommended by physicians, most of the doses taken even for potentially lethal symptoms such as chest pain were either OTC drugs or could not be identified by the older people. Such information raises serious concerns about the appropriateness of the self-treatment of these elderly people.

The findings about drug ingestion reinforce the increasing concern about the elderly and pharmacology (*Supplement to the Journal of the American Geriatrics Society,* 1982). People 65 or over are 11% of the total population, but they take 25% of the prescription drugs sold in this country and account for 50% of all adverse drug reactions (Institute of Gerontology, 1981).

One comprehensive review of drug misuse in older people identifies multiple problems:

- The elderly are more vulnerable than younger people to negative effects from drugs;
- recommended dosages are often established on the basis of the needs of younger, healthier people;
- older people take more drugs simultaneously, often mixing pre-scribed medications with OTC drugs, which are often abused;
- the elderly have many symptoms and take many drugs for sympto-matic relief, therefore using multiple drugs;

Table 5–3. Numbers and Percentages of Remedies for Mental

Type of Remedy	Normal Subjects								Functionally	
	Mental Health Remedies (n = 20)		Remedies for Worries (n = 28)		Remedies for Upsets (n = 22)		Total Remedies		Mental Health Remedies (n = 35)	
	No.	%	No.	%	No.	%	No.	%	No.	%
Nothing	6	14	21	30	6	15	33	22	33	23
Increased activities (social, chores, leisure)	14	33	13	19	6	15	33	22	22	15
Rest, sleep, decreased activity	8	19	4	6	6	15	18	12	39	27
Thought	6	14	9	13	8	20	23	15	9	6
Problem solving	—	—	16	23	6	15	22	14	2	1
All medications	2	5	2	3	4	10	8	5	16	11
Prescription medications	1	50	2	100	3	75	6	75	11	69
Over-the-counter medications	1	50	—	—	1	25	2	25	—	—
Unidentified medications	—	—	—	—	—	—	—	—	5	31
Crying, worrying	—	—	1	1	—	—	1	1	12	8
Contact with professional	—	—	1	1	2	5	3	2	1	1
Other†	6	14	3	4	3	7	12	8	11	8
TOTAL	42	100	70	100	41	100	153	100	145	100

*Mental and emotional symptoms were symptoms of mental illness such as depression, nervousness, anxiety, tension, and nightmares; worries, most often about their own declining health or that of family and friends, about the household and environment, or about money; and upsets, or reactions to specific external events.

Source: Reprinted with permission from "What Older People Do About Their Day-to-Day Mental and Physical Health Symptoms" by Elaine M. Brody, Morton H. Kleban, and Elizabeth Moles, in *Journal of the American Geriatrics Society,* Vol. 31, No. 8, August 1983, pp. 496–497.

and Emotional Symptoms* by Mental Status Group

| Disturbed Subjects | | | | | | All Subjects | | | | | | | |
| Remedies for Worries (n = 25) | | Remedies for Upsets (n = 22) | | Total Remedies | | Mental Health Remedies (n = 55) | | Remedies for Worries (n = 53) | | Remedies for Upsets (n = 44) | | Total Remedies | |
No.	%	No.	%	No.	%	No.	%	No.	%	No.	%	No.	%
13	18	17	34	63	24	39	21	34	24	23	25	96	23
10	14	12	24	44	17	36	19	23	16	18	20	77	18
8	11	5	10	52	20	47	25	12	9	11	12	70	17
14	19	3	6	26	10	15	8	23	16	11	12	49	12
19	26	9	18	30	11	2	1	35	25	15	17	52	12
3	4	1	2	20	8	18	10	5	4	5	6	28	7
3	100	—	—	14	70	12	67	5	100	3	60	20	71
—	—	1	100	1	5	1	5	—	—	2	40	3	11
—	—	—	—	5	25	5	28	—	—	—	—	5	18
2	3	2	4	16	6	12	6	3	2	2	2	17	4
—	—	—	—	1	—	1	1	1	1	2	2	4	1
3	4	1	2	15	6	17	9	6	4	4	4	27	6
72	100	50	100	267	100	187	100	142	100	91	100	420	100

†Other remedies included those used less than a total of 15 times: eating or drinking, going to bathroom, exercise or positioning, and applied treatment (heat, cold, baths, preparations, ointments).

- the number of adverse reactions increases with the number of drugs taken and the complexity of the prescription's directions (Atkinson & Schuckit, 1981).

Another review emphasizes errors made by older people in complying with prescribed drug regimens—their difficulties in understanding proper timing and dosage of multiple drugs, economic barriers to purchasing prescriptions, and the role of their limited knowledge and understanding (Levy & Glantz, 1981).

Misuse of drugs has been attributed to problems in doctor-patient communication and unclear explanations of how the medicine is to be taken (German et al., 1982; Wade, 1979), as well as to patient noncompliance, drug interactions or adverse reactions, and the prescribing patterns of physicians (Raffoul et al., 1981). Various research efforts have found medication errors among two-fifths to three-fifths of the older people studied (Raffoul et al., 1981; Schwartz et al., 1962). One of them (Schwartz et al., 1962), which studied chronically ill ambulatory outpatients of a hospital clinic, found that three-fifths of them made errors in taking their prescribed medications, with 25% making potentially serious errors. The types of errors, in order of frequency, were omission of medicines, inaccurate knowledge, self-medication (nonprescription drugs, home remedies, outdated drugs, drugs prescribed for other people, etc.), incorrect dosage, and improper timing and sequence. Those most prone to errors were the very old (75+), the widowed and divorced/separated, those who lived alone, and those with a large number of diagnoses.

Two recent reports concluded that almost 20% of the patients entering the geriatric service of a general hospital show evidence of disorders directly attributable to the effects of prescription drugs (Levy & Glantz, 1981). And in a large study in the United Kingdom, an adverse drug reaction was found to be solely or partly responsible for hospital admissions of older people in more than one in 10 admissions (Williamson, 1979).

At the least, the problems identified in this study confirm the need for concentrated attention by the pharmaceutical industry to matters such as dosages, labelling, and the effects of various drugs, the need for professional alertness to problems arising from multiple prescriptions, and the shortcomings of present monitoring.

Turning to what the older people in the study did *not* do about their day-to-day symptoms, it is notable that they did not report them to their doctors; only about 1% of all those symptoms were reported. This does not imply, of course, that all the symptoms should have been reported or that the physicians were unaware of the health conditions that produced their patients' symptoms. Other aspects of the project data had indicated that the vast majority of those diagnoses had been talked over with the older people's physicians at some time. As Chapter 7 will indicate, slightly less than half the symptoms on a checklist of potentially serious symptoms (experienced during the month preceding the interview) had been reported to physicians.

It may be that these older people view their doctors' awareness of their health conditions and recommendations for treatment as the limit of what is to be gained from professional health care. Their day-to-day symptoms and bothers may be regarded as not amenable to further professional intervention. At the least, however, these and the findings of others (Costa & MaCrae, 1980; Steinback et al., 1978) emphatically disprove the stereotype of the complaining, hypochondriacal older person. In fact, the evidence suggests the reverse—that is, there is considerable suffering in silence, particularly from unrelenting, unalleviated pain and other forms of chronic discomfort.

As pointed out in Chapter 1, other studies have documented the underreporting of the elderly's health problems to professionals and the existence of much untreated mental and physical illness (Litman, 1971). As the next chapter will indicate, among the reasons found for the failure of older people to report symptoms are their acceptance of discomfort as a normal and expected part of aging, pessimism about possibilities for relief, feelings that "nobody cares," reluctance to bother professionals or to worry their families, lack of appreciation of the symptoms' significance, and cognitive deficits that impair their capacity to communicate their experiences.

The two mental status groups of elderly people whose actions were reported in this chapter—those with normal mental functioning and those with functional mental disorders—were alike in the extent to which they took some remedial action for their symptoms rather than doing nothing. Chapter 4 indicated that group membership was, however, related to the degrees of discomfort reported; those with functional mental disturbances tended to rate their symptoms as causing more severe discomfort than did those with normal mental functioning. The functional group had also reported more day-to-day pain and mental health symptoms than the normal group. It merits repetition that professionals should be sensitive to the role of mental status in the health experiences of their elderly patients; the responses of those who have functional mental disturbances, however, should not be attributed to malingering or imagining. Rather, the relationships between psyche and soma are underlined: those with functional mental conditions may be vulnerable to mental health symptoms and to pain, and they may perceive such symptoms as causing them more distress.

It is emphasized that the data presented in this chapter are only part of the picture of the health behaviors of the older people. Other aspects are their responses to potentially serious symptoms which may not have appeared on the log data (see Chapter 6) and the measures they take to prevent illness or promote health (see Chapter 7).

These findings, however, begin to delineate a world of health experiences and remedies taken of which professionals should be aware. Considerably more exploration of that world is indicated to provide a rounded picture of the actions older people take to relieve their day-to-day discomfort, the processes by which those actions are determined, and the effects of their mental and physical well-being.

It is clear that it is important for health professionals to ask older people what they do for symptomatic relief in addition to (or instead of) what the doctor recommends—that is, to probe not only for the day-to-day symptoms they experience but also for the day-to-day remedies they apply. The findings also underline the established needs for health education for older people, for more aggressive outreach to them rather than reliance on their initiative in seeking help, and for health professionals to convey encouraging and patient attitudes.

6

The Twenty-Symptom Checklist and Whom the Older People Told about Their Complaints

As we have seen in the preceding chapters, most of the information about the physical and mental health of the elderly people studied was gathered from the baseline interviews and from the four logs completed for each individual.

An important section of the baseline interview was a checklist of 20 potentially serious symptoms. In gathering the log data, the participants had been invited to report "everything" they had experienced, using their own words. In using the baseline checklist, the older people were asked if they had experienced any of 20 particular symptoms named by the interviewer during the month preceding the interview. If the answer was affirmative, follow-up questions were asked: Did you tell anyone about it? If so, whom did you tell? If no one was told, why not?

The answers to those questions provided compelling information supplementing the data from the logs. The fact that more than half of the symptoms experienced at least once were not reported to health professionals is alarming to the extent that many potentially serious symptoms were among those not reported. It also points to the need for more generally available health education not only for older persons but also for members of their families (who are often more likely to be told of symptoms than health professionals). A common reason for failure to report symptoms was the feeling that no one cares or that nothing would or should be done. That fatalism can intensify health hazards affecting an already at-risk group.

This chapter describes the checklist findings and compares them with the findings from the information collected on the logs.

The checklist was intended (1) to supplement the medical history of diagnoses, (2) to capture the major symptoms of ill-defined conditions that are not clinical diagnoses per se but that suggest the possibility of a serious disorder, and (3) to identify the health experiences and symptoms that may not have been reported as part of a formal history or that may have occurred during the intervals between the four log interviews.

Some of the material in this chapter was included in the publication "Physical and Mental Health Symptoms of Older People: Whom Do They Tell?" *Journal of the American Geriatrics Society*, 1981, 29:442–449.

In order to select the 20 symptoms on the checklist (see Table 6–1), our research group first assembled a large number of items from four sources: the *International Classification of Diseases* (1978), Lawton's activity study (1978), the OARS questionnaire (1974), and the National Health Survey (1977). The exhaustive list was then shortened to 20 items by the use of two criteria: (1) the frequency with which the item appeared in the four sources, and (2) judgments made by a Ph. D. public health specialist and a master's level R. N. (who were on the project staff) as those most likely to be experienced by older people and which could be the most serious.

As was true in other aspects of the research, some of the older people with senile dementia were unable to respond or unable to respond fully to the question asking if they had experienced any of the 20 symptoms. The information they were able to supply was supplemented by responses from their caregivers.

The Incidence of the 20 Symptoms

The most common types of symptoms, each experienced by about half of the older people, were difficulty in sleeping, tiredness, nervousness, feeling blue, unsteadiness on feet, and forgetfulness. The proportions of older people in each group and in the combined groups who experienced the 20 symptoms at least once during the month preceding the interview are shown in Table 6–1. (The data do not indicate the severity or the frequency of each type of symptom.)

In comparing the three groups, there were no statistically significant group differences in the number of symptoms they experienced. The older people had experienced an average of 7.5 symptoms each, with a range among them from no symptoms to all 20 symptoms. There were six significant differences, however, in the types of symptoms experienced by the three groups. Those in the functional group were more likely than those in the other two groups to experience difficulty in sleeping, shortness of breath, and indigestion. Those with senile dementia were more likely to experience unsteadiness on feet and forgetfulness. And the normal group had less constipation than either of the other two groups.

The differences among the groups in the types of symptoms should not obscure the fact that large proportions of people in each group showed many types of symptoms. Thus, difficulty in sleeping was experienced by 43% of the normal people, 64% of the functionals, and by 32% of those with senile dementia. Similarly, tiredness, nervousness, feeling blue, unsteadiness on feet, and forgetfulness were experienced by at least 40% of those in each group. In the senile dementia group, a predictably high proportion of people (82%) exhibited forgetfulness, but about half of the normal group (47%) and of the functional group (53%) also reported that symptom.

Table 6-1. Proportions of Ss Experiencing Symptoms During Month Prior to Interview

Symptom	Normal Ss (Group 1) N = 51	Functional Ss (Group 2) N = 46	COBS Ss (Group 3) N = 35	Percentage for 3 Groups Combined (N = 132)	Chi-Square, 2 df.
Difficulty in sleeping	.43	.64	.32	.48	8.69, p < .05
Shortness of breath	.26	.59	.15	.35	19.38, p < .001
Pain or discomfort in chest when active	.24	.38	.15	.26	5.64 ns
Swelling of feet or ankles	.25	.33	.44	.33	3.20 ns
Coughing a lot	.42	.31	.38	.36	.88 ns
Loss of strength in arms and legs	.33	.56	.44	.44	4.80 ns
Tiredness	.51	.71	.59	.60	4.06 ns
Light-headedness or dizziness	.31	.41	.41	.37	1.30 ns
Headaches	.33	.42	.26	.35	2.18 ns
Other distressing aches and pains	.29	.49	.32	.37	4.31 ns
Leg cramps	.27	.29	.12	.24	3.73 ns
Nervousness, tenseness	.43	.67	.59	.56	5.95 ns
Periods of feeling blue	.51	.65	.53	.57	2.23 ns
Unsteady on feet	.39	.47	.68	.49	6.79 p < .05
Trouble passing urine	.06	.16	.15	.11	2.64 ns
Poor appetite	.10	.20	.26	.18	4.14 ns
Indigestion or gas	.27	.53	.18	.34	12.55, p < .01
Bleeding, other than a cut	.10	.04	.12	.08	1.54 ns
Constipation	.12	.38	.41	.28	11.60, p < .01
Forgetfulness	.47	.53	.82	.59	11.21, p < .01

Source: Reprinted with permission from "Physical and Mental Health Symptoms of Older People: Whom Do They Tell?" by Elaine M. Brody and Morton H. Kleban. in Journal of the American Geriatrics Society, Vol. 29, No. 10, October 1981, p. 445.

Whom Did They Tell?

In analyzing the information about whether or not the older people told anyone when they experienced a checklist symptom, the group of people with senile dementia was omitted because they were so rarely able to reply to that question. The normal and functionally disturbed older people are combined in reporting their replies because there were no differences between those two groups as to whether or not they told anyone or whom they told.

As Table 6–2 shows, a slight majority of people in the normal and functional groups told someone—either a health professional, family member, or friend—about their symptoms when they occurred. However, there were large proportions who did not tell anyone when they experienced dizziness, feeling blue, headaches, leg cramps, and shortness of breath. More than 30% did not report forgetfulness, constipation, indigestion, trouble passing urine, nervousness, tiredness, loss of strength in limbs, and difficulty in sleeping. The symptoms most frequently reported to another person were poor appetite (80%) and unsteadiness on feet (71%); the few incidents of bleeding (not from a cut) were all reported.

It was found that most of the symptoms were not reported to health professionals. Of the total of 697 checklist symptoms experienced at least once by the 97 older people during the previous month, 394 or 56% of them were either reported only to family or friends or were not reported to anyone. For example, about half of those with shortness of breath and almost 40% of those with chest pain on activity failed to inform a professional.

When another person was told of the symptom, the elderly individuals were as likely to report most types of symptoms (16 of the 20 types) to family or friends as they were to health professionals. Three types of symptoms were more likely to be reported to professionals: shortness of breath, chest pain on activity, and unsteadiness on the feet. One symptom—forgetfulness—was more likely to be reported to family or friends.

Why Symptoms Were Not Reported

The reasons the older people gave for not telling anyone of their symptoms were grouped into six categories. Table 6–3 summarizes the reasons offered for not reporting 221 (32%) of the collective total of 697 symptoms at least once. The largest category of reasons, given 86 times, was "no big deal," (this category includes knowing the reason for the symptom or being accustomed to it). Next in frequency was the "nobody cares" or "no one to tell" category (given as a reason 43 times), followed by "can't do anything about it, normal aging" (38 times), "don't want to worry or bother people" (23 times), "will tell the doctor at next appointment" (22 times), and "others know" (9 times).

Table 6-2. Symptoms Experienced by Normal and Functional Subjects, and Who They Told about Them (N = 97)

| Symptoms | [1] Number of Ss with Symptoms | | How Many Ss | | | | Whom the Ss Told | | | | [6] Number of Ss Who Didn't Tell Professionals | |
| | | | [2] Told No One | | [3] Told Someone | | [4] Family/ Friends | | [5] Health Professionals | | | |
	N	%*	N	%**	N	%†	N	%‡	N	%†	N‡	%**
Difficulty in sleeping	51	.53	18	.35	33	.65	19	.58	18	.55	33	.65
Shortness of breath	40	.41	17	.43	23	.58	5	.22	19	.83§	21	.52
Pain or discomfort in chest when active	29	.30	9	.31	20	.69	5	.25	18	.90§	11	.38
Swelling of feet or ankles	28	.29	5	.18	23	.82	7	.30	18	.78	20	.71
Coughing a lot	24	.25	9	.38	15	.63	5	.33	11	.73	13	.54
Loss of strength in arms or legs	42	.43	13	.31	29	.69	12	.41	20	.69	22	.52
Tiredness	58	.60	23	.40	36	.60	18	.51	21	.60	37	.64
Light-headedness or dizziness	35	.36	17	.49	18	.51	8	.44	17	.94	18	.51
Headaches	36	.37	17	.47	19	.53	8	.42	14	.74	22	.61
Other distressing aches and pains	37	.38	9	.24	28	.76	12	.43	22	.79	15	.40
Leg cramps	27	.28	12	.44	15	.56	6	.40	11	.73	16	.59
Nervousness, tenseness	53	.55	21	.40	32	.60	15	.47	19	.59	24	.45
Periods of feeling blue	56	.58	28	.50	28	.50	18	.64	12	.43	44	.78
Unsteady on feet	41	.42	12	.29	29	.71	8	.28	23	.79§	18	.44
Trouble passing urine	10	.10	4	.40	6	.60	3	.50	4	.67	6	.60
Poor appetite	14	.14	2	.14	12	.86	5	.42	9	.75	5	.38
Indigestion or gas	38	.39	13	.34	25	.66	12	.48	19	.76	19	.50
Bleeding, other than a cut	7	.07	0	.00	7	1.00	4	.57	4	.57	3	.43
Constipation	23	.24	7	.30	16	.70	5	.31	14	.88	9	.39
Forgetfulness	48	.49	13	.27	35	.73	27	.77	10	.29§	38	.79

*Based on total number of subjects, N = 97. **Based on number or subjects with symptoms in column [1].
†Based on number of subjects in column [3]; subjects who told someone.
‡This N equals the number of subjects in columns [2] and [4], i.e., those who told no one plus those who told family/friends. The figures do not equal the total in column [6] because a few subjects who told family/friends also told health professionals.
§Significant t-tests for proportions between family/friends vs. health professional (p ≤ .05): 1) shortness of breath (t = 2.449, 22 df.); 2) pain or discomfort in chest when active (t = 2.686, 21 df.); 3) unsteady on feet (t = 2.099, 32 df.; and 4) forgetfulness (t = 3.370, 40 df.).
Source: Reprinted with permission from "Physical and Mental Health Symptoms of Older People: Whom Do They Tell?" by Elaine M. Brody and Morton H. Kleban, in Journal of the American Geriatrics Society, Vol. 29, No. 10, October 1981, p. 446.

Table 6-3. Reasons Given for Not Reporting Symptoms*

Reason for Not Reporting Symptom	Number of Times Reason Given			Number of Ss Giving the Reason		
	normal	funct.	Total	normal	funct.	Total
"No big deal"; S knows reason for symptom; S is used to it	39	47	86	25	25	50
Nobody cares; no one to tell	13	30	43	8	12	20
Can't do any thing about it; why bother?; normal aging	15	23	38	9	12	21
Don't want to worry or bother people	16	7	23	10	6	16
Will tell doctor at next appointment	11	11	22	5	7	12
Others already know	4	5	9	4	4	8
Total	98	123	221	61	66	127

*Ninety-nine symptoms of the normal group and 148 symptoms of the functional group were not reported. However, reasons were not always given for not reporting, i.e., reasons were given in 221 instances for the total of 257 non-reported symptoms.

Source: Reprinted with permission from "Physical and Mental Health Symptoms of Older People: Whom Do They Tell?" by Elaine M. Brody and Morton H. Kleban, in Journal of the American Geriatrics Society, Vol. 29, No. 10, October 1981, p. 447.

Because the sample was small, caution is indicated in comparing the normals and the functionals in terms of the different kinds of reasons they gave for not reporting symptoms. There were no differences in the numbers of people in the normal and in the functional groups in the reasons they gave for not reporting symptoms. However, those in the functional group had a tendency to give the "nobody cares/nobody to tell" reason for not reporting more of the types of symptoms. Since family members are so often the recipients of reports about symptoms, such replies were consistent with the fact that fewer people in the functional group were currently married and fewer of them were in touch with an adult child. (See Chapter 3.)

It is also possible to look at the data in terms of the number of individuals offering each type of reason rather than the number of times the reason was given. At least once, 20 of the 97 older people (20%) stated "nobody cares"; at least once, each of 21 of them (22%) interpreted (or misinterpreted) a symptom as normal aging about which nothing could be done; at least once, each of 16 people was reluctant to "bother people" (16%); and at least once, each of 50 people (50%) felt that a symptom was "no big deal" or had become accustomed to it.

Comparing the Checklist Findings with the Log Data

By contrast with the log data, the information in this chapter reports the older people's responses to a one-time series of questions. These one-time questions asked the older people if they had experienced any of a predetermined list of 20 potentially serious symptoms during the month preceding the interview, while the log data were derived from open-ended invitations to report everything that had bothered them. A comparison of the two sets of responses offers some interesting contrasts.

Table 6–4 juxtaposes the responses to the checklist to the same or similar log symptoms, noting the percentages of people reporting each symptom. The percentages of people reporting certain kinds of symptoms were roughly similar in both analyses—namely, sleep problems, chest pain, head pain, digestive difficulties, and fatigue. Other kinds of symptoms had not appeared on the checklist (notably worries, upsets, and nocturia).

Still other symptoms were not reported at all or were reported by comparatively few people on the log but were elicited in response to the specific questions on the checklist: shortness of breath, coughing a lot, leg cramps, trouble passing water, forgetfulness, swelling of feet or ankles, nervousness/anxiety/tension, feeling blue/depression, and constipation. Forgetfulness is a dramatic example of this contrast. That symptom was reported spontaneously on the logs so few times by so few people (a total of six reports, two from each group) that it was subsumed under "worries" about

Table 6–4. Comparison of Checklist and Log: Percentages of Subjects Reporting Symptoms

Twenty-Symptom Checklist		Spontaneously Reported Symptoms (Logs)	
Symptom	Percentage of subjects experiencing symptom in month prior to interview	Symptom	Percentages of subjects reporting symptom during 4 sampled days/nights
Difficulty sleeping	48	Sleep problems	35
Shortness of breath	35	—	—
Pain or discomfort in your chest when active	26	Chest pain	26
Swelling of feet or ankles	33	Swelling of feet, etc.	08
Cough a lot	36	—	—
Headaches	35	Head pain	30
Other aches and pains that trouble you a lot	37	Pain in: extremities	58
		eyes or ears	18
		overall aches	14[a]
Leg cramps	24	—	—
Nervousness, tenseness	56	Nervousness/anxiety/tension	17

96

Period of feeling blue	57	Depression	21
		Loneliness	13
		Negative emotions	15
Trouble passing water	11	—	—
Poor appetite	18	Digestive discomfort	22
Indigestion or gas	34		
Bleeding other than a cut	08	—	—
Constipation	28	Elimination problems	10
Forgetfulness	59	—	—[b]
Loss of strength in arms or legs	44	Fatigue/weakness/unsteady on feet	67
Lightheadedness or dizziness	37		
Tiredness	60		
Unsteady on feet	49		
—		Worries	52
—		Upsets	43
—		Nocturia (3 × or more)	27

[a]39% of pain reports were rated by subjects as bothering them "a lot."

[b]The six reports of forgetfulness are included in "worries" (about subjects' declining capacities).

Source: Reprinted from "Day-to-Day Mental and Physical Health Symptoms of Older People: A Report on Health Logs" by Elaine M. Brody and Morton H. Kleban, in *The Gerontologist*, Vol. 23, No. 1, 1983, p. 83.

declining cognitive abilities (see Table 4–1 in Chapter 4). Yet 49% of the normals and functionals and 82% of the SDs stated they had been forgetful when asked specifically about that symptom on the checklist.

Discussion of the Findings

In the month preceding their interviews, the elderly persons in all three groups experienced many of the 20 distressing and potentially serious mental and physical health complaints on the predetermined checklist about which they were questioned. (It is emphasized that the checklist questions, by contrast with the logs, were asked once.)

One cannot avoid being impressed by the pervasiveness of symptoms such as tiredness, difficulty in sleeping, nervousness, feeling blue, unsteadiness on feet, and forgetfulness. The overall picture that emerges is one of depression, anxiety, and fatigue. Since the group of those with functional mental problems were reached through community mental health centers, the large proportion of that group with such symptoms was not unexpected. Similarly, those in the SD group, by definition, had mental problems. The normal group, however, also contained a large proportion of people with the same symptoms but who were not receiving mental health care. These normals were part of the large number of older people whose mental and emotional problems go unrecognized and untreated.

The majority (56%) of the symptoms experienced at least once were not reported to health professionals. When the symptoms were reported to someone, it was as likely to be a family member or friend as a health professional. The exceptions to that pattern were three types of symptoms that were more likely to be reported to professionals than to family or friends: that is, shortness of breath, chest pain when active, and unsteadiness on feet. Even those symptoms, however, were not reported to anyone by large proportions of the elderly respondents. One type of symptom (forgetfulness) was more likely to be revealed to a family member or friend. The fact that four-fifths of those experiencing that symptom did not report it to a professional suggests that older people often do not view forgetfulness as a health symptom.

Such data confirm the established need for health education for the elderly. Their knowledge about the kinds of symptoms that should be called to professional attention cannot be taken for granted. Most people (old and young) seek medical care for acute symptoms and the treatment of short-term illness (U.S. DHEW, PHS, 1977). The onset of chronic illnesses for which cures are not available may find older persons unprepared. Their orientation, like that of the health systems and most professionals, is to crisis care. The elderly often are not aware that their chronic illnesses and symptoms may be amenable to ameliorative treatment and relief from discomfort. Their need for medical counseling contrasts with the fact that such counseling constitutes the smallest proportion of therapeutic services received by all age groups during visits to physicians' offices, a proportion that does not rise with advancing age (prescription of drugs predominates during such visits for all age groups) (*Sourcebook on Aging*, 1979). The proportion of office visits in which a general history or examination is provided is lowest on the list of diagnostic services for all age groups and actually is slightly lower for those 65 and over than for younger people (*Sourcebook on Aging*, 1979).

The importance of educational programs for family members and significant others is also underlined. Not only do 80% of the elderly consult a relative in a health crisis (Shanas, 1961), but our data illustrate the major role of family members as the first-line recipients of information about important symptoms that may not be considered significant by the older people themselves. These family health confidants are therefore in a pivotal position to make appropriate referrals for professional care. Their role goes beyond that of being a critical link connecting the elderly to providers of needed treatment. Families are also the principal caregivers, providing the great majority of ongoing health services to older people (U.S. DHEW, PHS, 1972; U.S. General Accounting Office, 1977). They therefore should have a base of accurate information and should receive feedback on the effectiveness of their activities.

The reasons the older persons gave for not telling anyone about so many of their symptoms do not allow judgments as to whether or not the symptoms should have been reported. For example, the symptoms in the "no big deal" group—the largest category of reasons for nonreporting—may or may not have been a "big deal." There was a poignant frequency, however, of the feeling that "nobody cares" and in the helpless or hopeless acceptance of the symptom as part of "normal aging" or as a form of distress about which "nothing can be done." Some of these elderly subjects were silent about their complaints because of diffidence; they were reluctant to bother or worry people. And some "saved up" their symptoms, to be reported when they next would see a doctor. Whether or not the symptoms were "serious" enough to indicate a need for health care, at least the need is clear for the elderly to believe that someone does care. That need is particularly applicable to those with functional mental disorders, whether their feelings stem from lack of family or from psychological problems.

The comparison of the data from the checklist and the logs suggests that older people must be asked specific questions about particular symptoms and also be encouraged to describe in their own words the things that bother them. The comparison also highlights the failure of these older people to report many symptoms spontaneously even when they were urged to do so during the four yesterday interviews. It may be that an open-ended invitation to report everything provokes selective reports of complaints that are most bothersome symptomatically but results in omission of others that may be equally or even more important medically or psychiatrically. At the same time, however, a one-time inquiry (checklist) does not convey the frequency, continuity, or degree of bother and activity interference caused by certain symptoms.

In short, the data suggest that older people need to be asked periodically and in detail about symptoms specifically named by professionals and also to have opportunities to describe how disturbing, continuous, and disruptive to their daily lives those symptoms are.

Individual patients differ in their levels of health knowledge and styles of relating to health professionals. In the main, however, our findings support those in previous reports concerning the overall low levels of information among the elderly, their therapeutic pessimism about their ailments, and their feelings of not meriting attention. Large numbers of uncomfortable and distressing symptoms are borne in silence.

Health professionals differ, of course, in the ways in which they relate to their patients. They must evaluate for themselves the degree to which they are aware of the nature and number of symptoms their elderly patients experience. It is apparent from this study that older persons require an extra measure of effort, concern, and time so that the professional may elicit information, encourage the voicing of distressing complaints, give health/mental health counseling, and convey the feeling that someone is listening and someone cares.

7 Lifestyles

The research study used a number of approaches in attempting to obtain a picture of the health experiences and practices of the older people. The main body of data was derived from the logs (Chapters 4 and 5), and the checklist (Chapter 6) provided further information. There were, in addition, three small sets of questions that also bear on the mental and physical health of the people studied. They are reported in this chapter as follows:

1. *Regimens to promote health and prevent illness.* In addition to experiencing and responding to specific symptoms or ailments, many people routinely do some things to prevent illness or to maintain their health. At the close of the interviews with each older person in the normal and functional groups, each was asked several questions to elicit information about their health promotion and illness prevention behaviors. (Again, the responses of the SDs were too sparse to warrant analysis.) The goal of this aspect of the study was to find out what the older people were doing as a matter of routine. These actions would not always have appeared in the log data, since that instrument was designed to obtain information about specific symptoms and actions to alleviate the discomfort caused.

2. *Lifestyles of people with severe senile dementia.* Since a number of these older people were too deeply impaired to respond to any interview questions, a special questionnaire was administered to their caregivers.

3. *Enjoyable activities.* The elderly were asked about the enjoyable things they did in order to counterbalance in part the "down" picture of their lives on which the research focused.

Regimens to Promote Health or Prevent Illness

The open-ended questions asked were: What things do you do to improve or maintain your health? Why? and Who told you to do this?

There proved to be sharp differences between the people in the normal and functional groups with respect to the measures they took to improve or maintain their health. First, the normals engaged in more kinds of such activities: an average of 3.5 types of actions as compared with slightly less than

2.0 for the functionals. Most of the normals (59%) engaged in two or more kinds of health promotion activities, while 29% did one thing to promote health, and a few (12%) did nothing. An example of the few who engaged in five or six activities is the woman who exercised by shoveling snow, went out to get fresh air, walked, avoided orange juice (allergic), and made a Manhattan cocktail but didn't drink it. A man did yoga, walked two miles in the evening, watched his diet and drinking, exercised, and took his medications.

Second, the nature of the actions taken by the normals and functionals differed greatly in many instances. An overwhelming majority (84%) of the normals walked or did exercises compared with less than one quarter of the functionals. The normals also exceeded the functionals in watching their diets (48% versus 17%), keeping busy (25% versus 10%), socializing (23% versus 2%), and making conscious efforts to keep calm and avoid worrying (18% versus 2%). The functionals tended to emphasize medications (56% versus 39% of the normals) and visits to health professionals (17% versus 9% of the normals).

In reading the responses of the older people to this interview question, still another difference between the groups was apparent. The replies of the functionals often had an aimless quality. They might say, for example, "I just walked around," or "I ate breakfast"; the normals more clearly expressed their goal of walking or eating certain types of foods (and avoiding others) as a health promotion and illness prevention measure. And, as might be expected, there were a number of inappropriate responses from the functionals such as "I try to hide," "I try to be charming," and "I had the exterminator."

The next questions were "Why do you do this?" and "Who told you to do it?" The people in the functional group often did not respond to these inquiries; though some did, there were too few answers to produce any meaningful information. The reasons given by the people in the normal group for their various health regimens were, in the main, straightforward. Some examples follow.

- About two-thirds of their dietary regimens were adopted in response to or to prevent specific health problems (1) for their laxative effect; (2) to avoid stomach/bowel problems; (3) to control weight, blood pressure, or diabetes; or (4) to avoid cholesterol or caffeine. The remaining one-third were attributed vaguely to "It's good for you," or "It (certain food) doesn't agree with me."
- About two-thirds of the walking/exercise regimens were carried out because "it's good for you." Most of the remainder were carried out to "prevent stiffness."
- The "good thoughts/mental health" regimens (such as prayer, conscious avoidance of distressing thoughts) were the older people's attempts to keep themselves calm and to avoid worry or anxiety.

These normal subjects reported that about half of their health regimens were self-prescribed, while about one-third had been advised by their doctors. (The exception was the "good thoughts/mental health" category; all of these activities were self-prescribed.) Most of the remainder had been recommended by the media, and a few by relatives or friends. (Two people faithfully followed diets that had been recommended by their mothers long ago.)

It is interesting that many of the activities identified by these older people as promoting health or preventing illness were the ones that generally are regarded as treating illness—diabetic diets, for example. This suggests that the chronic ailments have become so much a part of their lives that treating existing illness is viewed as prevention. That is, while a young person may exercise to promote health, the old person often does so to ameliorate a health condition or to prevent it from worsening.

Overall, the older people with normal mental functioning were more involved in health maintenance measures in general and in self-help behaviors in particular than were the functionals. It is obvious that this reflects the mental status of the functionally impaired people and their greater dependency. However, it is a reminder to health professionals of the importance of involving caregivers or collaterals in the health care of such individuals.

Finally, about two-thirds of the health regimens practiced by the normal older people were either self-prescribed or had been recommended by the media. Undoubtedly, most of these were appropriate or innocuous. Nevertheless, it underlines the importance of professional awareness of all the various health activities in which elderly people engage.

Lifestyles of People with Severe Senile Dementia

As has been stated repeatedly, some of the older people in the group of those with senile dementia were so impaired that they could not reply to the research questions. All of these participants, of course, lived with other people who took care of them. A special questionnaire was developed for the caregiving collaterals of ten such deeply impaired older people. The information collected permits not only a glimpse of the lives of those older people but a glimpse of the lives of their caregivers as well.

These ten older people were very old—almost all of them were in their nineties. As could be expected, therefore, nine of the ten were women. (At ages 85 and over, women outnumber men in a ratio of 238 to 100.) Also as might be expected, nine out of the ten caregivers were women, and their average age was 60. Eight of the collaterals were daughters (three were married and five were widowed or divorced), one was an unmarried son, and one was a married female relative.

A summary of the questionnaires yielded the following information:

- *Sleeping rooms:* Eight of the ten older people had their own rooms; the remaining two shared their rooms with collaterals.
- *Where they spent most of their days:* Six of the ten older people spent most of each day in their bedrooms; the others also spent some time in living rooms or dining rooms.
- *Place of eating:* Six of the ten ate their meals in their bedrooms; the others ate in the dining room, kitchen, or living room.
- *Toileting:* Four of the ten older people were toileted by means of a bedpan or commode in the bedroom; three either were diapered or had a catheter.
- *Use of time:* Seven of the older people spent most of their days doing virtually nothing—that is, sleeping, lying in bed, talking to themselves, or just looking around. Two spent some of their time looking at family photo albums, magazines, TV, or listening to records. One person did dress and feed herself, listened to TV and radio, but spent most of her time in bed.
- *Communication of needs:* Six of the older people were able to communicate when they were in pain, uncomfortable, needed toileting, or were hungry or tired. Two people simply groaned, moaned, or became "fussy," and two did not communicate at all; in these situations the collateral would make some judgment as to what was needed and what to do.
- *Communication of moods:* A few of the older people were able to communicate when they were happy or unhappy. The rest smiled, sang, clapped, or laughed when happy and became quiet, sad, whined, or scolded when unhappy.
- *Length of time this level of care had been needed:* Six of the older people had needed this level of care for three to five years; one person had been this dependent for ten years, one for two years, one for one year, and one for only one month.

To summarize, most of these older people with severe senile dementia were spending their entire lives in one room which served for sleeping, eating, and toileting. Most did virtually nothing to occupy their time, spending most of their days in beds or chairs. Some were able to communicate their needs and moods, but in some instances the collateral had only her own judgment to go on. And most of these older people had needed this level of care for years.

Those reading the research protocols of these ten people (to say nothing of the interviewers who went into their homes) could not avoid being moved by the profound emptiness of their lives and the bleakness of the lives of their caregivers. The case studies in Chapter 11 describe some of these situations in detail.

It is now fashionable to denigrate institutional care and to extoll the virtues of community living for older people. The questions that must be asked are "For whom?" and "Compared to what?" And, of course, what can be done to improve the quality of life for both the recipients and providers of care?

Enjoyable Activities

At the end of each yesterday interview, the older people were asked "What especially enjoyable things did you do today?" One reason for asking that question was that the interviews were largely concerned with negative experiences—that is, symptoms and bothers. In addition, we wanted to dilute the impact on the older people of such an intense focus by ending the interview on an "up" note.

The spontaneous replies of the elderly participants (each had been asked that question on four days) were categorized by the research team. Overall, the normals reported the most enjoyable activities and those in the SD group the fewest. The normals averaged 6.3 activities named for the four sampled days (that is, about 1.6 per day), the functionals averaged 3.8 (about 1 per day), and the SDs averaged 2.3 (about 1 every other day). There were a number of statistically significant differences among the three groups:

1. The people in the normal group far surpassed the other two groups in socializing, reporting significantly more such occasions of activities such as visiting with their families and friends, and attendance at meetings. Such activities were the main category of the enjoyable things done by those in the normal group, representing 37% of all their responses.
2. The normal people reported significantly more instrumental activities as enjoyable (such as shopping and household chores) than either of the other two groups.
3. The principal sources of enjoyment for those in the functional group were solitary in-home activities, specifically, watching TV, listening to the radio, and reading (29% of their responses). They reported significantly more such activity than either the normals or SDs.
4. The people with SD responded that they had done nothing enjoyable to a significantly greater extent than those in the normal group, with the functionals falling between the other two groups.

The "nothing" responses of the SD subjects are another reminder of the psychological and social poverty of the lives of older people with that diagnosis and to a lesser extent of the lives of those with functional mental disorders.

More than half (52%) of the responses of the SD subjects were "nothing"—that is, more often than not, they could not name a single enjoyable activity as having taken place during the past 24 hours. Twenty-eight percent of the responses of the functionals but only 11% of the responses of those in the normal group were in the "nothing" category. Those with SD, in particular, lack the personal mental and physical resources to initiate enjoyable activities, and apparently little is done by others in their environments to either take them out or to bring social/recreational activities to them. Solitary media-at-home activities (radio, TV) rose in relative importance for the functional subjects.

These findings, of course, are not unexpected, since sheer competence plays a major role in one's ability to obtain psychosocial supplies. We interpret the small amounts of socialization activity of the SD and functional groups as a lack of opportunity rather than preference. In Lawton's study (in press) of how older people use their time, the more competent subjects spent greater amounts of time with friends and in out-of-home activities. And the U.S. General Accounting Office survey of the Cleveland area showed that only 8% of severely impaired older people received social/recreational services, compared to 26% of those who were mildly or moderately impaired and 33% of those who were unimpaired (U.S. Comptroller General of the United States, 1977, p. 29).

If the normal group in this study most closely approximates a model of what older people enjoy and find satisfying, it is obvious that attention should be paid to the needs of older people with mental problems (whether organic or functional) for opportunities to socialize and to get out of their homes from time to time.

8

Lay Consultation and Its Implications for Health Professionals

Anne-Linda Furstenberg*

A small substudy of the Health Practices project dealt with "lay consultation" by the older people interviewed for the project. That is, it explored the ways in which they talked to their friends and family about their health problems and the effect such conversations had on the way they took care of themselves. This chapter will describe such lay consultation as reported by the participants in the substudy and its relationship to their dealings with health professionals. The discussion will lead to some suggestions about how health professionals might take account of the lay consultation in which their patients or clients engage and some ways in which professional practice can be shaped to meet the needs of the older patient.

The substudy consisted of intensive case studies of 12 older people. It combined the formal interviews of the Health Practices project about health problems and the use of health care with semistructured questions about how the respondents went about making decisions about their health, how they had learned about remedies they were using for their ailments, and what they discussed with other people about their health problems. A second informant, a collateral who was familiar with the latter's health problems, was asked for the same information. The author spent an average of four hours with each participant.

The participants in the study were among those being interviewed in the pilot phase of the Health Practices project. Because these pretest subjects were recruited from a senior citizens center, they were all Jewish. They

*Anne-Linda Furstenberg, Ph.D., completed her master's degree in Social Work and her doctorate at the Bryn Mawr School of Social Work and Social Research. While working on her doctorate, she was awarded an Administration on Aging Research Internship at the Philadelphia Geriatric Center. Dr. Furstenberg now teaches in the areas of health and aging at the School of Social Work of the University of Pennsylvania, and is associated there with both the Center for the Study of Aging and the Rehabilitation Research and Training Center. This chapter is based on Dr. Furstenberg's doctoral dissertation, "Lay Consultation and Illness Management of Older People," Bryn Mawr College, 1979.

ranged in age from their sixties to their nineties, with half of them being in their seventies; they lived in their own homes in the community; and only four of the 12 were married. Since they were Jewish, this group of participants probably tended to be much more health conscious and more oriented to the use of professional care than the general population, since these characteristics are found to be much more common in that population (Antonovsky, 1972; McKinlay & Dutton, 1974; Twaddle, 1969; Mechanic, 1978). Moreover, the class composition of the study participants, half of whom were middle- or upper-middle class, would also tend to be associated with higher use of medical care (Mechanic, 1978; McKinlay, 1972; Suchman, 1966).

What Is Lay Consultation?

Lay consultation is a term that has been used to describe the way people talk about and look for information from nonprofessionals about a health problem they are experiencing. Many episodes of illness begin with symptoms that are ambiguous and that the sufferer must interpret. One might, for example, be forced to consider whether extraordinary weakness accompanying a severe upper respiratory infection betokens pneumonia or simply classic flu and whether one should wait it out or go straight to the doctor. People use information and corroboration from others to help them evaluate the nature of their own symptoms and decide what kind of action they should be taking. There are, of course, variations in the extent to which people do this and how they do it. But, in general, most people, at least those who are not isolated, probably carry on some discussions with someone when faced with a health problem.

Lay consultation is so named, of course, to distinguish it from the consulting of professionals. Even people who are well oriented to using physicians for help with health problems may engage in considerable amounts of conversation with lay people they know. These discussions may help to define the nature of the problem and to establish that it is a problem that justifies seeing or talking to a doctor. However, among groups with less access to doctors, with less ease in talking with them, or with less confidence in medical science, lay consultation may play an even larger role in influencing people's health behavior.

Most past research about lay consultation explored what people did when they were first experiencing health problems, particularly from the time they began to feel ill until the time they consulted a doctor (Suchman, 1965; Kasl & Cobb, 1966; Twaddle, 1969). Such research investigated the emergence of symptoms of acute illness and focused primarily on the process of deciding to consult a doctor. The little research that looked more closely at what happened once the patient had consulted a physician revealed, however, that people discussed health problems and asked for advice from other people not only *before* talking with their physician but they also told people what had happened when they saw the doctor, reported what was prescribed, and discussed the merits of the prescribed medication or regimen (Freidson, 1961). Lay associates, therefore, could influence not only how quickly people go to the doctor but also how they evaluated their physicians, how they interpreted the diagnoses and recommendations, and how they judged and complied with prescriptions.

Lay consultation for the chronic illnesses characteristic of older people had not been explored, however. Commonly, acute illnesses show a definite onset and demand short-term attention, sometimes including drastic changes in activity, such as bed rest and/or a short course of medication. By contrast, most of the illnesses of older people are chronic, common, and expected, but have gradual onset and ambiguous symptoms. The sequence of events in seeking care and following treatment measures may result at best in improvement but not in recovery. Patients have to live with, manage, and accommodate a chronic disease. Moreover, the treatments for chronic illnesses differ from those in acute illness, such as making long-term changes in lifestyle to retard the progress of the disease; managing, juggling, and remembering medications over a long period and judging whether they are doing any good; and generally continuing a course of action to take care of an ailment even when no clear or dramatic improvement results.

With this much ambiguity and with the need for continuing action facing those who suffer from chronic illness, the influence of other people has potential for being even more marked than in the case of acute illness. Little, if any, research, however, has examined whether older people discuss their chronic ailments and whether consultation with other people ever deals with continuing symptoms that have been under treatment for awhile. One aim of this study, therefore, was to understand in particular what kinds of conversations went on about chronic illness. Would these discussions influence how people felt about their chronic illness? Would the discussions influence the way in which they carried out self-treatment measures, both those prescribed and those not sanctioned by their physician?

What We Learned about Lay Consultation

In the dominant view of this culture, scientific knowledge is the best tool for dealing with disease, and the medical profession is seen to have the best command of that knowledge. In this substudy, all of the participants shared this attitude. All but one used medical doctors for their care and saw doctors as the primary source of information about what to do about their health problems. Nevertheless, all engaged in some conversations with lay people about their health problems. There were some important differences, however, in the reasons and ways they talked to people and in the use they made of their conversations. The styles of lay consultation can be grouped into four categories: reporters, consulters, the supported, and the nonreporters.

Reporters

Many of the participants reported carrying on a steady stream of casual conversations with spouse, relatives of the same generation, and/or friends about their symptoms, their illnesses, and the things they were doing to treat them. They call it "just reporting" or "just a formality" and seemed to use health simply as a form of social currency, something that one could talk about and exchange with other people. But there were differences in *whom* people would report to in this casual way. Men seemed to be able to talk only to their wives about health matters. Women who were married also "reported" to their spouses. Regardless of marital status, however, the women discussed health matters with one or more female intimates.

Unless the respondent depended physically on a younger caregiver, a group that will be discussed below, few conversations took place with children or other members of the younger generation. Respondents felt that an announcement to children was required only in the case of serious illness or when some weighty course of action was contemplated, such as surgery, or when help might be needed. The casual discussion of illness almost never occurred with children.

Many of these reporters seemed not to carry on this kind of conversation with the intent of gaining information; symptoms and remedies were simply the kind of thing they talked about with those close to them. Nevertheless, when people repeated or reconstructed their dialogues, it could be seen that even this casual discussion had important consequences for the person's way of thinking about and dealing with the health problem. Four discrete effects of discussions were observed in the respondents' reports.

First of all, just talking out loud about one's symptoms and actions helps a person to think about them—that is, the other person acted as a sounding board. Because listeners typically ask what the person is doing, reflection and evaluation of the actions being taken is encouraged.

Second, the listeners often responded with new information, such as their own experience with the same illness or the case history of someone else they knew. One woman told of listening to the details of someone else's surgery and knowing much better what to expect of her own. The listeners may describe the remedies they or others have used and how well they worked and make suggestions about what to do. Even information the person already possesses is reinforced and validated when someone else says the same thing.

Third, the reports in the interviews made it clear that the conversations transmitted models for coping—that is, they held up examples, good and bad, of how different people went about dealing with a vexing ailment. Even if the participants guided their actions primarily by what their physicians recommended, these conversations with friends and companions increased the participants' information about an ailment. This, too, provides them with important guidelines for their actions. Moreover, the knowledge of what other people have gone through and the sense that one's experience is not unique can be comforting and supportive.

Fourth, although the participants were not consciously seeking advice and influence, they receive some anyway. People reminded and coaxed the participants to try a remedy or a particular physician. Participants told of instances of having some course of action pressed on them or of being reminded to follow through on something the doctor had advised. For example, one woman urged the participant to go and "take the needles," to submit to painful injections of medication into her severely painful arthritic knees. Although a subtle process, it seems fair to assume that all this information and even prodding from other people has some influence on how people take care of themselves and their success and persistence in carrying out prescribed regimens.

Consulters

Though the reporters described above obtained their lay consultation as a part of a friendly conversation rather than with a conscious intent of gaining information, most voiced strong principles about using only professional advice and not listening to advice from lay people. One-quarter of them, however—the "consulters"—actively solicited information and advice from friends or associates when they were experiencing a health problem. One man, after several medical mishaps, refused to see a doctor at all but talked instead with two male acquaintances to get advice based on their own health problems. He explained it thus:

> See, when I am in doubt about what I should do I talk to someone to find out what his opinion is. So when you think something is wrong and the man went through it, you can talk to him about it, he can tell you out of his experience what's what.

One woman talked with a large circle of old and new friends before deciding to follow her doctor's recommendation of a liver biopsy and later for surgery.

It is important to note that the pattern of a real search for advice and information from nonprofessionals was observed only when the participant lacked a strong relationship with a physician, one in which they could get answers to their questions. These older people perceived their physicians as not giving them enough information to understand their condition and to be clear about what they were supposed to be doing. It seems likely that the reliance on lay advice resulted not only from poor communication from doctors but also from the older people's lack of skill in eliciting and understanding information.

The Supported

When the study participants were older and more frail, a very different pattern of conversation took place. These older people—"the supported"—required help with many of the activities by which they were maintained in their homes. That is, because of their decreased physical, sensory, and sometimes their cognitive capacities, they needed help with shopping, with keeping their homes cleaned and in repair, with meals, with transportation, and with handling finances. While most frail elderly people are helped by their adult children, this particular group of study participants happened not to have children and were helped by a nephew or a young friend.

Because the frail older persons depended on them and were cut off from friends and confidants of their own age, such supportive people were the ones to be consulted about health problems. Moreover, the caregiver's help included surveillance, shopping (including health supplies), and transportation; it therefore was difficult, if not impossible, for the older person to avoid revealing health problems and self-care regimens. The caregiver who helped the older person buy analgesics knew they were available, could monitor how quickly or slowly they disappeared, and could promote and encourage their use. Mrs. V's friend, for example, reminded her to take medications and advised her what to tell the doctor. She reported this exchange when Mrs. V was complaining about pain: "Do you have the medication? Take it," said the friend. "The medication's no good," replied Mrs. V. The friend then asked, "Why don't you call the doctor and tell him that the medicine doesn't agree with you?"

One feature of the pattern of support and care by younger persons was their role in taking charge when action seemed required. Because of the degree of responsibility assumed, the caregiver could authoritatively insist on a particular decision, particularly when it involved the need to see the doctor. For example, after Mr. K. made an unsuccessful attempt on his own to get clinic treatment for a painful condition in his mouth, he reported this to his nephew who simply said, "We'll find a doctor," and took him back to the hospital. Another informant, Mrs. E, reported the following exchange with her nephew: "How do you feel?" asked her nephew. She replied, "Not so hot, I got something the matter with my leg." He looked at it and said, "I'm going to call L" (the doctor). "Whatever the doctor will say, we'll listen to him."

When the doctor advised hot compresses, Mrs. E protested that this was too hard for her to do. Her nephew responded, "Yes, that's true. We'll get somebody to help." And he did. These caregivers assumed important roles in solving problems and deciding upon and executing courses of action. This was particularly likely when the caregiver perceived the older person as managing an illness poorly (as was the case in Mrs. V's situation) or as being at the limit of his or her resources for coping with a health problem (Mr. K and Mrs. E).

Knowing that their caregivers might feel compelled to take action, some of the older participants withheld information from them. Mrs. E, for example, claimed, "Always, always I say I'm good, I never say bad. . . . Otherwise, he would take me to the doctor every day." This seemed to be a response to the older person's embarrassment about being dependent, desire not to impose or to be a burden, and an exaggerated sense of the time and energy costs of the help their caregivers were providing.

Nonreporters

While every participant described some limits about to whom and about what they would talk, some engaged in almost no conversation with others about their health. Widowed Mr. K, for example, discussed nothing about his health with his wide circle of acquaintances and made only the most necessary disclosures to his nephew. One of the two married men studied reported only to his wife. The other males in the study engaged in no such casual discussions, only asking for help when making decisions. For the most part, the men disclosed very little about their health to anyone except their wives and physicians. This seems to be a gender-related pattern in which males engage in little intimate interaction or self-disclosure outside of the marital relationship (Hess, 1979; Powers & Bultena, 1976).

These different patterns with respect to the discussion of health problems makes it possible to identify varied consequences in terms of information received and support for health care actions. The older people who engaged in a lot of reporting and consulting received much information and advice. The men, who tended not to report or consult, received much less information about the regimens, symptoms, and coping patterns of others. Frail people who needed help with shopping, transportation, and other services were less able to hide their health problems; their caregivers were likely to be very influential and even to take the initiative in problem-solving. Those who were perceived as neglecting an ailment or to managing it poorly, whatever their conversation pattern, evoked strong efforts from others to persuade them to use treatment regimens or to visit professionals.

Since the participants' use of lay advice was related to their seeking of professional advice, the next step in the study was to examine the older people's accounts of their communication with their physicians.

Physician-Patient Communication

The reports of the participants suggest that there were great variations in the effectiveness of their communications with their physicians. Some excerpts from three case studies illustrate instances in which there were communication problems.

Mrs. C

Mrs. C's internist told her that a blood test had "shown something," and he wanted her to have a liver biopsy. She didn't know why she needed a biopsy and was unprepared for the risks involved. "Even the doctor didn't tell me anything until I got into the hospital, and they shoved a paper under my nose to sign it." When the consent form listing the risks in detail (including risk of death) was read to her, she wanted to sign herself out of the hospital but felt too embarrassed. She never did understand what the test revealed.

When Mrs. C was referred to a surgeon, he informed her in a rushed hallway conference that she would need an operation for polyps of the colon. Only from a lay source did she learn that the operation involved an abdominal incision. Her internist was helpful in reassuring her about the necessity for the surgery, but when she asked about the seriousness of the operation, he sidestepped the issue by responding that all surgery was serious.

Mrs. C was also taking a heart medication, which she thought was prescribed for "a rhythm." She reported no heart disease on the health history taken for the research project and apparently did not know that the medication had anything to do with her heart.

Mrs. D

Unlike Mrs. C, Mrs. D was told she had a heart condition. "I just told him I'm short of breath. He didn't say anything. He just said, 'Don't lift any furniture or heavy packages.' No explanation." She added, "I think it's connected with the heart. Or the lungs, I don't know which it is. I'm not a doctor." Later, she remembered, "He did tell me what's wrong with the heart. He said, 'You're very nervous, your heartbeat is like you're shaking, you're nervous inside.' I said to him, 'Does that mean that I don't have a good heart beat?' Then he turns around and says, 'Do you have pains in your chest?' "

Mrs. S

Mrs. S developed double vision shortly after beginning Dilantin therapy (for blacking out). She was convinced that the Dilantin was causing her problems, although her internist and neurologist did not agree with her. No one, not even the several eye specialists she saw, offered her any alternative explanation for the problems in her eyes.

These examples suggest the kinds of information that patients want. Basic, of course, is the need to know what to do. For the most part, the doctors gave instructions and prescribed medications. Unless they had some reason not to do so, the patients followed directions. When more far-reaching decisions had to be made such as changing activities (Mrs. D) or submitting to procedures (Mrs. C), patients seemed to need more information to make a judgment. Both women wanted to know something about the seriousness of their conditions; faced with a threat, they needed information to evaluate its seriousness and to know what to expect and how to respond. The patients' acceptance of their physicians' recommendations and the commitment they make to following them depend, to some extent, on such understandings.

Even if a condition is not serious, some patients still want an explanation for what they are experiencing. Thus, Mrs. S could not help but treat her vision problems as serious; when her physicians failed to provide an explanation, she created her own. As a result, she stopped taking a medication she may in fact have needed.

While the health professionals in the above cases could improve their communications with patients, other professionals were described who communicated well. The participants' reports about them suggest a variety of potentially effective techniques.

One doctor carefully reviewed each medication as part of his patient's visit. He asked her to tell him how well each medicine was working and how it was making her feel; he then acted upon this information. Another physician kept a special time free to return his patients' calls and still another set time aside for patients to walk in without an appointment. Each of these arrangements signalled the availability of the physician and his readiness to listen. They communicated receptivity to their patients' reports of their experiences and to their questions and uncertainties.

Conversely, the lack of any arrangement for unpressured time during which a patient could speak with the physician made communication difficult. Many of the older people had long waits to see their doctors and felt that others would have to wait if they delayed the physician. Some physicians conducted their consultations in a rushed way that conveyed that they did not have much time to spend with the patient—Mrs. C's hallway consultation with her surgeon, for example. Apart from the lack of privacy, such an on-the-run consultation does not encourage full discussion. Each of these situations led the patient to perceive the doctor's time as very scarce and inhibited the patients' freedom to report symptoms or ask questions. In such a rapid-fire exchange, a patient can easily become unnerved, confused, or intimidated.

The patients, as well as the physicians, varied in their contributions to the process of communication. Two better educated, more verbal, and more assertive patients obtained much more information. Each reported their physicians' efforts to inform or educate them. Mr. N was able to explain the readings on his arteriograms. Mrs. H described the dynamics of arthritis and the operations on her thumb joints in detail. "My doctors tell me everything; I guess they think I can take it." Indeed, these two patients could "take it"; they had sufficient information about their ailments and their bodies to be able to assimilate information given them by their physicians.

In contrast, Mrs. D and Mrs. C did not have a framework for understanding what they were being told. While their physicians might have gone further in explaining arrhythmia or liver biopsy, the women lacked basic information and therefore had difficulty assimilating what they were told. Unlike Mr. N and Mrs. H, they had difficulty in being assertive and asking questions. Their feelings of being intimidated and their relatively low self-esteem compounded their low level of health information. They were comfortable, however, in talking to lay associates and therefore turned to them with their fears and uncertainties.

Managing Drug Side Effects

The undesirable effects of medications or treatments was a crucial area of doctor-patient communication. The study participants were taking many powerful medicines, and several of them reported feeling worse or even quite ill following the initiation of a medication. Mrs. S, who attributed her double vision to a new drug, is one example. When a physician failed to attend to patients' reports of side effects, this was very disruptive. Four participants reported leaving a physician because of dissatisfaction with his handling of side effects. Mrs. M, for example, complained to her cardiologist that a heart medication had made her very ill, but he represcribed it, tripling the dosage. As she explains it:

> I trusted the doctor, I thought he gives me something else. I took the medicine the next morning. I got so nauseated, and I could not do things, so I called him right away. "Doctor, what medicine did you prescribe for me?" He said, "That's the same medicine you had before, 100 milligrams in the old one, 300 milligrams in the new one." I told him before I couldn't stand it. "You have to take it, otherwise you'll die." I said "No, I don't have to take it, doctor, thank you," and I hung up, and I never rang him back.

Even if the physician's response to side effects does not prove disruptive to the doctor-patient relationship, it serves as a paradigm for the communication and relationship that exists between them. Communication about this topic can convey the physician's commitment to the patient's need for understanding and responsibility for their own care. In the reports of the older people in the substudy, this was the exception rather than the rule.

The degree of patient participation required for the management of a chronic illness was mentioned above. When patients are gravely ill, physicians perform surgery or administer treatments to an essentially passive recipient. With chronic illnesses, patients (or their family members) must take much more responsibility for their own actions for a much longer time. The extensive literature on noncompliance speaks to the fact that physicians have less control in such situations. Some observers have proposed, therefore, that physicians adopt a more egalitarian or colleaguial relationship with chronically ill patients (Szasz & Hollander, 1956).

A few of the participants' reports illustrated some features of such a relationship. Physicians who elicited and responded to the patients' reports in effect invited them to be partners in the treatment, through encouraging them to observe and judge effects. On the other hand, doctors who ignored or did not deal with the patients' reports of unpleasant side effects adhered to a model of the doctor-patient relationship in which they, the physicians, had sole responsibility for decisions.

Sharing information about medications and regimens with the patient would have several important results. They would be more comfortable because uncertainty is reduced, and they would be able to make more informed decisions. The patients would be more likely to give a medication or a regimen a fair trial or to recognize dangerous effects more quickly. Some examples of ways in which doctors could share information follow.

When the patient's discretion about the dosage of a medication is warranted, the doctor could give guidelines about when and how to adjust dosages. Patients often did this on their own initiative, reporting to or checking with their physicians after the fact. If the physician judges it inadvisable to alter the dosage of a particular medication, he should tell the patient.

Patients should be informed ahead of time about what to expect from a medication, such as what delay might occur before a medication takes effect, what unpleasant side effects could be predicted, and whether the side effects are likely to be transient. Such preparation gives patients a framework for understanding what they are experiencing. If such effects cannot be predicted, more frequent communication might be planned until an acceptable modus operandi with a specific medication is struck. Doctors also may need to provide reassurance that the side effects will not be more harmful than the disease. Through such steps, physicians and patients could work more cooperatively, with consequent improvements in the use of medications.

Patients who receive such preparation are better equipped to judge and monitor the effects of the treatments they carry out. The variability and unpredictability of the older body's physiological response to medications and the need to monitor their effects carefully have been well documented (Rowe, 1977).

In following regimens as well, the cues and clues from the body may be the best guide to the patient about how much walking is too much, or enough, or how much rest is too little. Mrs. D and Mrs. C were both given instructions about changing their levels of activity but were not provided with guidelines to gauge the correct levels. Physicians can encourage the patient's observation and judgment through instruction about what might be desired or undesirable effects of a regimen, as well as through respecting the patient's description. Such methods can enhance patients' abilities to manage their own chronic illnesses.

Information giving is key to encouraging more patient responsibility for health management. The patient needs to know enough about what is wrong and what is being recommended to understand the reasons for recommendations, judge correctly the seriousness of the condition, make informed decisions, and monitor correctly the body's response.

Suggestions for Better Professional/Patient Communication

Many health professionals are aware of the need to elicit reliable data from their patients and, in turn, to provide their patients with information that can be understood and assimilated. Because of the special characteristics and needs of the elderly, such matters take on added importance. The participants in the substudy offered instructive examples of factors that encouraged or inhibited communication.

Office Procedures. Office procedures often convey a message about the availability of the professional to listen or instruct. Long waits and an office full of waiting patients, a rushed examination, and hallway conferences did little to convey the doctor's receptiveness to discussion. On the other hand, carefully scheduled appointments, call-in times, and unpressured time with the physician legitimated the patients' questions or revelations.

While such procedures are important for patients of all ages and some rushed situations may be difficult for busy professionals to avoid, the pacing of contacts takes on added importance to older people. Cognitive processes may be slowed, even if unimpaired. Lowered self-esteem may make it more difficult for patients to raise questions or to reveal that they have not understood. Health professionals, seeing older people bewildered, confused, or uncomprehending when communications are delivered too rapidly, may mistakenly assume that the older person is mentally impaired, or at best, not capable of independent and intelligent judgments. Unpressured time for discussion, geared to the pace of the patient, may be crucial for effective communication.

Alternatives to the Physician's Own Communication. For a variety of reasons, physicians may choose a style of practice incompatible with extended discussions with patients or responsibility for patient education. Among the physicians dealing with the case study participants, some used adjunct staff such as nurse clinicians or physician assistants to aid in communication. Such personnel could take charge of reviewing the patients' health experiences and symptoms since the last visit or of teaching and answering questions about the physician's recommendations. Mrs. C poignantly articulated the need for such a person: "There should be someone that you can come and talk to that you can tell these things to . . . that could sit and talk to you and tell you, but there isn't. A professional. Well, our agencies should be geared for that."

When there is a great deal of uniform or routinized information needed by an entire group of patients, health professionals can make use of educational pamphlets.

Assessing the Patient's Level of Knowledge, Fears, and Comprehension. Among even the few persons participating in this study, the variations in their communications with physicians were instructive. The health professional should make some attempt to assess the patient's level of health sophistication in order to judge how much patient education is appropriate and how information can be given in the way most comprehensible to that particular patient.

The study revealed another feature of the participants' thinking about health: the amount of background information gleaned from observing or hearing of the illness of others, from the media and from other sources. When symptoms occurred, or when changes in a continuing illness occurred, people used this background information to interpret and categorize what was happening to them. Depending on the individual's personality and sense of vulnerability, and, of course, on the nature of the symptoms, people can arrive at some frightening conclusions. For many of the study participants, a particular specter or fear attached itself to their symptoms. Most commonly it was of cancer, but the specter of heart attacks or strokes proved equally terrifying.

Even if patients do not experience such definite fears, they may approach the health professional with specific preconceptions or interpretations of the current condition. Asking what patients fear or believe they have, and what they expect to happen, will give the health professional some idea what preconceptions need to be worked with or corrected, and what the patient wants, needs to know, and will be most easily able to hear.

Even a carefully designed communication may be misunderstood or blocked. Sometimes patients are so upset and anxious about a new diagnosis that it is difficult for them to absorb the information. They may not have heard what was said to them because it does not yet seem relevant. Questions may not occur to them until they go home and begin to wonder if they should be doing something differently.

Health professionals attempting to gauge how much the patient has understood might ask the patient to repeat back what has been said. This is more likely to reveal areas of confusions, incomprehensions, or resistance than simply asking if the patient understands or has any questions. Communications that take place through an interactive process in which the patient can "try out" the new information will be much more successful than those in which the health professional talks and the patient listens.

Using Significant Others.   Another method by which the patients' information about their ailments and regimens could be supported is to include the patient's caregiver or significant other in discussions. As influential as these significant others were in discussing and reinforcing health actions, the study participants evidenced clear norms about privacy and self-responsibility. The appropriateness of such inclusion, therefore, is a delicate judgment to make; a very competent older person may smart at the inference that he or she is not capable of independent judgments, and a moderately disoriented person who truly requires support may object just as strenuously.

In the absence of clear indications of incompetence, the wishes of the patients are the best guide. The health professional should ask if the patient wishes the doctor to include the collateral or to inform the supportive person after the examination. If the professional judges it necessary to inform a supportive person, the reason should be explained to the patient. Doctors described in the study sometimes addressed their remarks *only* to the significant other; this undermines the self-esteem and sense of competence of the older patient. Even a disoriented patient should be involved to the maximum degree, and everything that will support the patients' autonomous management of their self-care should be tried. It might be easier for the patient's son to give the medications if his father is forgetful, but if a notebook in which the older man writes down every dose aids him to take medications successfully, that method is preferable.

Assessment of Health Information Resources

This substudy suggested that discussions with other people have some influence on the things people do to take care of themselves. For this reason, the assessment of older people might include exploration of the information resources available to them. People living in senior housing or a retirement community see and learn much more about health problems of older people from those around them. Those who remain actively in touch with one or more sources of information may be more likely to be reminded about the need for care of their health. Older people with no one to talk to may receive little reinforcement of health actions and might be considered in special need of health information and health education.

In summary, the substudy found that conversations with friends or family members were influential in determining how the older people dealt with their health problems. Such lay consultation carried more weight and was even sought actively when people felt ill-informed by their physicians. Of course, some kinds of information from lay sources, especially from those suffering the same ailment, may be useful, for it may reveal how others cope with the symptoms or special features of the disease. Even so, lay consultation is not a substitute for professional expertise. These elderly participants themselves preferred to have access to professional advice. The sharing of information by health professionals with their patients is part of a more egalitarian model of shared responsibility. Professionals can support self-care by providing information and by educating older people about their health and their diseases. The strengthening of patients' responsibility and decision-making is an important component of optimal management of the health problems of the elderly.

III Case Illustrations

The preceding chapters have reported the findings about the 132 elderly people studied mainly in terms of aggregated data. That kind of information about their mental and physical health experiences and practices, however, tells only part of their story. Each of the older people is an individual who differs from the others in many ways. They live and function in varied social and physical environments, in different socioeconomic and personal circumstances, and they have diverse lifestyles. Their personalities and histories differ, and they react and adapt to their health experiences differently one from the other. The selected case studies in the next three chapters place the health experiences and behaviors of these older people in the context of their daily lives.

The case studies also serve to illuminate another aspect of older people's health practices. The quantitative data spoke to their day-to-day symptoms (small and large), their responses to those symptoms, their diagnoses, and their relationships with the health systems and professionals. But, because the research questions focused on symptoms and bothers, they did not elicit information about the actions many of the older people took to prevent illness or promote health. Though the responses to the direct question about preventive actions did identify many such measures, additional ones often were mentioned as the participants chatted informally with the interviewers. These, too, are included in the case studies.

In the course of the study, the older persons became, in effect, hosts to the project interviewers who spent many hours with them in their homes. They shared details of their lives, sometimes with remarkable candor. Their relatives, too, were responsive, often displaying a concern about the purpose of the study and the possibly beneficial effects that could result for other persons in similar circumstances.

The mental and physical health of an older person inevitably affects the lifestyle, relationships, and even the physical and mental health of their collaterals—that is, the family, friends, and neighbors—who provide support and care. The older people had many different family constellations. Some had family collaterals who were close and supportive. At the other extreme, others had only friends or neighbors who, though interested and caring, could provide relatively little in the way of help. The case studies serve to provide a picture of the pressures often put on family members and others when an elderly person needs ongoing care and the interpersonal problems that may come to the surface. The behavior of family members—sometimes heroic, sometimes simply dutiful—constitutes further evidence of the commitment and responsible behavior of most families. The small minority who react with indifference or abuse of the older people (verbal or physical) are represented among the case summaries. And the selfless help sometimes provided by friends or neighbors of those older people who have no close family members is also illustrated.

The case studies are grouped as the older people were in the research study—that is, as normals, the functionally disturbed, and those with senile dementia. But there are many familiar themes common to all three groups. Among those themes are the multiplicity of chronic conditions and the efforts to deal with them, sometimes in eccentric ways; the unrelieved pain and fatigue which many of them tolerate; the intricately interwoven mix of physical and emotional problems; the widespread confusion about medications and frequent misuse of them; and the older people's complaints about health practitioners.

Each case is headed by a phrase highlighting a particular aspect or problem of mental or physical health or health care. However, because so many aspects occur in relation to each individual situation, those phrases were selected almost arbitrarily. Notes in the margin are, therefore, used to call attention to the various matters they illustrate.

9 The Mentally Normal Older People

A multiplicity of symptoms is demonstrated strikingly in many of the older people studied, among those with normal mental functioning as well as among those in the other two groups. The normals were referred to the research project mainly by senior centers where they were involved and active. But the study provides a behind the scenes look at their problems—including much mental and physical distress.

Mrs. Kind, for example, takes an almost awesome inventory of medications for her multiple symptoms and health conditions.

Mrs. Kind: Multiple Symptoms and Medications

Seventy-year-old Mrs. Kind is a native Philadelphian who lives with her husband in a suburban middle-class neighborhood. Their home is neat and tastefully decorated. The couple recently celebrated their 50th wedding anniversary. They report managing comfortably on their income of about $8,000 a year.

A beloved son died five years ago. Mrs. Kind says sadly that "God gives and takes." Mr. and Mrs. Kind are very close to their daughter, son-in-law, and two grandchildren. The daughter is in touch with Mrs. Kind twice a day by telephone. She and her family live about 25 minutes away and visit at least weekly. The daughter describes her mother as "a worrier," particularly about her own health, though Mrs. Kind has been in poor health for 30 years. For her part, Mrs. Kind feels her health is only fair and that she is afraid that she soon will not be able to take care of herself. "I pray to God that I don't want to become a burden and become senile."

A close family

"I don't want to be a burden"

Mrs. Kind says she experienced many physical symptoms in the month prior to her interview, including shortness of breath, swelling of feet, headaches, chronic tiredness, and nervous-

Multiple symptoms and nonreporting

125

ness. She did not report these to anyone because "after so many complaints, it's like a broken record." She also experienced difficulty sleeping, aches and pains, being unsteady on her feet, gas, and forgetfulness. These she reported to her husband. She told the doctor about the gas and her friend about her constipation.

Many chronic problems

Mrs. Kind's medical history includes many chronic conditions. Along with trouble seeing and hearing, she has had high blood pressure and heart failure for 40 years and diabetes for 28 years. She also is anemic and has circulation problems, trouble passing water, gout, constipation, and hemorrhoids. Three years ago, she had a stroke and lost feeling in her left hand. During her adolescence she had had "seizures." Though these ended 28 years ago, she claims to have taken phenobarbital ever since and feels that she is addicted to it.

Eleven prescription drugs

Medications currently being taken by Mrs. Kind include Aldactazide (hypertension), Diabinese (diabetes), Quinaglute (heart), Kondremul, Dulcolax (constipation), Phenobarbital, Persantine (angina), Slow-K (potassium), Inderal (heart), Isordil (angina), and Ascriptin (pain). She also takes self-prescribed vitamins "for good health," including vitamins B, C, and a combination of B and C, and One-a-Day vitamins.

An adverse reaction to a drug

During the past year, she had been hospitalized for ten days because of an adverse reaction to Pronestyl.

Because of her diabetes, Mrs. Kind is extremely careful about her diet, but she feels that she should get more rest.

Positive attitudes toward health professionals

Mrs. Kind travels the length of the city every three weeks to see her physician and calls him at least once a month to discuss a health concern. She is satisfied with the care she is receiving but complains that the ride to the doctor's office is too long. She sees a podiatrist every five weeks and a gynecologist and a urologist once a year.

Negative attitudes toward professionals

Though Mrs. Kind's attitudes toward physicians and other health professionals are highly positive, her daughter feels that hospital staff treat their patients inhumanely and does not think that doctors' advice should always be followed. She would like, for example, to see her mother's medications examined more frequently with a view toward decreasing them.

Despite her multiple health problems, Mrs. Kind is capable of self-care. Her daughter gives her much emotional support and often offers suggestions about activities and socializing opportunities for her mother's consideration. Mr. and Mrs. Kind are members of a couples club at the Y, which they

attend as regularly as they can. Mrs. Kind has several friends
from this club to whom she speaks daily.

Mrs. Kind strongly agreed with the statement that "Nowa-   The myth repeated
days, adult children do not take as much care of their elderly
parents as they did in past generations." She quickly added,
with pride, "But not in my case."

Though Mrs. Kind's chronic health conditions have permeated her own
thinking and that of her family for many years, to some extent she is able to
transcend them and remain cheerful and socially active. She receives comprehensive medical care and is fortunate in having (and appreciating) excellent
support from her family. Though she is satisfied with her health care, one
wonders whether the daughter may be justified in feeling that Mrs. Kind's
regimen of 11 drugs should be reviewed. Mrs. Kind is typical in believing
that nowadays adult children do not take care of the elderly as they did in the
past. She is also typical in believing that her family is an exception to that
rule.

Another project client, Mrs. Evans, resembles Mrs. Kind in that she is
similar in age and in experiencing multiple health complaints. By contrast
with Mrs. Kind, however, Mrs. Evans is so lonely and depressed that she
wept when her series of four interviews ended and she realized that the
interviewer would not be returning. She seems to be asking for sustained
attention from someone who is both caregiver and companion.

Mrs. Evans: Frail, Lonely, and Depressed

Mrs. Evans feels that her problems will be over only when she
is dead; she can barely "keep her sanity" and does not look
forward at all to the rest of her life. A 72-year-old widow, Mrs.
Evans lives alone in a small rented apartment. She feels   Poor environment
"claustrophobic" and says she was ready to leave it the day   and low income
she moved in three years ago. Since her present income is
between $3,000 and $4,000 (on which she "makes herself get
along"), she cannot move.

Mrs. Evans' closest social contact is her sister-in-law (the wife
of a deceased brother), whom she named as collateral. The
sister-in-law is in daily phone contact with Mrs. Evans and
visits at least twice weekly. Mrs. Evans depends on her heavily for emotional support, as well as for some specific instrumental supports. A sister who lives at the other end of the
city also manages to visit weekly and to call almost daily. One
of Mrs. Evans' two sons keeps in fairly close contact by phone
and visits several times a month; occasionally he and his wife
take Mrs. Evans out to eat. The other son lives 90 miles away
and is in less frequent contact.

Frailty limits activities

Mrs. Evans is petite, neatly groomed, friendly, alert, attentive, and eager to talk about her health problems. She walks slowly and deliberately because she is very fearful of falling, particularly when she is alone; she therefore tries to hold onto objects to support herself. Her poor health often interferes with her activities and seems to be the entire focus of Mrs. Evans' life.

Multiple physical
symptoms reported

During the month prior to her interviews, Mrs. Evans had experienced difficulty sleeping, foot and ankle swelling, loss of strength in her legs, tiredness, dizziness, headaches, other aches, weight loss, unsteadiness on her feet, trouble passing water, poor appetite, gas, constipation, and diarrhea. All of these symptoms were reported to her sister, her sister-in-law,

Emotional symptoms
not reported

her doctor, or all three. She had also experienced but had not reported nervousness and periods of feeling blue.

Anxieties

Most of the time Mrs. Evans worries about not being able to care for herself, and she feels that something bad could happen to her at night. She is afraid of being alone. Mrs. Evans described one incident when she felt ill and was going to call the fire rescue squad, but "it turned out to be diarrhea."

Mrs. Evans has cataracts which are ready to be removed. Her trouble hearing began four years ago and had been discussed with her doctor, but "it's just there" and nothing can be done about it. Mrs. Evans' doctor told her that her circulation "isn't that bad." Her hiatus hernia often causes a sensation which she describes as "like a tight band

Self-treatment

around the upper chest." She takes Maalox, doesn't eat fried food or roughage, and uses Rolaids (given to her by her sister) and ginger ale to relieve this feeling. She takes Dulco-lax tablets, Metamucil, or suppositories for chronic constipation. Though her physician recommended bran foods, Mrs. Evans eats dried fruits instead.

To compound her problems, Mrs. Evans claims that her bladder is "not in place," and she can't hold her urine, so that she's well all the time. Most nights she gets up to go to the bathroom as many as eight times. (This did not occur the night after she went out with her son; that night she slept straight through without incident.) This problem has existed for 30 years and,

A hysterectomy for
urinary incontinence

ten months ago, she had a hysterectomy when it was felt that her uterus might be pressing on her bladder, but Mrs. Evans claims that the problem has worsened since the surgery. She takes Ditropan to control her bladder and recently has begun to take Septra DS, an antibiotic, for a bladder infection.

Finally, Mrs. Evans suffers from severe arthritic pain in the neck, arms, back, and legs (which feel like they are "burning" most of the time). For these problems, she does exercises consisting of leg movements and bending at the waist. Her doctor also told her to take a hot bath, and she had her homemaker rub her legs and back with alcohol.

Chronic pain

Mrs. Evans has a great many concerns about doctors and what she perceives as poor medical service. She cried quietly when she talked about how doctors don't seem to care. She claims that after she had a fall, the doctor treated her brusquely, and a nurse had treated her as if she were senile, which made her feel angry and hurt. On another occasion, when she had surgery, she waited in the operating waiting room for four hours before her doctor came.

Complaints about health care and professional attitudes

Though Mrs. Evans has several good friends as well as family members, she states that she doesn't like to "live alone, eat alone, be alone." She feels "lost" all the time.

Loneliness

Mrs. Evans gets considerable assistance with her activities of daily living, primarily because she can't walk much or stand up for a long time. When she goes outside she needs help to get around and her sister, sister-in-law, or a paid homemaker help her. The homemaker and her sister-in-law buy her food, and Mrs. Evans' daughter-in-law sends her clothes. The homemaker does the housework, laundry, cooking, and helps her bathe. Mrs. Evans needs help dressing, and she either stays in her nightgown or gets occasional help from a neighbor.

Functional impairments and dependency

Mrs. Evans' major concern about her health now and in the future is that she not become a "cripple" or dependent.

Fear of dependency

Mrs. Evans is badly in need of companionship—a social contact that is consistent, permanent (unlike the interviewer, whose visits became so important to Mrs. Evans), and not based on meeting Mrs. Evans' physical needs. Her physical health is now the focus, not only of her interaction with others, but also of their contact with her. Mrs. Evans' problems seem to diminish when she is involved in social activities, as when she slept through the night after going out to eat with her son.

Despite her complaints about doctors, Mrs. Evans seems to have a fairly good rapport with her own physician, considering the fact that she calls him at least once per week and speaks to him personally each time. Her accounts of poor care may be due in large part to her vulnerability to what she perceives as slights and to her hunger for someone who really cares about her.

Mrs. Evans has nothing to distract her from sitting alone in her apartment, thinking about her health. She is frightened and panicky, as she proved when she considered calling the rescue squad for an unusual physical sensation, which turned out to be a minor intestinal disturbance.

Mrs. Evans desperately wants someone to take care of her totally— to walk with her, to eat with her, and to help her maintain her health. In spite of a dedicated and tolerant network of friends and relatives who seem to meet most of her physical needs, she wants more. One wonders whether a protected group living situation would provide the reassurance she requires in relation to her physical safety, as well as offering opportunities for contacts.

There are, of course, exceptions to the frequent pattern of taking multiple medications. Some older people, such as Mrs. Rowe, rely on folklore and the media for their health practices.

Mrs. Rowe: Nonmedical Care

Twice widowed, seventy-six-year-old Mrs. Rowe has a history of heart attacks and a stroke. Her present health problems include cataracts, arthritis, pain from a hip injured in a fall five years ago, and forgetfulness (which she attributes to age).

Antimedical care

She doesn't like to take doctors' medicines because of "the bad side effects they give you." Instead, drawing heavily from health magazines, Mrs. Rowe has adopted a conglomeration of preventive health measures. Even though her income is in the $3,000–$3,999 range, she adheres to an extensive regimen of vitamin and mineral combinations, including zinc with vitamins for health; bone meal for nerves and because "it puts marrow into the bones"; kelp for the thyroid and to help lose weight; vitamin C for general health; brewer's yeast which "builds you up and has all the vitamins in it"; cod liver oil, a laxative, and soy bean oil, which is "for every illness." She eats a raw onion at every meal and raw garlic at night to prevent colds and take care of high blood pressure. Recently, on a church trip to Pennsylvania, she purchased some black horseradish because "it cures arthritis." (She sometimes takes the horseradish in a mixture with whiskey.) Mrs. Rowe stands on her head because she read that this makes one look younger. She also soaks her legs up to the knees in cold water every morning for five minutes because one of her three health magazines advocated that practice as beneficial to the liver and kidneys.

Health advice from the media

Horseradish and whiskey

Mrs. Rowe's multiple health problems and busy illness- prevention regimen do not seem to limit her activities
very much. She has a part-time job that is a remarkable **Works and takes**
"fit" with her health views: she is a cleaning woman at **care of three other**
a health food store. In addition, Mrs. Rowe cares for three **people**
disabled people who share her home—a 49-year-old
daughter who suffers from the effects of lead poisoning,
a 46-year-old daughter with epilepsy, and her deceased
husband's 66-year-old aunt who is a former mental hospital
patient.

Mrs. Rowe is an example of the older person who rarely is in contact with
the professional health care world and does not appear to have suffered much.
She is active, happy, independent, and from all indications, pretty healthy.
She did hint at various times that her increasing forgetfulness is troublesome
to her, as is her arthritis (many of her curative measures deal with alleviating
arthritis).

Mrs. Rowe's preventive health behaviors are, to say the least, controver-
sial. From the financial standpoint her vitamins, minerals, bone meal, and
other health foods are probably more expensive than a complete, balanced
diet would be. While one is tempted to recommend nutrition counseling,
Mrs. Rowe seems to enjoy managing her own health and takes pride in her
excellent condition. She has a purpose that she feels has produced immediate
results. How can one argue against that?

Mrs. Jay's health situation offers a sharp contrast to that of Mrs. Rowe.
She has much contact with health professionals, but communication with
them leaves much to be desired. She receives attention from a strong network
of relatives but seems to need a thorough work-up and coordinated health
care.

Mrs. Jay: A Need for Coordinated Care

Mrs. Jay, 66-years-old, lives with her 70-year-old husband in
the nicely furnished row home where they have been for the
last 40 years. There are two adult children, both married. The
daughter phones almost daily and visits several times a week, **Good social supports**
as do an aunt and a cousin. Mrs. Jay's son visits weekly
and phones her several times between visits. Mrs. Jay
also has many friends and is in touch with one or more
almost daily.

Mrs. Jay was very much involved in volunteer work until her
husband was forced to retire at age 65. At that time, he told
her that he wanted her to stay at home. This was a big change **Problems with a**
for both of them, as Mr. Jay used to work at his service station **retired husband**

16–17 hours a day but now spends his time at home, reading. Mrs. Jay feels bored and says that her husband's retirement is not working out as they both would have liked. She regrets that she does not have a hobby and says that she and her husband do everything together. She still maintains her activities at the senior center, however, where she is involved in political lobbying to get various financial breaks for senior citizens.

Multiple mental and physical symptoms

Weight loss

Mrs. Jay worries constantly, particularly about her health, which often interferes with what she'd like to do. She reports anxiety, depression, and an inability to concentrate, to make up her mind, or to remember things. In the month prior to being interviewed, Mrs. Jay had experienced 18 physical and mental symptoms, including chest pain on activity and a loss of 22 pounds. She has arthritis of the feet, spine, and hands (for which she follows no regimen) and anemia, for which she takes self-prescribed vitamin B_{12} (though her doctor told her to discontinue this treatment).

Hears humming

Four or five years ago, Mrs. Jay fell and hit her head. She states that she bled internally and should have gone to a hospital immediately because she also was bleeding from the nose and mouth. She saw her doctor the next day, but he found nothing wrong. About a year and a half ago, Mrs. Jay started to hear a constant low hum that "sounds like water running." She has seen many ear, nose, and throat specialists who did not help her. Once, she states, a doctor said she "had a hole" in her right sinus passage and required surgery, but she refused the operation.

Gastrointestinal symptoms, including nausea, vomiting, and bleeding

Mrs. Jay has a hiatus hernia and diverticulitis and reports many gastrointestinal symptoms, including severe stomach pain. She takes antacids (Maalox, Mylanta) after every meal. She has frequent nausea and sometimes vomits after simply drinking water. Recently, Mrs. Jay had been vomiting almost constantly, including vomiting of her normal prescription of oral Compazine. She called the doctor who then prescribed a Compazine suppository for her nausea. During the interview period, Mrs. Jay also reported bleeding from the rectum. Her doctor has prescribed sitz baths. Mrs. Jay states that her hiatus hernia also interferes with her ability to swallow and that her husband has had to perform the Heimlich Maneuver on her numerous times to prevent her from choking.

Mrs. Jay complains that she gets no information from her doctor about her health problems. Her own family doctor stopped practicing three years ago and, since then, she's "been floundering." She had tests done in the hospital and asked for a written report but got none. She thinks that her present physician may leave his practice soon and is trying to pass her off to his nephew.

Mrs. Jay expressed frustration with the contradictory advice she receives. For example, when she went to the dentist for sores in her mouth, he said she has herpes and told her to gargle with salt water, use Orabase ointment with Kenalog, and to paint the sores with alcohol. She then called her dermatologist who told her to stop using the alcohol and prescribed tranquilizers four times daily. They made Mrs. Jay dizzy, so she cut the dosage and then skipped them completely.

Multiple sources of medical advice

Mrs. Jay thinks the medical profession is "lousing her up," that she needs better medical care and someone to study her more carefully. She feels that she has good rapport with her doctor but that she doesn't get the information she wants. Her husband agrees completely with his wife's assessment of her medical care and confirmed the details she provided.

Mrs. Jay has excellent social supports. Though these certainly are in her favor in helping her to deal with her physical health, they are not helping to solve her problems. Certainly, her husband's retirement and his demands that she spend her time at home with him could be aggravating her physical condition.

Despite Mrs. Jay's frequent medical contacts, she feels she is not getting better and is not getting any clues as to why she seems to be deteriorating. It is impossible to be critical of her medical treatment without getting all the details from the professional point of view. On the surface, it appears that she is being treated symptomatically, rather than by her conditions. For example, she takes Compazine for constant nausea but continues to experience this symptom. The chest pain, vomiting, bleeding, and radical weight loss may be signaling acute problems.

At the same time, Mrs. Jay gives evidence of seeking out many medical opinions but picking and choosing those she wishes to follow. We can only assume that this has happened in the past, and it is possible that she has declined treatment which would have improved her condition. We don't know the extent to which she has mixed opinions from more than one professional (possibly following conflicting regimens) nor whether she has informed each new professional contact of his/her predecessors. At the least, however, Mrs. Jay could benefit from a thorough evaluation, clear communication about her health problems, and coordination of care for her multiple conditions.

Like Mrs. Jay, Mr. Martin uses many nonprofessional sources of advice in his health practices, though these are supplemented by a doctor's recommendations.

Mr. Martin: Misinformation about Health

Poor family relationships

At age 70, Mr. Martin has been divorced for 27 years since his wife left, taking their two sons with her. He lives alone in a cramped, one-room efficiency apartment in a large center city apartment building and is capable of taking care of himself. He claims that he still has bad dreams about the separation from his sons. He sees them every few months or so but says that they resent him for trying to take them to court to obtain financial assistance years ago. Any present family involvement is only on occasions such as illness and funerals.

Mr. Martin is short, stocky, and barrel-chested. During his first interviews, he smelled strongly of sweat and after-shave lotion, but as the interviews continued his appearance and personal cleanliness seemed to improve. It was apparent to the interviewer that Mr. Martin looked forward to the interviews and enjoyed talking to someone.

Active at the senior center

For many of Mr. Martin's working years, he was a master painter. Now he occasionally does some painting at the senior center on a volunteer basis. His present income is about $3,600 a year, and he feels this is just enough to get along. He has almost daily contact with half a dozen close friends and is very active at the senior center. He is president of his group there and was proud that his name was in the newspaper because of his position.

Amputated toes

Constant pain

Inappropriate practices

Mr. Martin's most serious and bothersome health problem is the result of the fact that in 1947 he had all his toes amputated due to frostbite. He uses two canes to walk and has special implants for his shoes but is in considerable and constant pain. It feels like he is "walking on stones." In addition, his severe calluses cause a constant burning sensation. In the main, he treats himself, although he has discussed these problems with his doctor. He often soaks his feet in water with foot powder, files his calluses himself, and sometimes puts whole aspirin where his toes used to be. His major health concern in the future is his fear that he may become too weak to walk.

Mr. Martin takes Dymelor (for diabetes) but believes that his drug is "for blood pressure or urine analysis." He tests his urine for glucose daily with Tes-Tape and is on a special diet which requires him to avoid "eating sugar." He says, however, that he usually does not eat what he should because he can't afford it and because he finds it hard to get to the store.

Confusion about medication

Mr. Martin drinks alcohol because he "needs the taste and the feeling," and in order to stimulate his circulation and help his heart. He also often drinks with meals. After one incident of sharp left-sided chest pain, he treated himself by rubbing his chest and taking a shot of whiskey.

Whiskey for chest pain

Mr. Martin obtains most of his health-related information from friends and a variety of other sources. For example, at the suggestion of a friend, he had nine teeth removed to relieve bursitis in his arm. He takes certain preventive measures from books and magazines. For instance, he does arm and leg exercises in order to lose weight and takes ten breaths through each nostril separately in order to put himself to sleep.

Lay advice

Mr. Martin goes to a private doctor every two months at which time he reports his physical symptoms. With respect to his periods of feeling blue, however, "It's nobody else's business." Frequent periods of forgetfulness also go unreported because "it's a normal process," it might "degrade or belittle" him, and he would "make a fool of himself."

Ashamed of mental symptoms

Though Mr. Martin professes positive attitudes toward health professionals and following the doctor's advice, he is also influenced toward preventive health measures by outside sources, such as books, magazines, and friends. However, he lacks information about good care for his current conditions, particularly in relation to his diabetes. His understanding of the nutritional restrictions and demands of diabetes is inadequate; his use of alcohol could prove dangerous and has potential for resulting in a diabetic crisis. Appropriate and meticulous care of the feet is also an essential part of daily care for a diabetic. Because his foot problem is so severe, Mr. Martin is an excellent candidate for professional foot care on a frequent basis. Either there has been an absence of teaching or instructions have not been emphatic enough, since he seems willing to follow suggested procedures (whatever the source).

Mr. Martin shows a lot of courage in dealing with a major disability (his feet) and in dealing with constant pain. Unfortunately, he may be almost too willing to deal with pain, as evidenced by his self-treatment of chest pain. He needs to distinguish what requires professional attention from incidents which are self-treatable. His attitude of shame toward depression and forgetfulness is not unusual among older people and results in the nonreporting of such significant mental symptoms.

It is apparent that Mr. Martin gets great satisfaction from his senior center activities and, in the absence of real family involvement, seems to meet his social needs through his friends. He is an example of how a senior center can be important to an older person's self-esteem and sense of involvement.

In the course of the project, staff members were often in awe of the courage and resourcefulness with which the older people lived. At the same time, the low expectations many of them had with respect to the amenities and even necessities of life was often moving. Mr. Cooper is such a man.

Mr. Cooper: Low Expectations

At 79 years of age, Mr. Cooper has been widowed for five years and lives alone in his own home. He has four children—two sons and two daughters. One lives less than a half hour away, visits once a month, and phones several times a week.

Interested in finance

When Mr. Cooper worked, he operated his own lumber business. He was very active and loved to travel. His present income is between $9,000 and $10,000, some of which is the result of his active speculation on the stock market. He spends much of his time reviewing financial matters, reading the *Wall Street Journal,* talking to brokers, and writing finance-related letters. One of his sons indicated that his father has, at times, given him money. Whenever they talk, his father usually coaches him on what to do if anything happens to him, such as what stocks to buy.

Poor environmental conditions

Mr. Cooper has lived in the same house for the last 27 years in what now is a high crime area. Opening the door of the enclosed porch sets off a loud buzzer. There is a large mirror inside the house which affords a view of the entire porch, and there is a sign on the outside door which says "Beware—Bad Dog" although Mr. Cooper has no dog. Inside, the house is dirty and cluttered. There is a hospital bed in the dining room and a pair of crutches in the corner which Mr. Cooper uses to go upstairs several times during the day. When downstairs, he spends most of the day in his wheelchair, which he can maneuver very quickly. In 1974, for reasons that he never explained, his right leg was amputated, and three years later two toes were removed from his left foot.

An amputated leg

When interviewed, Mr. Cooper was always dressed the same way—in a loosely tied hospital gown, sometimes with a sweater over it. Some days his hair was combed; on others it was not. He often chewed tobacco, using a can in which to spit. He has no teeth because, as each tooth became loose, he just hit his mouth and pulled the tooth out. He does not wear dentures.

Pulled his own teeth

Mr. Cooper reports his health to be excellent, better than the health of his peers, and almost never interferes with what he wants to do. (The son feels his father's health is poor but agrees that Mr. Cooper almost never worries about it.) Mr. Cooper doesn't go out but claims to be "very content" in his own home. (The son disagrees here as well.) A homemaker does his food shopping from a list he makes, and he uses a catalogue for clothes shopping. He performs all other activities of daily living himself. Mr. Cooper states that he always eats what he should for good health. (The son, on the other hand, says that his father eats when he feels like it and eats whatever he wants—that he usually has one full meal a day and then snacks for the rest of the time.)

Claims to be content

Mr. Cooper reports no recent physical symptoms, except a slight loss of strength in his arms and leg. He denies any anxiety or depression, although he states that he worries a little about his family's welfare. In 1950, it was discovered that he had diabetes, and he was treated for a year, but he reports that he had not had diabetes since then. In 1961 he had a stomach or intestinal ulcer removed and, in 1973, cataract surgery on one eye. Mr. Cooper reports slight rheumatism in his wrists for which he takes Tylenol or aspirin. Otherwise, he takes no medication and hasn't seen a doctor since 1977. He doesn't trust them and has a highly negative opinion of health professionals.

Negative attitude toward health professionals

Mr. Cooper feels strongly that everything is in the hands of fate. He shares his philosophy on life—"be happy where you are, love your neighbor, and seek contentment and peace of mind." He appears cheerful, optimistic, and "greatly interested in life." The son worries that if something bad happens to Mr. Cooper, no one will be around. He would like his father to live with his own family (he is widowed and has two children), but his father's response is "Trust in God."

Kismet

Mr. Cooper's son wanted to get some help for his father but couldn't define what was needed. He asked, "Who could convince him that his lifestyle is not good?"

Mr. Cooper professes to be contented with his present living situation. A safe guess about his amputations is that they were related to his history of diabetes, a disease which requires frequent follow-up. He would be an excellent candidate for a visit from a public health nurse. His situation exemplifies a frequent dilemma of those who wish to help: How does one (and should one) help a client who does not want help?

Mr. Cooper, who claimed contentment, contrasts sharply with Mr. Frank, who does not.

Mr. Frank: "Down in the Dumps"

Seventy-nine-year-old Mr. Frank is an ordained minister who has been separated from his wife for 40 years. He lives alone in his own house in an extremely poor, almost deserted neighborhood. Though he is afraid to live there, he feels he has to "protect the house." On one occasion, there was evidence that his back door had been broken down, and he claims that his wallet was taken. Mr. Frank's home is dirty, with little furniture, and appears to be structurally unsound, as well as rat- and roach-infested. He wants desperately to fix up the house but is unable to do so financially and physically.

Poor environmental conditions

Rats and roaches

Mr. Frank himself appears dirty, and it is probable that he sleeps in his clothes, which are unkempt. He is extremely deaf and states that his hearing aid was stolen. Mr. Frank's closest ties are with a 50-year-old divorced niece, whom he named as his collateral. Though the niece lives close by, she sees Mr. Frank only every few months or less because she has crippling arthritis of the spine and is confined to a hospital bed most of the time. She does, however, call Mr. Frank almost daily, talking to him by phone for almost an hour. If Mr. Frank needs something, she sends someone to him.

A disabled collateral

At one point during an interview, Mr. Frank complained that he was tired of "all these questions about doctors and presidents" and wanted the payment given to participants in the study. He said that he cannot make ends meet on the $241 a month he receives from Social Security and SSI and doesn't eat as he should because he can't afford the food. He usually

Poverty and a poor diet

eats one meal a day, consisting of foods such as chicken wings, soda crackers and buttermilk, or corned beef hash. He has applied for meals-on-wheels but has not received service yet.

Mr. Frank has high blood pressure, a heart condition, and arthritis; he takes medication for all of these although he doesn't understand some of his medications and what they are for. For instance, during the interviewing period he was taking erythromycin (an antibiotic) which he said was to relieve his arthritic pain. He complained frequently of back and left-sided pain and a rash on his back, all of which he felt was due to a "bad medicine" given to him by the doctor. He thought that he might be allergic to one of his medicines but had not as yet told the doctor, and was afraid to stop taking the prescription. Mr. Frank attributes his back pain to arthritis but does nothing because he doesn't know what to do and "arthritis and getting senile are just part of getting older." *Misunderstanding of health and medications* *Ailments are "part of getting older"*

Mr. Frank reports emotional problems for which he takes medication he could not identify. He worries most of the time about being alone and what's going to happen to him. He gets lonely and "down in the dumps" often.

Mr. Frank claims to be satisfied with the medical care he receives, although getting to the doctor is a problem (partially due to poor eyesight).

Mr. Frank is an extremely impoverished man, badly in need of social and environmental supports which he does not receive. Technically, it seems that Mr. Frank's physical health is looked after, but his living environment, diet, and personal care are very poor.

Mr. Frank appears to be frustrated, desperate, and defeated. However, with an element of pride, he is trying to survive. This case, like many others, illustrates too clearly the interaction of health, mental health, and environment. It also underlines the frequent misunderstanding and misuse of medications, and the relationship between income and adequate nutrition.

As the cases above illustrate, the older people with normal mental functioning varied in the extent of their discomfort, the ways in which they adapted to their chronic illnesses, and in the support they received from family and from agencies. Being normal mentally—that is, free of a functional mental disorder or senile dementia—did not mean that their minds were at peace nor that they experienced emotional well-being. On the contrary, some were depressed, some were anxious, and some were lonely.

In many instances, it would be exceedingly difficult to sort out or sepa-rate their mental/emotional problems from those which were physical. Among those whose situations have not been summarized above was Mrs. Davenport who was in constant pain from arthritis. She wept quietly as she described her fruitless search for relief and her anger at the disinterest of various doctors. There were often obstacles to health care that relate to health professionals' attitudes and communication gaps between doctor and patient. Mrs. Appel, for example, did not report significant symptoms to her physician because she regarded them as normal and intrinsic to the processes of aging.

Though most of these older people had supportive relationships with their families, the relatives of others displayed a callous insensitivity. Mr. Smith, for example, discharged himself from a nursing home at age 82 against his children's wishes and struggles heroically to maintain his independence despite multiple disabling health conditions. They bring him food irregularly, have taken most of his household possessions, and depleted his funds which had been in a joint account with his son. When Mr. Smith jokingly said he would like to marry to relieve his loneliness, his daughter-in-law asked, "Who would want you?"

Many of the normal older people were gallant in their efforts not to bother people and to put up a good front. Mrs. Zinder, an attractive and a busy participant in activities at the senior center, was described by the center's staff as "well adjusted." But she had many troubling health conditions (shingles and colitis among them) and was constantly worried by the genuinely serious problems of her children and grandchildren. In an unguarded moment, she hinted to the interviewer that she has thought of suicide. But her sense of humor came through: after waiting in her doctor's office for three hours, she suggested to him that he put either a bar or a cot in his waiting room.

10 The Older People with Functional Mental Impairments

Many of the problems of the older people with normal mental functioning were age-related, such as their multiple physical ailments and functional declines in association with depression. While the older people with functional mental disabilities shared many of the age-related deficits of their normal peers, those new "insults" were imposed on a foundation of long-standing mental problems, deprivation, and unhappiness. Some of them struggle to manage, but most are angry, fearful, disturbed, and involved in painful interpersonal relationships.

Mrs. Samuels is one of the rare individuals in the functional group who exhibited a sunny disposition despite mental problems that occurred in the context of a developmental disability and early life hardships.

Mrs. Samuels: A Developmental Disability and a Hard Life

Widowed for 11 years, 67-year-old Mrs. Samuels was born with cerebral palsy, which she claims has shaped the events of her entire life. At age 16, she was "kicked out" by her father, a "perfectionist," and at 21 was married to a man who soon became ill. She sold light bulbs on the phone, ironed, sewed, and did other work to support an infant son and daughter. Mrs. Samuels says that because of her handicap, her family and society in general did not treat her as an equal, and she could not develop to her full potential. Aspirations to be a nurse, to go to college, and to study child psychology remained unfulfilled. *[margin: Born with cerebral palsy]* *[margin: Unfulfilled aspirations]*

Mrs. Samuels is tiny, weighing 73 pounds. She has no teeth, wears glasses, and a black eye showed under the glasses— the result of a fall. She chain-smoked throughout the interviews. Despite her many problems, she evidenced faith, warmth, and good humor.

Mrs. Samuels was told ten years ago to move to a first floor apartment but couldn't find one she could afford on her income of less than $4,000. Winters were particularly hard because she lived at the bottom of a steep hill. Recently, she was taken into her daughter's home. *[margin: Her daughter takes her in]*

141

Numerous mental
and physical
problems

Mrs. Samuels feels her health is poor, and often interferes with her daily activities. In the past month she has experienced symptoms too numerous to list, including shortness of breath, chest pain, nosebleeds, headaches, dizziness, coughing, and poor appetite. She reports no orientation problems, though she has some difficulties with memory and concentration, and experiences a great deal of anxiety. Her "nervous condition" dates back 50 years, and she still gets anxiety attacks. Though she takes Librium regularly, she takes only one per day instead of three as prescribed because it makes her feel strange. She is depressed most of the time.

A complex health
history

An extensive medical history includes hardening of the arteries in and around her eye (according to her doctor), causing "blind spells" every few days. These Mrs. Samuels treats by throwing cold water on her eyes. She gets headaches from reading and is afraid she is going blind. She fears not being able to complete an article she is writing for a handicapped people's magazine and would like a dictaphone. Her doctor wants Mrs. Samuels to come for treatment everyday but she can't afford it. In 1977, Mrs. Samuels had two strokes. She has arthritis in her right arm, which she soaks and exercises. A prescription for Tylenol with codeine is taken only when pain is severe, because she doesn't want to become an addict.

Admitted to a
psychiatric hospital

Fifteen years ago, Mrs. Samuels admitted herself to a state psychiatric hospital, an action which she claims was necessitated by a vitamin deficiency. She has had high blood pressure for 30 years and used to take medications but no longer does so. She just "tries to keep cool." She has had a heart attack and takes nitroglycerine as needed for chest pain. She gets B_{12} shots monthly for anemia, has circulation problems, and a history of stomach ulcers, kidney trouble, "female problems," and gall bladder trouble. Mrs. Samuels also has a pin in her hip for a two-year-old fracture. She lost all her teeth at age 27 and has a full set of dentures but does not wear them because they are too big. She has been plagued by both diarrhea and constipation all her life and has had hemorrhoids for ten years. Foot trouble dates back 20 years, resulting in three falls and about 20 cuts in the last six months.

Frequent falls

Mrs. Samuels feels very positively toward health professionals and sees her doctor every three months and her psychiatrist every two weeks. Her drugs are paid for by the multiservice center. She is not sure who pays her hospital and psychiatrist's bills and says she has a friend on the board of the hospital.

Mrs. Samuels has the support and love of her daughter and son-in-law with whom she lives in a third floor apartment above a drug store. A tiny bedroom is shared with a four-year-old granddaughter. Initially, Mrs. Samuels was anxious about having children around (there is also a four-month-old infant) but says that she doesn't get as depressed now that she is living with her daughter's family. At the same time, she has some concerns about her new residence. Her daughter forbade her to keep the bedroom door closed, and she has no privacy. Her own belongings are in storage, including the TV she bought for herself as a 65th birthday present. She feels she's worked hard all these years, and now she is left with nothing.

Good social support

No privacy or personal possessions

Mrs. Samuels feels her daughter doesn't understand old people. For instance, when her daughter invites her to go out, Mrs. Samuels is afraid of falling and doesn't feel an umbrella stroller is enough to hold onto. Her son-in-law gets up the same time Mrs. Samuels does and (according to Mrs. Samuels) monopolizes the bathroom for an hour and a half, which is particularly hard when she has diarrhea. She feels they don't do things deliberately, but "they just don't understand."

Mrs. Samuels' daughter expressed herself as being happy to have her mother living with her. Mrs. Samuels helps with the children and does some light household chores. The daughter describes her mother as very independent but in need of more socialization and activities.

Mrs. Samuels has had a life filled with deprivation and disability. Though she now lives with a loving and supportive family, she feels the loss of privacy and possessions keenly. Her living situation presents some problems for all concerned. Apparently, Mrs. Samuels does not follow through on any of her treatment plans, though she has a staggering list of health problems. She gives the excuse of not being able to afford certain drugs or treatments yet states that her bills are covered. Some socialization at a senior center might be beneficial, but she would need help with transportation.

Mrs. Brand's "nerves" are complicated by the conflict and hostility which characterize her marital relationship.

Mrs. Brand: "Nerves" and Marital Problems

"Nerves"

Mrs. Brand's major health problem is her "nerves"—anxiety, fatigue, and depression. She often cried during interviews, stating that her health interferes with doing things she likes to do (such as cleaning).

Marital problems

Mrs. Brand complained about her husband: he won't shave, he screams with the windows open so that the neighbors hear, and he doesn't do anything except watch television. Mr. Brand has been coughing since the fall, but she feels he is coughing to spite her. She feels embarrassed because she thinks people are making fun of him. After arguments with her husband, Mrs. Brand has episodes of fatigue and/or dizzy spells. For his part, Mr. Brand told the interviewer that he had very little interest in his wife and absolutely no concern for her emotional stress and pain. The couple's relationship is estranged and hostile. Mrs. Brand wishes she could be put away in a home, and Mr. Brand likes to go to the hospital because he gets good care.

Loneliness
Personal neglect

Mrs. Brand complains of loneliness. A married daughter doesn't visit, her friends have died, and she considers the agency homemaker her only friend. Obese and unkempt, she wears baggy housedresses, tennis shoes, and is completely toothless, and her hair is tousled and dirty.

A rough
neighborhood

Mrs. Brand dislikes her home and the neighborhood, which she says is "rough." She was mugged once and now is afraid to go out much. She thinks about "getting out of here, going to an apartment" and said, "I want to move . . . I feel entombed in this place . . . this is my coffin . . . I've got to get out of this neighborhood." She indicated several times that she would just like to be "put away in a home."

Mrs. Brand's medical problems include high blood pressure, a heart condition, and a thyroid condition. However, she claims not to worry about her health at all because she just neglects it. "I'm too tired and unhappy." She has medications for both the high blood pressure and the heart condition but doesn't take them. Other health conditions are trouble hearing and "urine leaking" which embarrasses her. The doctor suggested surgery for this problem but she refused.

Refuses surgery

During the month prior to the interview, Mrs. Brand had experienced a variety of symptoms, including difficulty sleeping, shortness of breath, chest pain when active, swollen feet/ankles, loss of strength in limbs, dizziness, headaches, other aches, unsteadiness on her feet, indigestion, and forgetfulness. Except for the last problem, she told no one about these symptoms mostly because "there is no one to tell, my husband doesn't pay attention." No one to tell of her symptoms

Mrs. Brand feels more angry, moody, and disappointed in life and less useful as the years go by. She feels strongly that everything is in the hands of fate and that she has little influence over things that will happen to her. At the same time she says, "I'd like to be contented, not have so much pressure—get out of this miserable situation." Disappointed in life

Mr. Brand claims his wife's nerves "have been acting up more." While he recognizes her need for special medical attention for her nerves, he offers no support to her to seek this care. He is extremely critical of Mrs. Brand's obesity and fears she may have a stroke as a result of her high blood pressure. Since his retirement from the post office ten years previously, Mr. Brand's health has deteriorated significantly. Because of his concern with his own poor health, he too gets attacks of "nerves" and anxiety three or four times a day. Husband's poor health

The director of the senior citizen center which referred Mrs. Brand to the project stated that the couple's marital difficulties have been long-standing but have become worse since Mr. Brand's retirement and his failing health. They had attended marital counseling sessions with a psychiatrist, but Mr. Brand withdrew. Mrs. Brand has been attending a group therapy session at the center twice a month for the past two to three years but has not been responding, and her mental health is deteriorating significantly. She is more fearful, feels more inadequate, and thinks people are talking about her. Her refusal to use medication is a major problem. No success with marital counseling

Mrs. Brand is a picture of deteriorating mental health and a shrinking social network. Her regular attendance in group therapy, a weekly Bible class, and senior center activities are offset by her poor marital relationship, the loss of all her neighborhood friends, and the noninvolvement of her only daughter. The poor marital relationship appears to have been exacerbated by Mr. Brand's retirement. Not only does Mrs. Brand not adhere to her prescribed medical regimen, but she ignores frequently experienced symptoms which could be related to major pathology. The intrapsychic and interpersonal relations are problematic, but the role of the environment is not helpful either.

While Mrs. Samuels and Mrs. Brand have some family members, Mrs. Young has only a friend. She receives some supports from the formal system.

Mrs. Young: Familyless and Hallucinatory

A creative life

Poverty and a
bleak environment

Though widowed and childless, 87-year-old Mrs. Young looks back with pride on a creative life. A college graduate, she had written poetry that was published in magazines, had been a reviewer for medical journals, and had taught school and sung professionally. Now, with an income of $315 a month, she lives in an efficiency apartment in a large building. No rugs are on the floor. There is a small bed with a nightstand and a radio on it, two small bookshelves filled with books, and two hardback chairs. The only decoration is a large oil painting, which Mrs. Young says is of her grandfather as a young man. The windowshades are torn, and the walls are dirty and marked with finger-prints.

Poor personal care

Mrs. Young is very frail-looking and uses a walker to move around. She has finely tailored, good quality clothes, but they are unbuttoned, dirty, and disheveled. She wears a scarf on her head and a red shawl tied around her waist. Her stockings are rolled down below her knees. Her cheeks are sunken, and one eye was inflamed and oozing. The symptoms she experi-enced in the past month include tiredness, weight loss, ner-vousness, and forgetfulness. Some of the time she is unable to make up her mind or to tell what day of the week it is. She worries about not being able to care for herself, but much of the time she feels "peaceful."

Hallucinations

Mrs. Young experiences visual hallucinations very frequently and asked the interviewer to check "what was occupying her bed now." When the interviewer found nothing, Mrs. Young said there were "female figures reclining on her bed" and asked the interviewer if she saw them. While she is not afraid of them, she said, there was always one thing or another with her in her apartment.

Men in her radio

A recent experience which bothered Mrs. Young a great deal had to do with her radio. The station she usually listens to was accidentally switched off. She was frustrated because she found herself listening to talk shows rather than music and couldn't understand how "those men" got into her radio. She decided they must be very short. She called her radio station to find out "what was going on" but had difficulty compre-hending the explanation.

Telephone checks

The social worker at the medical center which Mrs. Young frequents stated that Mrs. Young has been diagnosed as "involutional paranoid," mostly because of her reports of seeing "creatures" in her home. In group sessions Mrs. Young appears "proper" and independent. She calls in daily to the center and seems to be oriented to time, place, and person. She has a limited number of friends and talks a lot about the deaths of others.

Mrs. Young is "not overly fond of doctors." According to the social worker, Mrs. Young's health problems (besides poor nutrition) are centered around eyesight. She has cataracts and states that her doctor told her that her eyelashes are "growing the wrong way." The social worker also feels that new living arrangements are needed. Mrs. Young complains of head pains, resulting from two bad falls in the last three years, which she endures without treatment. She does stretching exercises to alleviate pains in her neck. Mrs. Young also has a herpes infection in her right eye and has a pin in her hip from a fall six years ago. Another vision problem is that Mrs. Young has no depth perception, and this confuses her.

Mrs. Young finds it difficult to cook because of her eyesight, and her nutritional status is inadequate. For breakfast on one particular day, she had raisin bread and butter and for lunch bread and peanut butter. Her dinner was brought "by some- *Receives community* one" (meals-on-wheels), and this was a balanced meal. The *services* Division of Adult Services of the Department of Public Welfare provides someone to do the housekeeping and some laundry for Mrs. Young. She also gets transportation to the medical center clinic 2–3 times per month.

Mrs. Young generally dislikes "senior citizens" and also dislikes the term. The collateral she named is a 27-year-old woman whom she has known for six years. This friend phones *A young* almost daily and visits about once a month. She is a profes- *friend cares* sional musician, has been married for less than a year, and has a graduate degree. She buys food and clothing for Mrs. Young, takes her out on special occasions, and has let Mrs. Young stay at her apartment. This young woman states that Mrs. Young is often depressed and could use companionship. She is concerned about Mrs. Young's fate because she will be moving soon. She has tried to get people at her church interested in Mrs. Young, but this hasn't lasted.

Mrs. Young is being followed by "the system." She has daily contact with her social worker and still manages to maintain her independence, although not always successfully. She needs more help with her meals, since it is clear that her only sound nutrition comes from the delivered meals. They do not always arrive on a daily basis, however. The radio incident demonstrates how confusing sensory deprivation and mental problems combined with complicated technology can be. Mrs. Young could not see her radio dial, and it might have been useless to explain technical matters to her in her current state. Unhappily, Mrs. Young will lose an important social support when her loyal young friend moves away.

Unlike the three preceding older people, Mr. Miller lives in a foster care situation—not unusual for ex-mental hospital patients.

Mr. Miller: In Foster Care

Foster care

Mr. Miller, at age 64, has been widowed for 25 years. He has not seen or heard from his daughter for several years and a close friend, whom Mr. Miller raised, visits only every few months. Mr. Miller has lived in the home of a foster caregiver, whom he named as his collateral, for the past year. She is a divorcee, who says her own health is poor because of a bad back. She is neatly groomed and cordial. Mr. Miller was previously in a boarding home but hated it because "it was dirty and the people were mean." His present residence is clean, with plastic covers on the furniture, and is gaudily decorated.

His shop closed up

Boredom and
uselessness

Mr. Miller claims that his SSI of $221 per month is barely enough for him to get along on. He had been a shoemaker with his own shoe repair shop until his brother, against Mr. Miller's will, "did me dirty" and closed it up when Mr. Miller had a stroke. His inability to work is now a source of considerable and constant unhappiness and boredom. Mr. Miller said he once had everything he wanted—his own house, a business, a family, and after working so hard for all those things, he now has nothing. He is also depressed about the fact that his daughter, for whom he "did everything," never contacts him. He feels of no use to anyone and less interesting to people than he used to be. The single most important thing which concerns him about the future is that he'll "be bored even more."

Eight
medications

Mr. Miller had a stroke a few years ago and says he's had trouble since then. He gets around the house easily but doesn't go outside often because his legs are too weak. In addition to his mental problems, he has trouble seeing, kidney trouble, arthritis, foot trouble, high blood pressure, and bronchitis. According to Mr. Miller, the medications prescribed by the doctor at the clinic to which he goes for care are Tylenol (as needed for pain), Combipres (for water), Darvocet N (for nerves), Dilantin ("don't know what they are for"), Uticillin (infection from a cold), Theragram (vitamins), Drixoral (doesn't know why he takes it), and Polymox (doesn't know why he takes it).

The foster caregiver seems to have equally poor knowledge of what his medications are and why he takes them.

Mr. Miller reported that in the past month, he experienced an inventory of a dozen symptoms, many of them mental or emotional, but told no one about them, because there is "no sense in telling anyone." He worries a good part of the time that he might lose his mind.

There is considerable confusion as to which medications Mr. Miller is actually taking and what conditions they are for. Some significant drugs are listed, including an anticonvulsant, two antibiotics, an antihistamine, an antihypertensive, and two analgesics, one of which he is using for the wrong reasons. All of the symptoms he reported in the past month could easily be side effects of these medications (two of which are contraindicated for use together). Is there a lack of medical follow-up on the drug regimen? Is Mr. Miller continuing to use medications which are no longer necessary to his current health status? At the same time, many of the symptoms he reports often are regarded as part of normal aging by professionals and by the elderly themselves. The reports of both Mr. Miller and his collateral give evidence of this misinformation.

Mr. Miller's social environment is clearly deprived. With adequate physical assistance and transportation, he probably would be a good candidate for socialization programs which might help his depression and boredom.

11 The Older People with Senile Dementia

The cases of the uniquely deprived older people who are afflicted with senile dementia illustrate several themes that arise over and over again in the literature about them. First, the fact that senile dementia usually occurs in combination with physical illness was clearly demonstrated by every one of the members of that group who was studied. Second, the demands on those who care for such elderly people often means full or nearly full-time commitment. These caregivers are, in the main, women who are themselves aging or already old (daughters and wives). Often the caregivers have health problems of their own, and there often is severe tension in the households. The behavior of the caregivers ranges from selfless devotion to outright abuse of the elderly person. The lives of the older people themselves are bleak almost beyond description. It is in relation to such individuals that the prospect of institutionalization arises most often. These afflicted elderly may seem almost totally unaware of the world around them or, at the other extreme, they may be painfully sensitive to their situations.

In the following case, the emotional equilibrium of the caregiving daughter was upset when a physician advised her to put her 85-year-old mother in a home on the grounds that the around-the-clock care she provided was performed solely out of guilt rather than compassion or love.

Mrs. Horton: Improvement with Skilled Care

Withdrawn

Mrs. Horton, now 85 years of age, had helped her husband in his clothing store but was always "introverted" and uninvolved in outside activities. This pattern became more exaggerated 12 years ago, when Mrs. Horton's home was burglarized and a great deal of money was taken. Mrs. Horton became withdrawn, and her daughter consulted a psychiatrist who recommended electroshock therapy. The family decided against this treatment, however, and Mrs. Horton remained passive even when her husband was dying of cancer. The daughter nursed her father throughout his illness.

Moves to daughter's home

When Mr. Horton died, Mrs. Horton moved to her 55-year-old daughter's home where she has been for seven years. Also

150

living in the household are the son-in-law, a granddaughter, and Mrs. Horton's son. The latter is unemployed, and his sister took him in after his broken marriage and attempted suicide. He contributes nothing to the support of the family and is considered by his sister to be "a bum," although he is Mrs. Horton's "shining light." Another strike against her brother as far as the daughter is concerned is that he induced Mrs. Horton to sign all her assets over to him when Mr. Horton died.

Early sibling rivalries persist

Mrs. Horton has her own bedroom on the second floor of the house. The room is clean and furnished with personal belongings. For the past three years, Mrs. Horton has spent most of her days there, sleeping or just lying in bed. She eats in bed as well. She has stopped performing all activities of daily living by herself and now needs to be fed, toileted, groomed, bathed, and given medication by her daughter.

The daughter is under so much pressure that she says "I've stopped living . . . the atmosphere in the family is morbid . . . I can't go out and socialize . . . I can't plan ahead." The situation has caused many mental conflicts and problems with the granddaughter as well. A nursing service had come in for a while, but the daughter felt the nurses were incompetent. She also felt that she does things a certain way and, perhaps, expects others to do things the same way, leading to dissatisfaction when they don't.

Severe caregiver burden

Despite her heavy burdens, the daughter believes she is doing the right thing for her mother, and this gives her a good feeling. She was advised to institutionalize Mrs. Horton but says she couldn't do that, denying that she is being a martyr. The daughter is not satisfied with her mother's medical care, stating that the doctor's attitude toward Mrs. Horton is "she is an old lady . . . you can't do anything for her, and she should be in a home." He tells the daughter that she is crazy and is "doing it out of guilt." He comes to the house every four to six weeks to see Mrs. Horton.

Institutionalization is advised but refused

The doctor makes house visits

Mrs. Horton's health is poor, she is always worried about it, and she has an impressive list of symptoms. She forgets what meals she ate and is confused about the time and the day. She hallucinates at times, saying people are going to kill her and are coming through the wall. (The daughter says that her brother, who sleeps in the adjoining room, keeps the TV on all night and that those sounds may be causing the hallucinations.) When the interviewer saw her, Mrs. Horton would not answer any questions saying her head hurt and she did not want to be bothered.

Hallucinations

Multiple health problems

Mrs. Horton has a history of major medical problems: trouble hearing; circulation problems (for which she takes Pavabid); stomach problems (for which she takes Maalox); arthritis, which has crippled one hand; and both constipation problems and diarrhea at times, for which she has a variety of prescribed medications and over-the-counter preparations, including enemas. Mrs. Horton also has had parkinsonism for the last four years, resulting in severe tremors when she doesn't take her medication, Symmetrel. However, according to the daughter, this drug causes hallucinations so that the daughter has stopped giving it to Mrs. Horton (her own idea).

Incontinence and falls

Mrs. Horton wears rubberized panties for "incontinence." She also takes Haldol and Benadryl elixir for her mental state. In the past six months, she fell from bed and cut her scalp, requiring eleven stitches to close the wound. Mrs. Horton also experiences transient ischemic attacks which have left her without body coordination or normal speech for parts of the day. She perspires heavily during these episodes. The daughter says they happen often but pass in time.

Improvement with skillful care

During the interviewer's last visit, it was noted that the situation in the home had improved greatly. The daughter has answered an ad in the paper and hired an aide who apparently is skillful in providing firm but gentle care for Mrs. Horton. In a short time, the aide has been able to encourage Mrs. Horton to do more things for herself, including feeding herself and coming downstairs for some meals. Her speech has improved, she has "perked up," and she even asked to

Relief for the caregiver

prepare her own meal. The daughter is ecstatic about the improvement in her mother's condition and in the changes in her own life. She looks more relaxed and has been able to go out with her daughter and husband.

The intervention of a skillful aide not only improved Mrs. Horton's condition but relieved the daughter's burdens. Apparently, the physician and the daughter had underestimated Mrs. Horton's potential. This suggests that both women might benefit from a complete assessment of Mrs. Horton's health (mental and physical) and from an active treatment program. It is possible that her drug regimen may be causing some of her physical symptoms. In addition, the family could probably benefit from counseling, since they all seem to be having many difficulties. The recommended institutionalization of Mrs. Horton might have created as many stresses for the daughter as keeping her mother at home, but a time may come when such a solution will be indicated.

Unlike Mrs. Horton's family, the family of Mr. Prince has decided to place him in a nursing home. His situation illustrates how family attitudes and behavior can contribute to depression and poor functioning.

Mr. Prince: Giving Up

Mr. Prince, 84-years-old, is awaiting admission to a nursing home. In the meantime, he and his wife continue to live in a luxury high-rise building. Two daughters and two sisters each visit and phone two or three times a week. Mr. Prince has a master's degree and had taught Latin for most of his working years. He enjoyed teaching and learning, and he especially loved to read. Books, he says, were his "friends." Now, however, he would like to read but can't because he forgets what he has read as soon as he closes a book.

A Latin teacher awaits nursing home placement

Mr. Prince is severely impaired mentally and has great difficulty recalling details such as his own address. He is well aware of his memory failure, however, and was fearful of "failing" the mental status questionnaire. He feels that life holds no successes for him now.

Anxiety about his mental condition

Mr. Prince still can express himself eloquently despite his mental status and slurred speech (a remnant of a stroke). He feels alienated because he "isn't really living"—there is something missing, and he is no longer a real person to anyone. He sees "living people" all around him—his wife, his visitors—but he feels alone and "unalive." He does virtually nothing all day because "there is nothing of importance to do."

Depressed and helpless

One consolation for Mr. Prince is that "it won't last too long." He says his time is limited, he has lived a good life, and now his experiences with living are over. He doesn't belong here anymore. At times when he is all alone, he thinks about "leaving the world," although he didn't mention suicide because his strong faith prohibits it.

Mr. Prince confided to the interviewer that his wife contributes to his sense of loss of knowledge and responsibility. She often talks of him in the third person, saying to others in front of him, "See, he didn't eat everything." However, Mr. Prince loves his wife, and he spends his day doing what she tells him to do because he knows she is taking good care of him. He knows it is hard on his wife because "she has desires and needs of her own, whatever they may be."

A wife's attitude contributes to depression

Mr. Prince takes Pro-Banthine (for bladder spasms) and wears an external urinary catheter attached to a drainage bag. (His wife attributes many of her husband's problems with

A catheter and skin problems

"giving up" to that device.) He also has high blood pressure (for which he takes Apresoline), circulation problems, and psoriasis. Three weeks prior to the interview, he developed shingles.

Mrs. Prince believes that her husband's doctor has a good understanding of Mr. Prince's condition and temperament but that her husband is indifferent and feels that treatment is futile. She says that he is almost always depressed, only talks about his health saying, "I'm no good," forgets everything, and is almost always confused.

According to Mrs. Prince, her husband's "will is gone," and he has given up. She feels trapped, shut in, and that she has given up her entire life to care of her husband.

Despite his senile dementia, Mr. Prince probably would benefit from psychological help. He has not resolved his deep problems with increased dependency, and his loss of self-esteem is poignant. The urinary catheter was a real blow to his body image. Real physical conditions have contributed to his depression which has, in turn, caused him to give up completely. There is no known physical reason, for instance, why Mr. Prince should have his food cut for him, yet he will not eat unless this is done.

The loss of books as companions has also been devastating because of Mr. Prince's past involvement with them. His self-worth has always relied on intellectual achievement, and that does not exist for him now.

Though Mr. Prince's care by his wife is complete, she has not left him with responsibilities or decisions to make. He needs goals, and though he has expressed this quite clearly, no one has responded. Mr. Prince certainly seems to need a complete assessment of his real capacities and a plan of care that will encourage him to utilize these to the fullest extent possible.

Like Mr. Prince's wife, Mrs. Norton's daughter feels ready to institutionalize the older person. Interestingly, however, this plan is being blocked by Mrs. Norton's son-in-law.

Mrs. Norton: To Institutionalize or Not?

Lives totally in one room

Ninety-five-year-old Mrs. Norton has been living in the two-story twin home of her 57-year-old daughter for the last four years. She has her own bedroom on the second floor of the house and spends all of her days there. Supplies in the room include a hot-pot, a thermos, a salt shaker, candy, cereal, and crackers. The bed is messy, and the room is sparsely furnished.

On a typical day, Mrs. Norton wakes up, sits on the side of the bed awhile, puts on her robe, goes to the bathroom and washes, returns to her bedside, makes her own breakfast, rinses out the dishes in the bathroom, lies down, and rests in bed until lunch. She repeats this pattern all day and does not read, watch TV, or listen to the radio. She says she feels dead.

Stays in bed and feels dead

Mrs. Norton is small and frail, with her white hair pulled into a tight, neatly secured bun. Her dentures clatter when she speaks. Her arms are thin, and her ankles are swollen. She complains frequently of being cold.

Mrs. Norton's senile dementia is severe. She is confused about people and time, including her past personal history. She could not identify a photograph on her bureau and does not always know who her daughter is. She seemed frustrated that she couldn't answer questions and, when asked how old she is, she responded by saying "That's a very good question, I wish I knew."

Severe confusion

Mrs. Norton remained in a fetal position during the interview, saying she is just tired, old, needs to rest and to be alone, and that "the main thing is to avoid aggravation." Her daughter recalled that when Mrs. Norton's two-and-one-half-year-old great-grandson spent the weekend, Mrs. Norton did not respond to him at all. The child stroked her arm, watched her eat, and seemed to adore her, but Mrs. Norton "preferred not to be bothered."

Unresponsive to a child

Mrs. Norton is most afraid of falling and being left alone. She does fall occasionally, but her daughter tries to encourage her to walk by herself, particularly to the bathroom. She spends some time alone when her daughter is at work and her retired son-in-law leaves the house. Recently she became very agitated and concerned about where her daughter was, although the daughter was not yet due home from work. Mrs. Norton could not be consoled or placated until her daughter returned.

Fear of falling and of being alone

Her daughter stated that Mrs. Norton experiences numerous symptoms, including difficulty sleeping, shortness of breath, swollen ankles, coughing, loss of strength in her arms and legs, weakness, dizziness, tiredness, leg cramps, nervousness, loss of weight, poor appetite, depression, unsteadiness, indigestion and gas, constipation, and forgetfulness. Her medical history includes trouble hearing for the past year; circulation problems for the past ten years, for which she takes Lanoxin (digitalis), Hydergine (used in cerebral arterio-

A long inventory of health problems

sclerosis), and Dyazide (a diuretic); trouble with dentures which fit poorly since she has lost weight; stomach or intestinal problems for the past 20 years; and constipation for the past 30 years, for which she takes Senekot and mineral oil. At one time she had skin cancer. She also has had foot trouble for the last 30 years for which she sees a podiatrist.

Mrs. Norton goes to a private doctor for her medical care, usually about five times per year. This is almost always difficult because Mrs. Norton has trouble walking and cannot use public transportation. Her daughter is not satisfied with the care Mrs. Norton gets, claiming that the doctor ascribes all ills to getting old.

Competing claims on a daughter

Mrs. Norton's daughter says she is ready to send her mother to a nursing home, but her husband doesn't want to do this. She gets no help or support from her brother, who hardly ever visits their mother. She feels like she is leading two lives and has to be one person for her husband and one for her mother. She is always tense and anxious and becomes very upset when she hears people talk about children who can't care for their parents and abandon them in nursing homes. She feels that her mother is a "nonuseful, nonproductive" person and asks "Who has the priority on life?"

"Who has priority on life?"

While Mrs. Norton undoubtedly has organic mental problems, depression may be compounding her condition. At the least, she deserves a thorough multidisciplinary work-up. It is obvious that the daughter also is in need of help with her feelings of guilt and ambivalence about nursing home placement for Mrs. Norton. One wonders why the son-in-law reinforces the bind of competing demands in which he places his wife by resisting institutionalization of his mother-in-law. This situation illustrates the vital necessity for counseling help for an entire family when the presenting problem is an older person's impairment. The daughter tersely states an issue that often arises in relation to the question of institutionalization of an elderly person: "Who has the priority on life?"

In another family, total care is provided without family conflict. Mrs. Unger's 62-year-old daughter and 68-year-old son-in-law uncomplainingly provide care that would tax the strength of people decades younger than they are.

Mrs. Unger: Loving Care for "A Vegetable"

At 93, Mrs. Unger is so severely impaired mentally that (according to her family) "she is a vegetable." Following

multiple strokes, she has become completely crippled. A
year ago, she developed gangrene in both legs, resulting in
bilateral above the knee amputations. She is incontinent of   Bilateral amputations
feces (diapers are used) and has a catheter which drains her   Incontinence
urine. She is fed through a nasogastric tube every four hours   Nasal feeding
with a blenderized mixture of eggs, pureed meat, orange
juice, strained carrots, skim milk, strained peaches, strained
cereal, sugar, oil, and Brewer's yeast (a formula prescribed
by a hospital dietician). Mrs. Unger is probably blind,   Blindness
although her daughter is not certain. Mrs. Unger shows no
sign of recognition and does not communicate her needs or
feelings in any way, except to groan when uncomfortable.
She spends all her time in bed, moved only by the home   A home health
health aide who bathes, feeds, and rotates her daily between   aide helps
9:00 and 11:45 a.m. She is presently being treated for a
bladder infection and is given Dilantin to prevent seizures. A
nurse comes to the home routinely to tend to Mrs. Unger's
medical needs, such as her decubitus ulcers.   Decubiti

Mrs. Unger's room looks like a hospital room. Next to her   A one-bed hospital
hospital bed is a double bed covered with disposable pads,
clean sheets, and extra nightgowns. There are containers of
powders, lotions, and creams. A string on the wall displays
many greeting cards, and family pictures also hang on the
walls. For medical check-ups, Mrs. Unger is taken by ambu-
lance to a clinic at the local hospital once a month. The
daughter is completely satisfied with the care her mother gets
there. Mrs. Unger has needed this level of care for the last 25
months and appears well cared for.

The daughter's own health is only fair. She sees a physical
therapist at her union twice a week for her arthritis and reports
extreme fatigue. She is completely tied down and unable to
go out socially or to attend church. Nevertheless, she has no   An uncomplaining
major complaints, is happy to have the homemaker service,   caregiver
and feels that nothing more can be done for her mother. She
does most of the work involved but gets help in grooming,
toileting, and bathing her mother from the homemaker. Her
own three daughters often help with cooking.

By most criteria, Mrs. Unger is a candidate for nursing home care. Yet,
her daughter has managed to cover all bases in providing adequate day-to-day
care for this semicomatose woman, with effective coordination of outside
services making it possible to avoid institutionalization. Though the daughter
is uncomplaining, the effect on her life is apparent. Ironically, the daughter
believes that most older people have the same health status as her mother.
How many other people believe this stereotype of aging and health?

A sharp contrast to the behavior of Mrs. Unger's family is that of Mrs. Tobias's family.

Mrs. Tobias: A Case of Parent Abuse

Seventy-eight-year-old Mrs. Tobias, who has a moderate degree of senile dementia, was discharged from the nursing home in which she had been living because she constantly wandered away. Her 60-year-old unmarried daughter set up an apartment for her mother over the barber shop she owned.

Wandered

Though Mrs. Tobias complains of deafness, high blood pressure, constipation, confusion, and blood cancer, the daughter claims that her mother's health is better than her own. Bottles of medicine shown to the interviewer included Pavabid (for cerebrovascular insufficiency), Aldomet (an antihypertensive), Festalan (an agent to replace deficient digestive enzymes), Valium (an antianxiety agent), and an antidepressant. The daughter states she gives her mother only Atarax, however, and that the doctor who sees Mrs. Tobias monthly simply "throws pills at you."

Medicines not taken

The daughter is upset about Mrs. Tobias' forgetfulness, inability to make decisions, and occasional incontinence. She believes the incontinence occurs "out of spite" and hits her mother when it happens. She also strikes Mrs. Tobias for what she views as "pretending" to forget things. Mrs. Tobias herself is described as "fast with her hands"—that is, she strikes people.

Physical punishment for forgetting

The daughter says she often gets very "nervous" and needs some time away from her mother. In a one-week period, Mrs. Tobias had left the bathroom sink water running, turned the gas on in the kitchen, and wet herself. For her part, Mrs. Tobias told the interviewer that her daughter is "hateful" toward her, had hit her "upside her face," didn't care about her, and will someday kill her.

Dangerous behaviors

The daughter is often overwhelmed by her caregiving responsibilities. During daily visits to her mother, she cooks, does the housework and laundry, manages finances, dispenses medication, and makes decisions about her mother's apparel. She tries to take Mrs. Tobias for a daily walk and allows her to spend time in the barber shop while she works, but Mrs. Tobias's behavior is embarrassing.

Caregiver overwhelmed

While "parent abuse" occurs only in a small minority of cases, it is an important issue for health professionals. As is so often true in abuse cases, there are hints that the older person had been physically aggressive toward her daughter at an earlier stage of their lives. In any event, the daughter is clearly under severe and unrelieved strain and is ignorant of age-related difficulties and how to cope with them. She seems not to understand that some of the behaviors and symptoms her mother displays are pathological and require follow-up by health professionals. It is obvious that the daughter needs to be relieved of some of her responsibilities and, certainly, to have other relationships and opportunities for socialization and recreation. Services such as respite care, homemaker service, and diversional activities for both women are conspicuous by their absence.

IV Toward Practical Application

12

Practical Health Education of Older People: The Philadelphia Geriatric Center Training Aids

The findings of the study reported in the preceding chapters reinforce professional consensus that many older people lack knowledge about aging and health and that lack of knowledge is a major barrier to effective health care.

That research and the studies of others indicate that the elderly often

- are unable to perform simple procedures basic to many treatment plans;
- fail to seek professional care when needed;
- do not follow prescribed treatment plans;
- are not aggressive enough in seeking information about their conditions or treatments from professionals;
- misinterpret the signs and symptoms of pathology as expectable aspects of normal aging, resulting in delayed treatment or even no treatment.

Ideally, to improve that situation, education about such matters should begin early in life; early, ongoing education would prepare people for their old age. Moreover, people who already are old rely for their care to a significant extent on younger family members (see Chapter 7). A good deal can be done, however, to educate adults who are already in the aging phase of life.

The Training Aids Project

This chapter presents one method of educating older people about their mental and physical health. It will describe the development by the Philadelphia Geriatric Center of a specific set of training aids that can be used

The work described in this chapter was supported by AoA Grant #90–A–1229. The overall director of the project was M. Powell Lawton, and the director of the training aids subproject was Elaine M. Brody. Acknowledgment is given to Rhona Cooper, R.N., B.S.N., M.A., for her major role in the development of the training aids.

with groups of older people in a variety of settings. The training aids themselves appear as Appendix B, together with detailed instructions for those involved in running such a program.

As a basis for developing the training aids, a first step was to gather appropriate information. This phase of the project involved a literature search, a survey of various groups of health professionals, and interviews with older people and their designated collaterals.

The survey and interviews were not intended as a research study but were designed to guide us as to what the content of the training aids should be. The professionals, older people, and collaterals who were our respondents in this effort did not constitute a representative or random sample. By contrast with the older people in the health practices study, the older people with whom we talked were all intact mentally.

Based on the information gathered, the content and format of the training aids were developed. The aids were then reviewed, revised, field-tested, and again revised and put in the final form (Appendix B).

Since some interesting and relevant information emerged from the survey and interviews, the findings will be reported here, before the training aids themselves are described.

Information-Gathering

This phase of the aids project included the following activities:

1. *A search of the literature* was conducted to review current knowledge about existing health care educational programs for the elderly, existing training aids and materials, patterns of self-care and family caregiving, health service utilization patterns of the elderly, and the needs and preferences of older people for services and training, based on their major health problems and concerns.

2. *A survey of health professionals* was carried out to elicit their experiences in treating older people and their views about what older people needed to know. This questionnaire was mailed to 250 health care professionals whose professional memberships and affiliations indicated frequent contact with older clients. One hundred and four people, or approximately 42%, responded. The respondents were primarily nurses (42%) and physicians (30%). The remainder were occupational therapists, social workers, psychologists, physical therapists, podiatrists, optometrists, and dentists. Most of these health professionals considered themselves to be practitioners (rather than administrators or educators), and slightly more than one-third indicated specialization in the field of aging. On the average, they reported that elderly people comprised 67% of their clientele.

The questionnaire included items related to the respondents' opinions on how treatment plans were implemented by older people, the professional-client relationship, and the extent of the older people's health knowledge. They were also asked to identify areas about which older people and their caregivers lack sufficient information to make sound health care decisions.

3. *In-depth interviews* were conducted by project staff with 25 elderly volunteers (whose mean age was 73) and 17 of the collaterals they named. The older people were accessed from a variety of community settings in the Philadelphia area, including senior citizens centers, the Philadelphia Geriatric Center outpatient services, and support groups of family members who provide assistance for their own elderly parents.

The interviews with the older people included closed and open-ended items about their demographic characteristics, medical history, selected aspects of medical knowledge, preventive health behaviors, problems with professional care (attitudes, satisfaction, need for information, adherence to medical regimen), and major concerns about their own health. The interviews with the collaterals included similar items, with additional questions about their opinions and suggestions relative to the older people's care.

Findings from the Preliminary Survey

The older people interviewed had an average age of 73, and two-thirds were female. About half of them lived alone, and the remainder were divided between those living with spouses and those living with other family members. Eighty-four percent were white, and 16% were black. About one-fifth were or had been professionals (such as teachers, lawyers), about half were white collar workers, and 30% were blue collar. Their incomes ranged from $3000 up, with the median being between $7,000 and $8,000 a year.

Although two-thirds of these older people considered their health to be good or excellent, the median number of health conditions they reported was four per individual. The most often reported conditions were arthritis (44%), heart conditions (36%), high blood pressure (32%), and hearing problems (32%).

The 17 collaterals interviewed ranged in age from 34 to 85. About half shared a household with the older person. Almost half of them were adult children (mostly daughters), and one-third were spouses.

The most interesting findings are reported here.

On Decisions to Seek Health Care

Table 12–1 indicates the poor opinion held by many professionals about older people's decisions to seek health care. Three-fourths of these professionals agreed that older people often misinterpret treatable illness as part of normal aging, and about the same proportion agreed that older people resign themselves to symptoms of chronic illness. Two-fifths felt that older people rely

Table 12–1. Health Professionals' Opinions about Older People and the Seeking of Health Care (N = 104)

Statement	Strongly Disagree %	Mildly Disagree %	Mildly Agree %	Strongly Agree %
1. In my opinion, older people often misinterpret treatable illnesses as part of normal aging.	7	17	41	35
2. My older patients/clients tend to resign themselves to symptoms of chronic illness.	7	19	39	35
3. In my opinion, older people rely more on folklore and home remedies than on professional advice.	10	48	32	10
4. Most older people do not visit professionals as often as they should for adequate care.	6	14	38	42
5. It is difficult to convince older people that they will benefit from professional treatment plans.	6	34	42	18

more on folklore and home remedies than on professional advice, and four-fifths agreed that older people do not visit health professionals as often as they should.

Most of the elderly people surveyed believed that health professionals cannot do much to prevent disability in old age. And more than half of them felt that home remedies usually work better than professional advice. Yet all had seen a physician in the past year, almost all the health conditions they had listed had been discussed with a professional, and one-third of those conditions were being treated by prescribed medications and/or regimens such as diet or exercise.

When presented with a list of 12 symptoms of chronic or acute illness, the older people stated that when they had experienced those symptoms, most of the physical symptoms had been reported to either a doctor or a relative, but the vast majority of mental symptoms (80%) had not been reported to anyone. (These included feeling blue, forgetfulness, confusion, and nervousness.) The reasons given for nonreporting were similar to those described in Chapter 6: not important, didn't want to bother anyone, it's normal, part of growing older.

The collaterals agreed with the older people that health professionals cannot do much to prevent disability in old age, but only one-quarter of them preferred home remedies to professional advice.

On the Professional-Client Relationship

The older people and their collaterals were asked questions to elicit their attitudes toward professionals, their satisfaction with the care they were receiving, and reasons why they were or were not satisfied. Sixty percent of the older people and almost the same proportion of collaterals agreed that "health professionals rarely tell you the whole truth about your health." Large minorities (44% and 35.8% respectively) also felt that most health professionals do not take a real interest in their patients/clients.

At the same time, more than two-thirds of the older people and three-fourths of the collaterals expressed satisfaction with the professional care the elderly individuals were receiving. When dissatisfaction was expressed, reasons given were most often attributed to some form of professional failure which included lack of professional follow-up, not enough time taken by the professional to explain the treatment, poor instructions given, failure to assess individual needs adequately, or failure by the professional to reinforce appropriate behavior by the subject.

When health professionals were asked about their problems in their relationships with older people, almost 60% of them agreed that it is difficult to convince older people that they will benefit from professional treatment plans.

On Adherence to Treatment Plans

More than three-quarters of the health professionals indicated that they had problems with older people's adherence to treatment plans or professional advice. Among the problems (each identified by large majorities) were mis-understanding, difficulties in understanding or reading instructions, mental status (including confusion, memory loss, inability to integrate information), and access problems such as the older person's inability to obtain needed supplies or services.

The health professionals were asked what would be needed to help older people adhere to professional treatment plans. Among their answers were (1) education about his or her treatment or condition (almost 40% of the professionals mentioned this need), (2) involvement of the family in the educational process (almost 25%), (3) adequate and clear verbal instructions (22%), (4) taking individual needs into account (20%), (5) professional follow-up (14%), (6) written instructions (10%), (7) and good client-professional rapport (10%).

From the nonprofessional perspective, 80% of the older people and 60% of their collaterals felt that a person should always follow the professional's advice. Yet almost half the elderly individuals admitted that there were times when they had not done so. When asked to explain why, more than half said they disagreed with advice that was given. All but one of these disagreements were medication-related: either the older people felt they were taking too many medications or that the medications were producing uncomfortable side effects. More than one-third of those who had not followed the professional's advice felt that the treatment conflicted with their lifestyles. A typical example is that of the man who was told to take three oatmeal baths per day for a skin condition; since he was employed, he found the treatment difficult to maintain.

On Knowledge about Health

The professionals, the older people, and the latter's collaterals were asked to rate the knowledge of older people about 14 aspects of health care. The topics which health professionals felt represented the largest gaps in knowledge appear on Table 12–2. Most of those topics were rated as "knowledge lacking" by large majorities of all three groups. It is notable that 94% of the professionals, 88% of the older people, and 100% of the collaterals rated "common emotional problems of older people" as a gap in knowledge.

Performing Simple Health Procedures

The professionals were asked if they thought their older patients could perform certain techniques or procedures basic to health care. As seen on Table 12–3, about half thought that the older people would not be able to take

a pulse or stop bleeding but that they would be able to take an oral temperature. More than one-fourth did not know if their older patients could perform
the first two procedures at all.

The older people themselves were asked to describe the same techniques that the professionals had rated, and their responses were evaluated by
the project staff. As Table 12–4 indicates, very few older people showed an
excellent understanding of any of the three procedures. Taking a pulse was
understood least; 80% had minimal or poor ratings. One-fifth of these elderly
individuals could not explain how to take an oral temperature and even fewer
could not describe how to stop bleeding.

Discussion of the Findings

In preparation for the development of the health educational materials for
older people, the perspectives of professionals, elderly people, and collaterals
were sought about seeking health care, the professional-client relationship,
adherence to professional advice, and knowledge of health.

Though only 25 older people were interviewed, they resemble the
general population of elderly in age, sex distribution, living arrangements,
income, and prevalence of chronic conditions. In contrast to the older people
in the research study reported in the earlier chapters of this book, all of these
25 older people were intact mentally. The 104 health professionals who
responded to the questionnaire represent members of a special group who
were selected because they had significant involvement with geriatric patients.

While the ultimate goal of this small study was to gather information
relevant to health education for older people and their families, the findings
raise an important point from the perspective of professional providers. The
information suggests that some professionals may assume too much about
their patients' lifestyles and knowledge regarding health. This was the case for
the older people who were given more medications than they were willing to
take or who decided without professional advice to discontinue medications
that produced uncomfortable side effects. Further, skeptical attitudes were
expressed by the older people and their collaterals in their expectations of
professional behavior.

Several of the findings were directly relevant to the development of
programs of health education for older people and their supportive others.

First, with regard to seeking professional care, the health professionals
agreed that older people may misinterpret or resign themselves to physical
and mental ailments as normal to the aging process. The older people themselves believe that little can be done to prevent the disabilities of old age and,
therefore, that there is little use in consulting professionals after the initial
diagnoses of chronic conditions are made. Further, there is strong evidence

Table 12-2. Gaps in Older People's Knowledge: Opinions of Health Professionals, Older People, and Collaterals

	Health Professionals (N=104)		Older People (N=25)		Collaterals (N=17)	
	Knowledge lacking	Knowledge adequate	Knowledge lacking	Knowledge adequate	Knowledge lacking	Knowledge adequate
	% Totals*		% Totals*		% Totals*	
Proper self-administration of drugs	65	34	64.0	32.0	71	30
Nutrition for older people	77.5	22.5	68.0	28.0	82	18
Emergency first-aid	80	20	84.0	12.0	76.5	23.5
Foot care for older people	81	19	64.0	28.0	59	35
Dental Care for older people	72.5	27.5	64.0	32.0	65	35
Common personal care procedures (e.g., bathing feeding, grooming)	32	68	64.0	32.0	53	47

Topic						
Vision loss and aging	70	30	64.0	32.0	65	35
Hearing loss and aging	72	28	72.0	24.0	76.5	23.5
Common emotional problems of older people	94	6	88.0	8.0	100.0	0.0
Short-term memory loss and occasional confusion associated with aging	81	18	76.0	20.0	88	12
Signs and symptoms to report to the professional	74.5	24.5	64.0	32.0	76.5	23.5
Removing environmental barriers in the home	79	20	76.0	20.0	88	6
Preventing acute illness	84	15	68.0	28.0	59	35
Normal processes of aging	85	14	84.0	12.0	88	6

*Totals may not equal 100% due to missing data and rounding errors.

Table 12–3. Health Professionals' Assessment of Older People's Ability to Perform Procedures (N = 104)

Procedure	Can Perform %*	Unable to Perform %*	Don't Know %*
Taking a pulse	20	53	25
Taking an oral temperature	48	31	20
Stopping bleeding	19	51	28

*Totals may not equal 100% due to missing data and rounding.

Table 12–4. Older People's (N = 25) and Collaterals' (N = 17) Scores on Descriptions of Procedures as Assessed by Project Staff

Procedure	Poor S %*	Poor C %*	Minimal S %*	Minimal C %*	Satisfactory S %*	Satisfactory C %*	Excellent S %*	Excellent C %*
Taking a pulse	20	18	60	47	20	29	0	6
Taking an oral temperature	20	6	36	18	36	65	8	12
Stopping bleeding	16	6	40	30	40	53	4	12

*Totals may not equal 100% due to missing data and rounding.

that older people, at least initially, report physical symptoms to close relatives and professionals. However, this clearly is not the case with mental or emotional symptoms, virtually none of which the older people reported to anyone.

A second issue is that of the relationship of professional and patient. The older people and their collaterals thought that health professionals rarely tell the whole truth about their elderly patients' health, and many believed that health professionals are not interested in their elderly patients. Paradoxically, however, most of them were satisfied with the professional care the older people were receiving. When dissatisfaction was expressed, it was usually related to some form of professional failure such as no follow-up or poor explanations of conditions or treatments. Apparently, good professional-patient rapport is much desired by the elderly, despite the absence of cures for chronic illness.

Adherence to professional advice or regimens is clearly a central issue. Most professionals indicated that they had difficulty convincing older people that they would benefit from treatment plans and that there were definite problems with adherence. Professionals identified misunderstanding, poor mental status, and access problems as major barriers to adherence.

Though the older people themselves believed they should always follow professional advice closely, they confirmed that they had problems adhering to treatment plans. Among those who indicated that they had not always adhered to professional advice (about half), most cited disagreement with the advice as the most important factor. More specifically, virtually all such disagreements were related to problems with medications.

The final issue concerned knowledge about health. Professionals prescribe treatment plans based on the assumptions that their clients and/or supportive others can perform certain basic procedures or techniques (such as being able to take one's pulse). But the professionals *and* the older people indicated a low level of practical knowledge among the elderly about simple health care procedures.

The professionals, the older people, and the collaterals were in clear agreement that there are many gaps in the health care knowledge of older people and their families. The common emotional problems of older people and the normal processes of aging were outstanding examples, with almost all members of all three groups identifying those subjects as not being understood.

A Description of the Training Aids: Putting Principles into Practice

Having gathered information from the literature and the survey/interviews described, the next step in the project was to decide on the form the training aids should take. The people toward whom the training was to be directed were older adults living in the community. The goal was to strengthen their capacities to provide themselves with appropriate day-to-day health care.

To accomplish that objective, the staff aimed to develop a training package that would be

- simple to understand,
- ready to use,
- capable of being presented in one-hour segments,
- usable by a medical or nonmedical professional group leader,
- applicable to small groups of older people (12 to 20 per group) in community settings which they frequent and in which they feel relaxed,
- flexible enough to meet the needs of different groups of older people regardless of their levels of sophistication about health information.

After the project staff developed a draft of the aids—called "Self-Care Training for Older People—Ways to Keep Healthy"—it was reviewed by a multidisciplinary panel of health professionals at the Philadelphia Geriatric Center, including a physician, a nurse, a social worker, and a physical therapist. The aids then were revised and field-tested at two training sites with 73 elderly trainees.

The final form of the training package is a four-unit program which will be described below and is appended in full as Appendix B. The units were I. Stereotypes and Aging, II. The Body and Aging, III. The Mind and Aging, and IV. Organizing for Better Health Care.

In order to instruct the group leaders in the use of the aids, each unit is accompanied by a summary of its objectives; a list of reference books, articles, and pamphlets; a list of materials and audio-visual aids needed; and a handout for the participants in the group.

A glance at the aids indicates that suggestions to the group leader about teaching methods appear in regular type accompanying the text of the lecture (in italics) so that the group leader has page-by-page cues throughout each session. (It is recommended that a health professional be available on a consulting basis to deal with complicated questions that participants may ask.)

A brief description of each unit is as follows:

Unit I. Stereotypes and Aging

A. What Is a Stereotype?

Participants are asked to respond to the question "What comes to the minds of most people when they hear the word 'old'?" Words with negative connotations, such as "cranky," "demanding," "senile," or untrue generalizations about entire groups are shown to be stereotypes. Stereotypes are learned in childhood, from television or other news and entertainment media, and from personal experiences.

B. How Stereotypes of Older People May Influence Health

Aging affects everyone differently rather than with stereotyped uniformity. Participants are urged to learn all they can about aging and health to discover which things are true and which are false expectations. They are also asked to keep their eyes and ears open during the following week for examples of how older people are stereotyped in television, newspapers and magazines, or in their own experiences.

A handout, which is a single-sheet, hand-printed message, challenges stereotypes and says: "You are *not* as old as you feel; you are as old as you expect to be!!! So learn how to expect to feel good as you are."

Unit II: The Body and Aging

A. Normal Physical Changes

The group is asked: At what age are many athletes considered past their prime? The answer, 30–35 years old, may seem young, but there seems to be some loss of muscle strength and functioning at that point and most athletes retire by the time they're 40. The loss of muscle strength, it is explained, affects digestive processes, the pumping of the heart, and other bodily functions in nonathletes as they become older. But such changes can be anticipated and dealt with positively. For example, the heart can be helped by taking actions to reduce blood pressure when the heart is forced to work too strenuously when pressure is needlessly high. Stroke may be averted, as well.

B. Some of the More Common Problems of Aging

The distinction is emphasized between rheumatoid arthritis (which causes inflammation of the joints, often starting with small joints and then affecting larger joints and sometimes the entire body) and osteoarthritis (a wear-and-tear of joints, especially the ones that do the most work). Self-treatment and good health practices are described.

The handout declares: "With a little know-how, good health is possible at any age. No two people are alike in how aging affects them. What is the same is the need to know *what is normal* and *what is not normal*."

Unit III: The Mind and Aging

A. Normal Cognitive Changes

The frequent use of the word "senility" is challenged on the grounds that only a small percentage of older people are actually and irreversibly "senile." Many conditions called "senility" can be treated or reversed, especially when the changes have come on quickly. Examples of long-lived celebrities who have maintained their mental abilities throughout life are given, elicited, and discussed. The key to maintaining intelligence is given as "What you don't use, you lose." Learning is possible at any age; forgetfulness does occur frequently in the later years of life, but memory aids can be useful. Personality and judgment can improve with age, but only if minds are open to improvement.

B. Depression

People who suffer from this disorder—called "the Great Masquerader" because people who suffer from it may be aware of physical problems but not of mental changes—may cause its victims to experience extreme fatigue, sleepless nights, headaches, lack of appetite, and constipation. While it is normal to have some periods of "feeling blue," "real depression is a lowering of spirits that is deeper and longer. . . . It interferes with the ability to function in everyday life. Yet . . . many people feel that getting professional help, such as from a psychiatrist, makes them 'crazy.' "

The handout states: *Depression requires professional help* which can be provided at your *community mental health center* at little or no cost. . . . Many famous people have shown that *it is O.K. to get professional help for emotional pains, just as it is O.K. to get professional help for physical pains*.

Unit IV: Organizing for Better Health Care

A. The Personal Health Care Chart

This session is built on the premise that it is necessary to be a well-prepared patient in order to get quality professional health care. The doctor can function adequately only when given complete information from the patient and vice versa. The focus of the session is on a "personal health care chart" designed to provide the care provider and the patient with an organized picture of the treatment plan. A sample page of the chart is reproduced in Appendix B. Great care is taken during the discussion of the chart to assure that all participants are at precisely the same point on the chart as the leader and that they can read every word on it. The leader suggests that follow-up discussion on an individual or small group basis be conducted to help the participants become proficient in the use of the chart.

B. How to Use Medications and Ask the Right Questions about Them

During the discussion of the columns in the chart dealing with medication, special attention is given to questions that should be addressed to the prescribing physician. Many people, for example, believe that if a little medicine is good, more must be better. But the doctor can readily answer questions on why variations from the prescribed dose can cause problems. The older person should also ask how long the medicine takes to work. Only in this way can the person know how soon to expect changes in the way they are feeling. They should also be clear about what the medication is intended to *do*. If, for example, a medication is intended to reduce fever when the patient is expecting pain relief, confusion and resentment can occur.

The handout urges participants: *"Be a Smart Consumer: Ask Questions!"*

A final note: These training aids are not intended to be definitive and unchangeable.

It is highly desirable that the aids be modified as needs dictate in different situations. Moreover, new units should be developed in response to the concerns of various groups. The older people with whom the aids were tested had suggestions for new units—such as How to Get Along Better with the Doctor, Exercise, Nutrition, Effects of Medications on the Elderly, and Dependency Problems. They also expressed an interest in sessions about specific ailments such as diabetes and circulatory problems.

Nevertheless, the package in Appendix B has proven useful as it is. The vast majority of the older people with whom it was tested found it helpful, wanted classes to continue, and were capable of using the Health Care Chart. The group leader (a social worker) was able to conduct the sessions with ease. And a by-product of the training sessions was that they offered the trainees opportunities to socialize.

13 Working with Older People and Their Families: A Note for Health Professionals

As all health professionals know, there are many aspects of the mental and physical health care of older people that are in need of improvement. This chapter does not undertake to be a comprehensive treatise on that subject. Nor does it presume to tell various health professionals how to practice their respective professions. Rather, based in part on the findings of the research described, but also on other experiences and research of the authors, some suggestions will be made for ways in which professionals can work effectively with older people and their families.

Each aspect of the information gathered about the attitudes, health experiences, and practices of the 132 older people studied was discussed in the relevant chapters. Each of those chapters included a discussion of the implications for professionals of the particular set of findings described. Certain main themes emerged repeatedly. The first part of this chapter, therefore, will summarize those themes in terms of what they imply for practical application by health and mental health professionals who work with older people.

The second part of the chapter will discuss the families who are partners to professionals in providing health care to the elderly, since families are becoming more and more prominent in professionals' day-to-day work. Just as mental and physical health professionals find themselves involved with older people to a greater extent than ever before in history, they are much more involved with such patients' families as well. The older person's family members—spouses, adult children, siblings, or others—more and more often are present in the health professionals' offices, in the home, or at the hospital bedside. And they may make multiple (often repetitious) phone calls. Many of the offspring making the calls and tending to their parents or parent may themselves be in their 60s or beyond. Such involvement inevitably will increase in the future.

The geriatric imperative (see Chapter 1) is the major reason for this trend. Since about eight million older people (roughly 30% of the total 65+ population) now need some amount of help and the very old and most frail are increasing at a rapid rate, there will be more old people in the future who depend on their families. Those family members may be involved in every aspect of the older person's health care from the initial provision of the health history through the practical implementation of the prescribed treatment regimen.

Working with Older People

It bears repetition that older people (like younger people) are extremely heterogeneous and that no one finding about their health experiences applies to all. "The aged" include the young old and very old people who have a wide range of physical and mental health situations and capacities to function in their daily lives. Their socioeconomic situations and family resources vary widely as do their life experiences and personalities. Some are extremely diffident in their relationships with professionals, while others are more assertive. And they vary in levels of knowledge and attitudes about health and in their adherence to professional recommendations. The suggestions presented here, therefore, reflect *tendencies* revealed by the research and must always be seen in relation to such diversity.

Awareness of Older Persons' Feelings and the Professionals' Responses

The ways in which older people feel about their mental and physical health problems, their attitudes toward health professionals, and their perceptions of health professionals' attitudes and opinions about them are major factors influencing their health behaviors. While this is true of all age groups, there are special and additional considerations at work with older adults.

Information from the research underscored the pessimistic attitudes held by the older people toward their own potential for improvement. Moreover, they often viewed their ailments as due to the processes of aging per se. Those attitudes acted as constraints on what they reported about their health and what they did (or failed to do) to maintain health, to prevent illness, and to follow professional recommendations. The natural anxiety one may feel about one's health may be intensified for elderly, who are aware of their relative closeness to the end of life.

Because negative attitudes toward the elderly are so common and because some professionals share those attitudes, the elderly person is likely to be especially sensitive to any real, implied, or imagined expression of such ageism. This was illustrated by the substantial minorities of the older people studied who were dissatisfied with their medical care because they felt that doctors have impersonal attitudes, are cold or abrupt, do not pay attention to them, do not take an interest in them, give better treatment to younger patients, and do not always tell them the truth about their health.

Again, despite those feelings, the majority of these older people expressed themselves as generally satisfied with their medical care, and the vast majority thought that people should always follow the doctor's advice! Those seemingly conflicting feelings suggest that the older people respect professionals and want their advice. But they want good rapport with them, they want to feel cared about, and they are sensitive to any implication that they are not valued.

Awareness of such feelings, therefore, should lead professionals to self-examination of their own attitudes and behaviors so that they do not communicate any negative attitudes they may have. Indeed, an extra measure of thoughtfulness should be extended to the elderly. Older people need to retain a sense of dignity (so necessary to the integrity of the human personality) and to feel that they are respected. Professionals should avoid doing things that could be interpreted as belittling. Many older people, for example, resent being called by their first names when they have not invited someone to do so. On the other hand, like all of us, they appreciate and respond to warmth, consideration, interest, and encouragement.

There should be full and patient explanations to the elderly about, for example, the nature of their illnesses, what they can expect, and what the recommended treatment and health regimens can accomplish. Many of the current generation(s) of older people have had limited education and are not sophisticated about health matters. In addition to their anxiety, many have sensory deficits (vision and hearing) that interfere with rapid or complete understanding of what the professional is saying. But they may be embarrassed to say so or not be sufficiently assertive to "bother" professionals by asking them to take the needed extra time for explanations.

Obtaining Health Information

What *are* the health experiences of older people and what do they *do* in response to those experiences?

Health professionals need a complete picture of those matters if they are to provide appropriate care. The different sources of information in the research made a clear statement of the fact that the picture is multidimensional, tapping many different aspects of health experience and behavior. Each portion of the data supplemented and augmented the others, providing new information that had not come to the surface in the others. For example, the log data (Chapters 4 and 5) and the checklist data (Chapter 6) each revealed experiences and practices not illuminated by the other. The baseline information (Chapter 3), the open-ended question about other health practices (Chapter 7), the case material (Chapters 9, 10, and 11), and the exploration of lay consultation (Chapter 8) added still more information.

Traditional health histories and thorough examinations yield essential information, but other important information should be sought, such as the following:

1. Whether the older person has experienced various "significant" or potentially significant symptoms;
2. What day-to-day symptoms or bothers are experienced, whether or not the patient considers them to be important (inquiries should be made about symptoms that are not spontaneously reported);
3. What the older person does about day-to-day symptoms—whom they tell and what steps they take to relieve discomfort;
4. What the older person does to implement professional recommendations and what treatment advice is ignored;
5. Whether or not the professional advice helped and the reasons it may not have worked (such as adverse reactions to drugs);
6. Whether the older person is seeing other professionals and what other medications and regimens may have been prescribed;
7. Whether the patient is receiving and following advice from non-professionals, such as family members, friends, neighbors, or the media (newspaper columns, magazines, television commercials);
8. What the elderly individual is doing to prevent illness or to maintain health—that is, general practices rather than specific responses to diagnoses or symptoms.

Do Older People Complain a Lot?

One of the most interesting findings from the study speaks to the issue of the older person as a complainer. That stereotype was thoroughly disproved (as it had been in other research as well). To the contrary, rather than badgering their doctors (or other professionals) with phone calls, all aspects of the study revealed that the elderly people *underreported* their symptoms—even those that were potentially serious.

One could speculate as to why the elderly have the undeserved reputation of being complainers. Certainly, they have more real complaints than younger people. It is possible that professionals are uncomfortably aware that cures cannot always be effected and that the complaints, like the ailments producing them, are chronic. Since most professionals genuinely want to help older people, their own frustration may make them feel impatient with reports of discomfort. That is, annoyance may result when a health provider feels unable to respond by removing the offending symptom.

Of course, some older people, like some younger people, do indeed call much too frequently. This may be the expression of a long-standing personality trait, or it may be due to extreme anxiety or fear that leads to repeated pleas for help. Each individual who behaves this way deserves thoughtful consideration to try to identify the causes of his or her constant entreaties.

An interesting study by Lipsitt (1969) offers a clue for the management of people who constantly and unnecessarily phone or come to the clinic or office. A special clinic was set up for demanding people (of all ages) who were called "thick-chart" patients. Any number of appointments were made for them on request. The result was that their utilization of services dropped off, an outcome attributed by the researchers to the fact that the flow of dependency satisfaction was not shut off but was gratified in a way "that does not divest the patient of his autonomy, self-control, and therefore self-esteem." That kind of response may be worth a try when professionals are confronted with such a person.

Unreported Symptoms and Lifestyles

Health professionals are, of course, interested in relieving discomfort as well as in treating the ailments that cause that discomfort. Yet the study revealed that the vast majority of bothersome day-to-day mental and physical symptoms were not brought to professional attention by the older people who experienced them. Of course, many of those symptoms may have been reported to professionals at some time, and it is possible that many need not have been reported. But if the older people had phoned in relation to even a small proportion of their symptoms, the health professionals would have been overwhelmed.

Apart from the significance of some symptoms (which may signal serious illness requiring investigation), it is important for professionals to be aware of the unrelenting discomfort that continues when the patient is at home. Moreover, those symptoms interfere considerably with the older people's day-to-day lives and activities. There is evidence that the search for relief does not stop with professional advice. Nonprofessional advice is sought and used; nonprescription drugs (some of which may be appropriate) and unidentified drugs are taken; prescriptions are not always taken because of adverse effects or the prescribed dosage is reduced or increased; and a variety of home remedies are tried, some of them innocuous, some bizarre, and some potentially harmful.

These older people endure (often with remarkable fortitude) continuing symptoms that have a profound effect on their lifestyles. We do not know from the study data whether relief can indeed be afforded. As stated in the previous chapters, however, professionals must judge for themselves the extent to which they are aware of those matters and exert every effort to improve the day-to-day comfort of their elderly patients.

Mental and Emotional Health

The connection between mental and physical conditions that is so prominent a feature of older people's ailments is well known to professionals and was discussed earlier in this book. The nature of the most prevalent and frequent symptoms experienced by the older people studied—pain, fatigue/weakness, and mental/emotional bothers of various types—again underline the intimate relationship between body and mind. Professionals cannot afford to ignore, for example, the role of daily pain or fatigue in producing depression. Conversely, we do not know the extent to which mental health problems manifest themselves as or increase vulnerability to those physical symptoms.

It is significant that, in general, mental/emotional symptoms (when they occurred) were rated by these older people as causing more bother ("a lot") than physical symptoms (Chapter 4). Yet these symptoms were scarcely ever reported to professionals (Chapter 5). Moreover, in the training aids project, the emotional aspects of aging headed the list of subjects about which older people were judged to have inadequate knowledge; virtually all the health professionals, older people, and family members studied agreed in that respect (Chapter 12).

Certainly, health professionals must be alert to the emotional/mental repercussions of physical illness. They also should make special efforts to elicit from their elderly patients a description of what mental/emotional symptoms they experience and that so rarely are mentioned spontaneously.

Elderly patients should receive the message that health professionals are interested in each of them as a whole person. Even if all possible therapeutic measures are being taken, sympathetic interest and understanding can provide real emotional support. At the least, such professional attitudes can mitigate feelings so destructive to one's self-image—feelings that nobody cares and that the reporting of the older person's mental/emotional bother is a bother to the professional.

Mentally Impaired Older People

The mental-physical relationship is true, of course, regardless of the patient's mental status. There were many similarities between the three groups studied in the symptoms they experienced. There were also some differences to which professionals should be alert.

It was expectable, of course, that the older people with a history of functional mental disorders experienced more mental health symptoms. They also reported more diagnoses, more symptoms, and more pain and rated their symptoms as more bothersome than did those with normal mental functioning. We interpreted these differences not as malingering but as indicating their increased vulnerability to distress. The people in this group more often lived alone or with nonrelatives—that is, they less often had someone close who cared about them. Their relationships with professionals may, therefore, be more important to them.

Older people afflicted with senile dementia present some special problems for professionals. Many in the study were unable to articulate their health experiences at all. Others described their negative feelings and amorphous anxieties in phrases such as "my mind is confused," or "I feel in a fog." Still others expressed vague fears—of going to bed or sitting on the toilet, of thunder, or of going out, for example. Yet many of them were indeed capable of describing their day-to-day symptoms.

It is tempting for busy professionals to talk only with the caregiving relatives of old people with senile dementia. Communication with those who have cognitive impairments is often difficult, slow, and incomplete. Nevertheless, people with that diagnosis range widely in the degree to which they are impaired and therefore in the degree to which they can communicate and relate to others. Bypassing such individuals contributes to their already low self-esteem and feelings of being wiped-out and worthless. Equally important, they can be the professionals' best informants about what they are experiencing mentally and physically. The effort of relating directly to such patients, therefore, can pay therapeutic dividends.

Those with organic mental disorders who are so deeply impaired that they cannot communicate at all pose a unique challenge to professionals. Piecing together their health problems and experiences from examination, observation, and information from caregivers makes special demands on those who would help such people. But if this is not done, much of their suffering may go unmarked and unrelieved.

Health Education

Many aspects of the study spoke to the older people's need for health education. Chapter 12 detailed one possible model of an educational program for groups of the elderly.

While group programs serve a very useful purpose, they do not substitute for ongoing individual education by professionals. Each older person has a unique constellation of ailments, an individual personality, a particular life history and culture, a specific level of health knowledge, a personal style of adapting to illness, and an individual pattern of complying (or not complying) with professional recommendations. Each, therefore, requires complete explanation of the nature of his or her ailments, the reasons for whatever treatment(s) is prescribed, and what can be expected. Each must have the opportunity to ask questions. And each must be encouraged to call and "bother" the professional if the treatment fails to have the hoped-for outcome or has adverse effects.

The Context of the Older People's Lives

The most meticulous attention to the older person's condition, the most careful diagnosis and treatment plan, can be sabotoged if the professional is unaware of the life situation of the patient. As the data and the case material illustrated, the making and implementation of the health plan depends on many factors such as money to buy medicine, nutritious food, or supportive services; access to transportation to go to the sources of care; and appropriate housing and safe living conditions.

Attention to factors such as those mentioned is a necessary part of the professional's care of mentally and/or physically impaired older people. However, busy professionals cannot be expected to explore these matters in depth, to have detailed knowledge about the availability and eligibility criteria for various sources of help and to make referrals to the appropriate agencies, or to monitor them over time. The complex array of services, facilities, and entitlements includes income maintenance programs, specialized housing, posthospital Medicare benefits, homemakers, home-delivered meals, day care and day hospitals, and recreational services. (Availability of these varies, of course.)

What professionals can do is to be aware of such needs and act as gatekeeper to connect the older people to the world of services of which they often are unaware. That is, the professional can make a referral to an agency in the community whose job it is to be informed about what services and facilities exist and to help to mobilize those services. Examples of such agencies (and most communities have one or more) are area agencies on aging, family counseling agencies, and hospital social service departments.

Working with the Family

A vast amount of clinical and research literature, as well as the findings of this study, emphasize the major importance in older people's health care of the family involved in caregiving.

One factor that determines the extent and depth of the family's involvement is, of course, the level of care needed by the older person. Thus, the group of people in our study whose mental functioning was normal were largely independent from a functional standpoint. Despite this independence, they depended on family for emotional support, for help at times of illness or emergencies, and for day-to-day socialization. Significant minorities of those with a history of functional mental impairment needed help with instrumental activities such as shopping, transportation, and housekeeping chores. Those with senile dementia were the most dependent, with many needing help with personal care and almost all of them with instrumental activities; some were totally unable to care for themselves in any way.

Many other factors influence the ways in which family members help older people. Among them are the quality of past relationships, the helping person's competing responsibilities, and the health and capacities of the caregiver. The behavior of various families cannot be evaluated by the same yardstick.

As stated above, however, it is a reality that families are full partners with professionals in the health care of the aged. Whether those partners are regarded as allies or nuisances or whether they are competent or not, they are there. In fact, family members have been shown by many research studies (including the well-known study by the U.S. General Accounting Office, 1977) to provide 80%–90% of the services needed by older people. That care includes medically related services (such as bandage changing and injections), home nursing and personal care, household maintenance, and transportation. It can be stated with assurance that families *invented* long-term care of the aged long before that phrase gained wide currency. The services provided by the formal system of government and agencies constitutes the tip of the service iceberg. It is also the family that (as best it can) mobilizes, coordinates, and monitors those formal services.

Moreover, family members often are the first-line recipients of information about older people's health complaints. The vast majority of the elderly consult a relative in a health crisis and, as Chapter 6 indicated, even potentially serious symptoms are as likely to be reported to family members as to professionals.

Health professionals, then, should understand the roles and experiences of the caregiving families of older people if the partnership they must forge is to be effective. The remainder of this chapter, therefore, will discuss the ways in which caregiving differs at this stage of life from caregiving at earlier phases of a family's history. It then will review the record of families as caregivers, describe trends that may affect family caregiving in the future, identify some problems families often experience when an elderly person requires care, and offer practical suggestions about the ways in which professionals can relate to families.

Family Caregiving at the Aging Phase of Life

Family caregiving to older people should be seen in the context of the differences between the ways the family can manage health care of the aged and the ways in which family care of members at other stages of life can be managed.

Apart from the multiplicity and chronicity of the ailments themselves and the dependencies they induce when a person is old, the symptoms of older people's ailments can be extraordinarily disturbing. Forgetfulness, confusion, emotional lability, incontinence, and an inability to communicate are high on the list of distressing symptoms that may lead to disruptions in the lifestyle of family members and to anxiety about their own future and their own aging processes.

The family's anxieties may be expressed in behavior that is especially difficult for the health professional—multiple and repetitious phone calls (sometimes from several family members), overdetailed questioning about the patient's condition and prognosis, inappropriate requests for specialty consultations, "shopping" among many doctors, or pleas for medical cures that are nonexistent. Though such behavior by some families represents their usual pattern, it may be exaggerated at this time; for most, it relates more directly to their current situations. The family members who are affected by the older person's condition and who affect his or her care must therefore be understood in the light of their own roles and their own life situations.

Throughout the family life cycle, interdependence of family members is a constant, but the nature and number of each individual's dependencies shift over time. The routine involvement of young parents in the health care of their children is expected and accepted. During young adulthood and the middle years, the main pattern is that people relate directly to the professional, with the family participating primarily at times of acute illnesses.

When an individual is in the later stages of life, the family may again assume a major caregiving role. By contrast with the dependencies of the child, however, the older person's dependencies are chronic rather than temporary or transitional, they foreshadow increasing dependency rather than growing independence, and they appear with greater variability and irregularity and in different sequential patterns. Moreover, the physical care of an impaired older person requires strength, stamina, and nursing in a different and more difficult way than the care of a young child.

Aged people also vary with respect to the number and kind of relatives who are involved or available. Younger people are generally members of a nuclear family and caregiving patterns are relatively clear-cut: parents care for children and for each other. The principle caregiving relative(s) of the older person may be a spouse, an adult child, a sibling, or even a niece, nephew, or grandchild (or a combination of such family members).

Elderly Spouses as Caregivers

When the older person is married, the spouse is the principal provider of care. Elderly men are much more likely than elderly women to have a spouse on whom to rely at times of illness. This is due to the differences between the sexes in life expectancy and the tendency of men to marry women younger than they are. Most widowed elderly people are women (there are nine million widowed older people): at age 65 and over, most older women (52%) are widowed, and most older men (77%) are married. Rates of widowhood rise sharply with advancing age, and the imbalance in the proportion of women to men increases. Between the ages of 65 and 74, the ratio of women to men is 131 to 100; between 75 and 84 the ratio rises to 166; and at age 85 and over there are 224 women to every 100 men (Allan & Brotman, 1981).

Whether they are husbands or wives, older people exert efforts in caring for an ill spouse, but their capacities are constrained by their own ages, reduced energy and strength, and age-related ailments. Compared with other relatives who provide care, they experience the most stress (Horowitz, 1981). Elderly wives caring for disabled husbands, for example, have been found to suffer from low morale, isolation, loneliness, economic hardship, and "role overload" due to multiple responsibilities (Fengler & Goodrich, 1979).

Elderly caregiving spouses, therefore, require attention to their own needs for respite, concrete helping services, and emotional support. The physical strain may be accompanied by tremendous anxiety and by fear of losing one's partner in a marriage that may have endured half a century or more. Since more couples nowadays survive together into advanced old age, such situations are likely to occur even more frequently in the future.

Adult Children as Caregivers

When an elderly couple has children, the children assist the well spouse in caring for the impaired marital partner; when the older person is widowed, the bulk of care is given by adult children (Shanas, 1979a, 1979b; Sussman, 1965; Tobin & Kulys, 1980). Despite widespread myths to the contrary, research findings have systematically disproved the notion that contemporary adult children are alienated from the aged and do not take care of them as used to be the case in the "good old days." The accumulated evidence documents the strength of intergenerational ties, the continuity of responsible filial behavior, the frequency of contacts between generations, the predominance of families rather than professionals in the provision of health and social services, the strenuous efforts of family members to avoid institutional placement of the old, and the central role they play in caring for the noninstitutionalized impaired elderly (Brody, 1978).

Most older people realize their preference to live near but not with their children (Shanas, 1962; Beyer & Woods, 1963), sharing households primarily when reasons of health or economics make it necessary. Only about 18% of the elderly live with children, but (counting shared households) about 84% of those with children live less than an hour away from one of them (Shanas, 1979b). As stated above, the vast majority of home help services are provided not by professionals but by family and friends (U.S. General Accounting Office, 1977).

The five percent of those 65 and over who are in institutions at any one time are outnumbered two to one by equally disabled noninstitutionalized old people who are cared for by their families (Brody, S. et al., 1978; U.S. Comptroller General, 1977), a proportion that did not change between 1962 and 1975 (Shanas, 1979a). The role of families is highlighted by the fact that the vast majority (88%) of the institutionalized aged are not married (being widowed, divorced, or never married); more of them are childless than are the noninstitutionalized (Brody, 1981); and those who have children have fewer children.

Trends Affecting Caregiving by Adult Children

The well-documented responsible filial behavior has persisted despite two broad influential trends that affect the capacity of adult children to provide care.

The first trend, of course, is the radical demographic change that has led to a vast increase in the demands for parent care. During the same time span in which the number and proportion of older people in the population increased dramatically, the birth rate fell sharply. People who are now in advanced old age, therefore, have fewer children to share caregiving responsibilities than used to be the case. In addition, since parents and children age together, the adult children of the greatly increased number and proportion of people in advanced old age most often are in middle age and some are in their sixties or seventies. At present, about 40% of people in their late fifties have a surviving parent (some have both parents) as do about 20% of those in their early sixties and 10% of those in their late sixties (NRTA-AARP, 1981). Many adult children are grandparents; the four-generation family has become commonplace, with about 40% of older people with children being at the pinnacle of a four-generation family tree (Shanas, 1980).

Demands for parent care, then, occur at a time of life when the adult children on whom the old depend themselves may be experiencing age-related interpersonal losses, the onset of chronic ailments, lower energy levels, and even retirement. Their responsibilities often extend both upward to the old and downward to the young.

The second broad trend—the rapid entry of middle-aged women into the work force—also is placing an additional burden on family caregivers. Most of the family members with whom health professionals come in contact are women in the next generation down from the elderly patient. In addition to confirming the responsible behavior of families, research has identified daughters (and to some extent daughters-in-law) as the particular family members who are the principal caregivers to the old (Sussman, 1965; Tobin & Kulys, 1980).

The need to care for an elderly parent or parent-in-law arises for many middle-generation women at a time when they and their husbands had expected to have "empty nests"; they now often find that those empty nests are refilled physically and figuratively in terms of responsibility by impaired older people in need of care. As women advance from 40 years of age to their early 60s, for example, those who have a surviving parent(s) are more and more likely to have that parent be dependent on them, to spend more and more time caring for the parent, to do more difficult caregiving tasks, and to have the parent in their own households (Lang & Brody, 1983).

Middle-aged women, then, may not only be experiencing their own age-related problems, but their responsibilities may peak rather than diminish at this stage in their lives. Their traditional roles as wives, homemakers, parents, and grandparents have been augmented to an extent greater than ever before by the role of caregiver to an elderly person. Many such women now have an additional role as paid worker in the labor force (some because of career commitment, but most because the money is needed). Sixty percent of women between the ages of 45 and 54 work, and even more surprising, 42% of women between the ages of 55 and 64 are in the work force (U.S. Department of Labor, 1981).

Effects of Caregiving on the Family

The physical and emotional effects of caregiving on family members qualify the way in which they can care for the elderly parent. Professionals' expectations of them, therefore, require a perspective that includes a good picture of their unique family constellation and an awareness of family members' anxieties and symptoms of stress. Though different families react differently to the demands of parent care, genuine concern and affection for the older person are generally at work. At the same time, however, there is a concern about themselves, other family members, and the duration and intensity of the caregiving efforts they will need to exert.

Depending on their own personalities as well as on the reality demands, family members may feel guilty about not doing enough for the older person. Some are angry (though they may not be aware of their anger or able to express it) at finding themselves in the predicament of needing to do more than they feel able. Unresolved relationship problems (and most families have at least some vestiges of such problems) may be reactivated so that the older person becomes the focus of exacerbated latent and overt problems—between elderly spouses, among the adult siblings who are their children and with their spouses, and across several generations (Brody & Spark, 1966; Spark & Brody, 1970). In some families, bitter conflicts erupt about such issues as the fair sharing of caregiving responsibilities, with whom the older person should live, or who should help with money.

The middle-aged women in the elderly person's family—the principal caregivers—are often under considerable stress from their multiple competing responsibilities, a situation that had led to their characterization as "women-in-the-middle" (Brody, 1981). Those pressures, compounded by emotional conflicts related to the need to set priorities, may place them at high risk of mental/physical breakdown. Many who seek health care for themselves may be doing so in the context of such "role strains." Since what affects them inevitably affects their husbands, children, and other family members, the ripple effect operates to involve the total family.

While adult sons are not remiss in affection or in a sense of responsibility, our culture thus far has designated parent care as well as child care to women as being gender-appropriate. When sons do become principal caregivers (usually when a daughter is not available), they are helped by their wives and seem to experience less stress (Horowitz, 1981). This may be because they were socialized to view work as their main role, so that they do not feel conflicted and pulled by parent care responsibilities.

Hidden Costs of Family Caregiving

The cost/benefit approach toward establishing the dollar costs of formal services often overlooks costs that could be incurred if the stress on middle-aged, aging, and elderly caregivers triggers *their* physical and mental break-down. The classic Sainsbury and Grad studies in England (Grad and Sains-bury, 1966a, 1966b) and more recently Gurland's study of older people in New York and London (Gurland et al., 1978) found that care of ill older people negatively affects the mental/physical health of the family caregivers, increasing neurotic symptoms (such as insomnia, headaches, irritability, depression), restricting family social and leisure activities, disrupting household and work routines, causing family conflict and strained family relationships, reducing income, and adversely affecting young children.

As responsibilities peak in middle age—particularly for working women—how do they manage? A New York City study (Cantor, 1980) showed that working caregivers did not relinquish their responsibilities to the old, or to other family members, or to their jobs. What they did sacrifice was their own free time, opportunities to relax, socialization, recreation, and the like. Two-thirds of the respondents reported a great deal of emotional strain, and almost half reported a great deal of physical strain.

This situation is not unique to the United States. Even in Austria, for example, where a great deal of support has been given to the development of social/health services, there is widespread dependency on the family for services (Oriol, 1982). A recent survey involving 14,000 interviews in that country reported that more than a third of the offspring giving aid to an older person expressed feelings of burden (Horl & Rosenmayr, 1982). Similar information is emerging from other countries (Gibson, 1982).

Many other relatives also find themselves in the caregiving situation, such as daughters-in-law, sons, grandchildren, siblings, and even nieces and nephews of the elderly. And those older people without relatives to be placed in the middle are uniquely deprived and require special attention from professionals.

The mix of formal and informal health/social supports is changing, but not always in ways that help the family caregivers (see Chapter 2 for discussion of public policy issues). It is amply clear that such help is needed if the ongoing efforts of families to care for their elderly are to be strengthened.

Practical Suggestions for Professionals

Balancing their relationships with the older person and with caregiving family members makes special demands on health professionals. While family members need to feel that their feelings and practical efforts are appreciated, it is important to preserve older people's right to manage their own lives to the fullest possible extent. An implication that such control has been transferred to others can be detrimental, intensifying feelings of helplessness, hopelessness, and negative self-image, all of which are stimulated by the realities of eroding functions. Professionals and family members should be collaborators in fostering older people's autonomy, participation in treatment planning and decision-making, and in encouraging them to follow rehabilitative regimens that can improve functioning and independence. For those adult children who tend to take over too much, the professional's attitude can communicate the respect due the older adult.

It has been pointed out that doctor, patient, and adult child constitute a "triad" (a small group consisting of three people), and that triads always have potential for becoming coalitions of two against one (Rosow, 1981). Patient and child may unite against the doctor, for example, in expecting—even demanding—that he or she perform a magic cure. The patient may be left out if the doctor and adult child talk together about him or her; a child wanting to control the situation may subtly enlist the doctor in supporting his or her position. Or, the doctor and patient may be allies in defending the patient against his or her adult child's power and control. These tendencies can be minimized by health professionals in contact with older people and their families, since the professional is in the best position to maintain objectivity.

Listening to the Patient

The professional's behavior in listening carefully to the older person's complaints and in taking them seriously can signal therapeutic optimism to the family as well as the elderly individual. Even victims of senile dementia who appear to be withdrawn to the point of apathy sense when they are being "written off" when despair and hopelessness are expressed in subtle or overt ways by family members. The professional, by exhibiting sensitivity to the ricochet effect of such negative forces, can help the family to overcome them.

Concern for the Family

Because of the circumstances in which many family members find themselves and because of the pervasive effects of caregiving on their lives, it is of paramount importance that health professionals have a family perspective. That is, it is imperative to evaluate the care needed by an older person in the light of the family's capacities, the family's problems, and the potential mental and physical health effects on family members.

As stated above, different families react differently to the caregiving demands placed on them but in the main behave very responsibly. On another level, however, family members are often silently asking another set of very human questions: How will this affect me and my family? Will I be able to help my parent in the way the doctor recommends? Will this situation go on and on? Will it improve? Will it get worse?

It is enormously supportive to the family when the doctor conveys concern for their well-being as well as understanding of their feelings and difficulties and an appreciation of their role in caring for the patient. And it is particularly important to avoid any implication that they could do more; most already are doing the best they can—and even overextending themselves.

Giving Information

The extent to which family members understand the nature of the elderly person's illnesses should be evaluated. Apart from their need for accurate information in order to carry out the treatment plan, lack of information or misinformation can increase a family's distress. Communication of factual information, on the other hand, can enhance care and stem a flow of anxious phone calls. Families also need a straightforward explanation of the possible course of the older person's illness and a realistic discussion of what they can do.

The professional can also be especially helpful in dispelling incorrect notions about various ailments. For example, families of older people with senile dementia may be embarrassed to articulate beliefs such as absolutely nothing can be done, the patient is "crazy," the disease is contagious or is inherited, all old people become "senile," or even that the patient is being deliberate in creating problems and could control his or her behavior if he or she wished. Few families are aware that positive effects on such a patient's well-being can result from meticulous medical care, a supportive environment, and skillful and sensitive treatment by the people around him or her.

The Elderly without Close Family

A significant minority of older people do not have a close family member on whom to rely. The proportion who are deprived in that respect rises with advancing age. At age 75 and over, for example, 68% of women and 24% of men are widowed. An additional 9% of women and 7% of men are divorced or had never married.

About 20% of people who are now 65 and over have never had a child, and an undetermined number are childless because they have outlived their children (Allan & Brotman, 1981). Although the vast majority of those with children see them frequently, 11% (almost two million old people) do not see a child as often as once a month (Shanas, 1979b). For most of these, geographic distance precludes the availability of a child for supportive health care; for a minority, little or no help can be expected due to long-standing alienation.

While spouse and children are the first to be relied on, other family members of those who are without a spouse or children (such as siblings, nieces, and nephews) and their neighbors and friends also play an important role in helping older people (Cantor, 1980). The health-related help they give, however, does not approach in level or duration the help given by family (Cantor, 1977). The assistance friends and neighbors provide to those without close kin is particularly important to them. Nevertheless, the elderly individual without family or whose family is not close at hand and whose illness or disability is severe or likely to be prolonged is at high risk. It is especially important that health professionals connect such older people with sources of formal services.

The Professional's Role in Planning

The role of health professionals often includes providing help in decision-making and planning, since they are viewed as being objective and not caught in the emotional upset of the older person and the family. This is an exceptionally demanding situation. There are no simple rules to follow, since each individual and family present a unique set of personal and social circumstances. It can be helpful, however, to have an overall goal. A noted British geriatrician states the goal as enabling old, impaired people to live where they would wish to live if they were not disabled. For the great majority of old people, he states, this means living in a private house with no undue sense either of being insecure or being a burden to others (Evans, 1981).

Achieving that goal depends on factors in both the informal and formal support systems. Family supports to be evaluated include the nature of the living arrangements of patient and family; the number, ages, health status, proximity, and availability of family members; the historical quality of family relationships; the emotional support given to the caregivers by his or her own spouse, siblings, children, and other relatives; the changing nature of the older person's condition and the length of time the care has been necessary; and the effects on family members of the effort involved.

There are many formal services, programs, and entitlements that can supplement the family's services, though many are in short supply and availability varies from community to community. Examples are respite care (to give the family temporary relief when needed), in-home services (such as personal care, nursing care, homemakers, home-delivered meals), day care, counseling services, income maintenance programs, specialized housing, posthospital Medicare benefits (such as home health aides), day hospitals, and recreational services, to name just a few.

When continuation of the past living arrangement is not possible, decision-making may focus on whether the patient should move to, for example, specialized housing, a senior citizens apartment building, a retirement community, or a nursing home or other type of institution.

As stated above, health professionals can and should act as gatekeepers to introduce patient and family to the complex and confusing array of programs that constitute the formal support system. It is particularly important to seek services that can help the caregivers *themselves* in their own often arduous efforts to care for the impaired elderly family member. The cases presented in Chapter 11 illustrate the prolonged care given by some and the almost unbelievable stress and lifestyle disruptions they may endure without respite. These strains are particularly evident when the older person is mentally impaired, with those who have senile dementia making especially heavy demands.

Services that focus on the needs of caregivers are by no means plentiful. Chapter 14 will list some that should be developed through social policy.

14 From the Researchers' Perspective: A Comment for Health Professionals and Policymakers

The frontispiece of this book was a quotation from Richard M. Titmuss about the importance of listening to the elderly. The quotation was chosen for a very specific reason. As the project proceeded, we held periodic debriefings of the interviewers who were in personal contact with the older people being studied. During those sessions, we often asked them, "Based on what you see and hear, what is the main piece of advice you wish you could give health professionals?"

The answers were consistent and clear and can be summarized in one word: LISTEN!

The interviewers said over and over again:

Listen to what the older people are *really* saying.
Listen to the families.
Listen not only to the words, but to cries, whispers, and even silences.
Really listen so that the older people know their concerns and feelings are being recognized.

We viewed the research as a way of listening. Each approach to listening added additional pieces to the information mosaic being assembled. These different aspects of the study have been reported and discussed in various chapters in this book. They included the baseline questionnaires about the older people's health histories, diagnoses, and relationships to professionals and to the health systems; the log data on their day-to-day symptoms and remedies; their responses to the 20-symptom checklist and whom they told about those symptoms; and their replies to open-ended questions about their routine illness-prevention and health maintenance practices. These were supplemented by information that was confined informally to the interviewers by the older people and their collaterals during friendly discussions. And the detailed in-depth study of a small number of mentally intact older people gleaned information about the lay consultation they obtained in the course of their day-to-day conversations with relatives and friends.

Obviously, there are many paths to the development of a complete picture of multilayered health experiences and practices. There are many ways of listening. This comment offers some overall impressions of what we heard.

The differences in the mental statuses of the three groups studied did indeed account for some differences in the nature, frequency, and severity of their day-to-day mental and physical symptoms. The older people with histories of functional mental disorders, for example, reported more pain and more mental/emotional problems. And the same group tended to experience more distress from symptoms of various types.

Despite the differences of the groups one from the other, however, there were some striking similarities. Those with normal mental functioning (few of whom were severely impaired in physical functioning) resembled their mentally impaired peers in that they experienced pervasive, distressing mental and physical bothers that permeated their day-to-day lives. They too endured a dismaying amount of unrelenting pain, fatigue, and mental/emotional suffering, most often without complaining either to health professionals or to relatives and friends. Their courage and their struggles to go about their daily activities and chores command respect.

Many of these normals were busy participating in the happy activities of the senior centers, which was one of our referral sources. Like the vast majority of older people as reported in national data, they were functioning well. But such data give very little indication of the private worlds of mental and physical discomfort. The phrase "functioning well" often erroneously conveys an impression of overall well-being, when in reality the quality of life may be affected by many factors other than those related to functional level.

The bleakness and deprivation of the lives of the members of the two mentally impaired groups was, of course, more to be expected. Nevertheless, we were not prepared for their virtually unrelieved desolation, particularly that of the people with senile dementia. The mental symptoms of the latter group were particularly poignant because of the amorphous nature of their fears and anxieties and because of their frequent inability to articulate their distress clearly. Contrary to popular belief, however, many were able to tell us what was bothering them. Certainly, at least some of them could have benefited from some recreational or diversional activities and from breaks in their dreary routines. Yet mentally impaired and housebound older people, who cannot obtain such psychological supplies on their own, are also the ones who are most neglected by agencies whose mission is to deliver recreational services.

Information about the emotional and mental symptoms of the older people underlined the general neglect of such problems. Their physical problems were often bothersome and were not always well understood or treated adequately. But mental and emotional symptoms caused more distress ("a lot" of bother) to the older people than physical symptoms and were virtually unreported to professionals. Moreover, in the Training Aids project, the "common emotional problems of older people" were identified almost unanimously by the older people themselves, their collaterals, and health professionals as a glaring gap in the knowledge of older people in general.

The research also reinforced the well-known facts about the intimate relationships among the chronic mental and physical problems experienced by older people and the chronicity of those problems. Though such knowledge has been available and has been emphasized by gerontologists and geriatricians for many years, there continues to be an imbalance between funding for acute care and the chronic care that is needed, including supportive health/social services. Integrated care and support is also impeded by the different delivery systems. Medical services for the most part are financed federally, for example, while the responsibility for health/social services is primarily state and local. And the mental health and physical health systems are separately organized despite the interlocking of those two spheres.

The fragmentation of care in the case of many of the older people studied spoke to the need for some way of putting it all together—social care, as well as medical and/or psychological care. Though the service agencies which referred many of them to us were doing what they could, they were limited by the scarcity of services and by systems problems. As a result, none of our 132 older people could be said to have been receiving comprehensive, coordinated care.

The known facts also have pointed consistently and emphatically to the need for multidisciplinary assessment, a process experienced by none of the people in our study. Such an evaluation would not take place even if nursing home admission was being considered; all that would be required would be a medical certification of need (often a paper review), and even that would be required only for those who would need to apply for Medicaid. The reason for neglect of assessment is that it is not fundable through third-party payments, private or public. Furthermore, legislation and policy operate so as to prevent that approach.

Various other themes were reiterated by the research that has been reported before by researchers and professionals but that almost always has had inadequate response.

For example, negative attitudes of some professionals and family members contribute to the poor mental health of the aged. Ageism and the loss of meaningful life roles lead elderly people to a negative self-image and low self-esteem. This is exacerbated when they are treated without concern for their wishes, when they are deprived of control over their own lives, and when they are talked about as though they are inert objects. These matters, too, must be addressed if health is to be promoted.

Most of the older people studied expressed overall satisfaction with their medical care and faith in their doctors ("You should always follow the doctor's advice"). Yet this trust existed side by side with noncompliance and feelings that home remedies usually work better than professional recommendations; with complaints about health professionals such as their impersonal or cold attitudes, abruptness, not paying attention, lack of interest, preferences for younger patients, and lack of honesty; and with feelings of futility, hopelessness, and helplessness about the potential for improvement in their health.

Caregiving families often experience severe strain when prolonged and/ or considerable help is needed by an older family member. Such situations were illustrated in the case material and were most dramatic when the older person suffered from senile dementia.

Experts agree that concrete services from the formal network are required and that the net effect would be to strengthen and support the family's efforts. Examples of such programs are respite services, day care, transportation, in-home household maintenance, personal care services, and service-supported housing. Relief from financial strain on families could be in the form of such mechanisms as tax rebates or direct payments for caregiving or for purchasing care. Despite these needs, current social policy lacks provision for family-focused services. Thirty years of gerontological research and practice have produced definitive evidence that families behave responsibly in caring for their aged. However, the increased demand for more care for vastly increased numbers of older people has potential for exceeding the caregiving capacities of families. Moreover, the traditional caregivers to the aged—their daughters, and sometimes their daughters-in-law—have entered the labor force at a rapid rate. That trend calls into question their ability to carry out the caregiving role to the same extent as in the past and causes concern about the effects of "role overload" on the women themselves.

The need for concrete help in the form of services and/or money does not obviate the need for counseling, as the case studies amply demonstrated. At the time of this writing, there is much emphasis on developing methods of connecting older people with resources and mobilizing services. This is certainly important, but the counseling aspect of the service is often lost. "Information and referral," "case management," "channeling," or whatever label is given to the coordinating function must be accompanied by individualized attention to the psychological problems older people and families have in relation to using the service, to their emotional/psychological reactions to illness, and to the intra-psychic and interpersonal problems that exist or are exacerbated at such times. The case situations spoke to the need for counseling on a variety of issues ranging from marital and intergenerational relationship problems that interfered with health care to conflicts resulting in the outright abuse of an older person. Unfortunately, counseling, like assessment, is not a reimbursable service.

The negative effects on the mental and physical health of older people of socioeconomic and environmental factors such as low income, dangerous neighborhoods, inadequate health/social supports, and lack of transportation have been well documented. Those matters have not received the necessary remedial attention by social policy, however. Consequently, some of our older people, like some older people everywhere, were handicapped by deficiencies in their physical environments, by their inability to purchase medications or nutritious food, and by transportation problems they experienced in getting to the sources of health care.

The integral relationship of mental and physical health to the basic social and environmental conditions of older peoples' lives cannot be overemphasized. Although illness may be an impediment to social functioning, the degree of incapacity depends not on the actual impairment alone, but on individual and family resources and on the availability, acceptability, and utilization of social and medical resources.

To underline: To a significant extent, the old person's capacity to function at a decent level of health and well-being depends to a significant extent on the willingness (or unwillingness) of society to provide needed supports. Attention to those matters must go hand-in-hand with measures focused on particular medical or psychiatric conditions.

The limitations of the research have been identified earlier in the book but bear repetition here. First, the study focused on one aspect of the older people's lives and must be seen in that context. We were asking about mental, emotional, and physical symptoms—that is, the things that bothered and distressed them. Except for the questions about enjoyable activities in which they engaged, we did not ask about the positive aspects of their lives. The picture drawn, then, necessarily represents the "down" side. Nevertheless, the distress recorded by the research often clouded other aspects of the older people's existence—witness the interference with their activities.

Second, two of the three groups of elderly individuals studied were selected because they had serious mental problems: in one group, each had a history of functional mental disorder; in the other, each was afflicted with senile dementia. Thus, the selection process itself ensured that most of the older people were a problem population and were not representative of the total elderly population. Only the group whose members were intact mentally had characteristics that approximated those of average older people.

Third, the small sample of people studied had (as a group) relatively low socioeconomic backgrounds. For many of them, their interpretations of their symptoms and the steps they took to alleviate their discomfort undoubtedly were affected by the cumulative effects of mental illness, low income, poor environments, and social deprivation.

Fourth, the information was gathered from self-reports by the older people themselves and therefore reflects their perceptions. (This was, of course, the intent of the study.)

It is obvious that much more research is needed with other populations of older people and with larger samples. Suggestions for biomedical research are beyond the scope of this book, though the research pointed most emphatically to the need to prevent and mitigate the ailments that cause so much human misery—Alzheimer's and related disorders and arthritis, for example.

Throughout the duration of the study the major frustration of the staff was that we were *studying* but not *helping*. We would have liked to intervene in many of the older people's situations—that is, to utilize a skilled multidisciplinary team to assess and evaluate the older people and then to treat their ailments in a concerted way, to mobilize and coordinate available social supports, to educate the older people and their families about their health and health care, and to counsel those whose interpersonal problems and conflicts were exacerbating their mental and physical health conditions.

The message of this and other research to health professionals who are in direct contact with older people is clear. But there is another level of listening.

Titmuss asked, "How do we . . . institutionalize the listening role and in ways which signal to those concerned that the message has been received?" (1970).

Professionals can perform their listening function more effectively by making their voices heard not only in their practice but also in the public arena.

The task of social policy is to listen and to signal that the message has been received by taking effective action.

Appendixes

Appendix A
Referring Agencies

Philadelphia Geriatric Center
In-Home Service Program
Community Housing
  for the Elderly
5301 Old York Road
Philadelphia, PA 19141

YWCA-Center for Older
  Adults, N.W.
5820 Germantown Avenue
Philadelphia, PA 19144

Marconi Senior Citizen Program
c/o South Philadelphia
  Community Center
2600 South Broad Street
Philadelphia, PA 19145

Hillside-Hilltop Senior
  Citizen Center
470 Green Lane
Philadelphia, PA 19128

Germantown House
(Public Housing Authority)
5457 Wayne Avenue
Philadelphia, PA 19144

Upper Darby Multi Service Center
7000 Walnut Street
Upper Darby, PA 19082

Riverview Congregate Meal
  Service Center
Riverview and Garrett Roads
Drexel Hill, PA 19026

Watkins House
326 Watkins Avenue
Upper Darby, PA 19082

Deliverance Church
4732 North Broad Street
Philadelphia, PA 19141

Horizon House, Inc.
1405 Locust Street
Philadelphia, PA 19102

Hahnemann Geriatric Services
1421 Arch Street
Philadelphia, PA 19102

Philadelphia Center for Older
  People (PCOP)
1336 Lombard Street
Philadelphia, PA 19147

The Coffee Cup (part of PCOP)
248 South 11th Street
Philadelphia, PA 19107

Catholic Social Services
c/o Community Services for the
  Aging Department
222 North 17th Street
Philadelphia, PA 19103

St. Ann's Senior Citizens Center
Catholic Social Services
2607 East Cumberland Street
Philadelphia, PA 19125

Hall-Mercer CMHC
8th and Locust Streets
Philadelphia, PA 19107

Weinstein-Hillman Geriatrics
  Center
2115 Sansom Street
Philadelphia, PA 19103

Salvation Army
701 North Broad Street
Philadelphia, PA 19123

West Philadelphia Community
  Mental Health Consortium
c/o Older Adult Services
6080 Woodland Avenue
Philadelphia, PA 19142

Tasker Center for Older Adults
3101 Morris Street
Philadelphia, PA 19145

Jewish Y's and Centers
Broad and Pine Streets
Philadelphia, PA 19102

Jewish Y's David Newman
  Senior Center
6600 Bustleton Avenue
Philadelphia, PA 19149

Jewish Y's Multi-Service Center
Marshall and Porter Streets
Philadelphia, PA 19148

Jewish Family Service
Division on Aging
1610 Spruce Street
Philadelphia, PA 19103

Benjamin Rush Center for Mental
  Health and Mental Retardation
10125 Verree Road
Philadelphia, PA 19116

Family Service of Philadelphia
  North
5700 North Broad Street
Philadelphia, PA 19141

Eastern Montgomery Meals
  on Wheels
c/o Abington Memorial Hospital
Abington, PA 19001

Northeast Community Center for
  Mental Health
The Gathering Place for
  Senior Citizens
6726 Rising Sun Avenue
Philadelphia, PA 19111

Interac-United Methodist Church
470 Green Lane
Philadelphia, PA 19127

Northwest In Home Service
c/o Philadelphia Electric Company
41 West Chelten Avenue
Philadelphia, PA 19144

Lower Merion-Narberth Coalition
75 East Lancaster Avenue
Ardmore, PA 19003

Department of Welfare
Adult and Aging Services Division
1405 Locust Street, Room 1918
Philadelphia, PA 19102

Lower Merion Counseling Service
551 West Lancaster Avenue
Haverford, PA 19041

Appendix B

The Philadelphia Geriatric Center Training Aids: Self-Care Training for Older Adults—Ways to Keep Healthy

INTRODUCTION TO THE USE OF MATERIALS

These training materials* are designed for use by community-based agencies which provide direct services to the elderly, such as senior centers, senior housing complexes, and area agencies on aging. With minimal amounts of preparation and guidance as contained in each unit, personnel of these agencies are provided with ready-to-use lesson plans which can be presented as separate sessions or as one continuous health education program for their clients.

Areas of discussion include:

Unit I: Stereotypes and Aging
   A. The meaning of stereotypes
   B. How stereotypes influence health

Unit II: The Body and Aging
   A. Normal physical changes
   B. Some of the more common problems of aging
      1. Arthritis
      2. Heart disease
      3. Hypertension

Unit III: The Mind and Aging
   A. Normal cognitive changes
   B. Senility
   C. Depression

Unit IV: Organizing for Better Health Care
   A. The Personal Health Care Chart
   B. What to ask your doctor

---

*These training aids were developed through the support of the Administration on Aging Grant #90–A–1229.

Each unit contains a brief introduction and summary of objectives; a list of references including books, articles, and easily obtained pamphlets which are all recommended for use by the group leader before and during the unit; a list of the materials and audio-visual aids required, including sample handouts, to present the unit to a group of older people; the teaching methods which are employed during the session; the actual lecture (*in italics*) and accompanying easy-to-follow instructions (in regular type); suggested group assignments; and ways that the success of each unit can be evaluated.

Groups should be kept small (12–20 participants) for maximum interaction between the leader and the participants.

It is also highly recommended that a health professional be available on a consulting basis to deal with complicated questions that participants may present.

Emphasis has been placed on accomodating agencies where educational resources are limited by lack of personnel and/or training funds. The units which have been developed were designed with simplicity and brevity in mind and should fit even the most disadvantaged situations.

UNIT I: STEREOTYPES

Time: 50–60 minutes

I   Introduction
        This session is a very general introduction to the topic of aging. It is designed to establish a relaxed, informal atmosphere which allows for give and take and for fun. It encourages active participation by group members, using their experiences to build to the major points of the lesson.

        If a course pretest is to be given, it would be most appropriately and conveniently done before this session.

II   Objectives of Lesson
        A.   General
             1.   Participants will recognize myth versus reality and stereotypes in relation to the aging process.
        B.   Specific
             1.   In discussion, participants will distinguish between specific myths and realities of aging.
             a.   health versus illness
             b.   mental competence versus senility
             c.   personality growth versus personality deterioration

2. In discussion, participants will define stereotypes as they relate to aging.
3. In discussion, participants will challenge stereotypes as they relate to aging.

III   References
    A.   Books/articles
       1.   Dangott, L. R. & Kalish, R. A. *A Time to Enjoy*. Englewood Cliffs, New Jersey: Prentice-Hall, Inc., 1979.

IV   Materials and Aids
    A.   Blackboard and chalk
    B.   Handout (Figure B–1)
    C.   Chairs in a semicircle
    D.   Large sign with word "STEREOTYPE" in large letters
    E.   Attendance sheet

V   Methods
    A.   Lecture
    B.   Question and answer
    C.   Large group discussion

VI   Procedure (see pp. 209–215 for special procedure steps)
    A.   Introduction of self and group warm-up exercise
    B.   Introduction to the session
    C.   Large group discussion and exercise
    D.   Handout (Figure B–1)
    E.   Assignment

VII   Evaluation
    A.   Ongoing participation in large group discussion
    B.   Attentiveness
    C.   Completion of assignment

Unit I Procedure

Introduction of Self and Group Warm-Up Exercise

Exercise optional depending on how well participants know each other. Just having them say hello is a nice way to start a session. Repeat directions if necessary.

Group leader can meet persons sitting at the ends of the row.

1. Before we start today's session, I'd like each of you to turn to the persons sitting to your right and to your left, say hello, tell those people a little about yourself, and find out a little about who they are. We'll take about five minutes to do that.

Introduction to the Session

1. *Today we're going to talk about the aging process, in general, and we'll start thinking about what growing old really means.*

Large Group Discussion and Exercise

Wait a few seconds for participants to think. Repeat question if necessary. Have participants call out–one-word responses, one at a time, and write these responses on the board.

Responses to expect: cranky, stubborn, wise, experienced, helpless, demanding, grandmotherly, cute, wrinkled, perverted, kind, proud, senile, confused, forgetful, etc.

Continue until most people have contributed at least once, or the group's responses have slowed.

1. *Think about the word "old." What comes to the minds of most people when they hear the word "old"?*

Call for answers from the group and try to build their answers into a correct definition.

2. *All of these descriptions are part of the stereotype of aging. What is a stereotype?*

Put up stereotype sign, pointing to it frequently when appropriate throughout the lesson.

Wait for participants to respond to each question with common stereotype.

3. *A stereotype is what some people think of others—it may be untrue, but it is applied to a whole group—usually because of race, religion, sex, age, or job. For instance, if I ask "What are teenagers like?," you might say, "They're all wild" or "They're all inconsiderate." If I ask about "fat" people, you might say they are all "jolly." Many people think all blondes are dumb. Many men think women are weak or emotional while many women think the opposite is true of most men.*

Expect and encourage spontaneous responses from the group to these questions!

Do you know people who don't fit those stereotypes? Can you think of teenagers who are not wild? What about fat people who are not jolly? Blondes who are not dumb? Women who are not weak? Men who aren't strong?

Call for answers from group, then expand on appropriate answers as stated.

4. *Where do we learn stereotypes?*

Use examples from the group, if they are offered.

a. *Parents pass stereotypes to children and, very often, the children never know why the parents formed their opinions originally. An example of this is the woman who used to cut the ends off her pot roasts because her mother did that. And her mother got that idea from her mother. One day the granddaughter found out why grandmom cut the ends off her pot roasts—she never had a pot big enough to hold the roast!*

b. *As children we also learn stereotypes from our friends or peers.*

c. *We may have personal experiences ourselves with different kinds of people.*

d. *Newspapers, magazines, and books may present a slanted view or one which could be misinterpreted by a reader.*

e. *TV is a rich source of stereotypes. Think about the kinds of stereotypes of old people we can find on TV. We see commercials for dentures, laxatives, vitamin tonics, and lemonade, but*

Wait for responses from the group
and for further examples.

*none for perfumes, clothes,
most foods, laundry deter-
gents, or shampoo. Don't
older people use these pro-
ducts?*

*What about some of the
characters on popular TV
shows who are older? How
are they portrayed? The
grandfather on "The Wal-
tons" is wise and experi-
enced. He's an example of a
good stereotype. On "The
Jeffersons," the old woman
was cranky, stubborn, and
meddling—a bad stereotype.*

Get responses from the group and
expand on them.

5. *Why do people **need** stereotypes?*
   a. *It may be easier to classify
      people in groups rather than
      to get to know them.*
   b. *It may be easier to explain a
      bad experience by blaming
      someone else.*
   c. *Many people are afraid—it is
      a way to cope with fear (of
      getting old, for instance).*

Get responses from the group and
expand on them.

6. *When **you** are stereotyped because of your age or color or religion, how might you act?*
   a. *You may get angry; try to
      prove you're not that way; get
      depressed; withdraw; feel
      hurt.*
   b. *You may act the way you are
      expected to act, especially if
      you believe the stereotype.*

This point must be fully understood
before moving on, as it establishes
the basic premise of the session and
lays the foundation for discussion in
later sessions.

*If you believe that older peo-
ple are supposed to be sick and*

Evaluation of whether participants understand this point may be achieved by asking for further examples from the group, or simply by the leader's sense that the group is attentive and following the discussion.

needy or forgetful and confused, you might begin to act that way. If you believe all old people become crippled from arthritis, you might not get proper care for yourself because you think that nothing can be done for your arthritis. And that's wrong! If you think that being older means aches and pains, and you have chest pains which you think are normal, you might not look for the help you need for a very serious problem, which could be treated.

Point to blackboard. Wait for responses from group, prompting by emphasizing various words on board which are negative.

7. *Now, let's look back at the list of words we used to describe old people. What do you notice? They are mostly negative. People expect aging to be a negative experience. Yet, can you think of older people who do not fit these descriptions, such as old people who are not confused or sick? In one study, most of the older people who were interviewed felt that their health was better than the health of most other older people. They felt that they were exceptions to the fact that when you get old, you get sick. But they can't **all** be exceptions, so maybe what they expected to happen as they got older doesn't always happen!*

Get responses from group.

8. *What conclusions can we draw from all of this?*
   a. *The descriptions on the board are not true—they are stereotypes.*
   b. *Everybody is different; everyone is an individual.*

9. *Aging affects everyone differently—that is the most important point we can make today. Successful aging depends
   on many different, individual
   factors. Your health and your
   financial situation are very important. Your expectations of
   how you will grow older may
   be just as important. Very
   often, if you expect the worst,
   it may become reality.*

10. *Most of you have heard the ex-
    pression "you're as old as you
    feel." We're going to change
    that to: "You are as old as you
    expect to be."*

    *And one way to expect to feel
    good as you age is to learn all
    you can about **aging and
    health,** both physical and
    mental.*

    *You need to discover which
    things are true and which are
    just false expectations or
    stereotypes of aging. You must
    learn that people have the pow-
    er to change or prevent illness
    just by knowing what is normal
    and what is necessary to report
    to a doctor.*

11. *In the next few sessions to-
    gether, we will discuss aging
    and health. We'll consider
    some of the ways to stay heal-
    thy in both mind and body, in-
    cluding diet, exercise, taking
    your medicines correctly, and
    just relaxing. We'll also try
    to help you get a picture of
    your own health care so that*

Write this on board for emphasis.

Point to stereotype sign.

when you leave the doctor's office next time, you'll have a good idea of what you are supposed to do to take care of yourself, what to look out for, and how to ask the right questions.

Handout

Distribute handout (Figure B–1) for session and review briefly. Either the leader or one of the participants can read it out loud to the group. Call for any questions at this time, trying to keep the group focused on the handout and not on personal individual health problems.

1. *Today's handout contains the major points of today's discussion. Let's take a look at it now.*

2. *I hope that you will use this handout in the next weeks to review today's discussion.*

Assignment

Be sure everyone understands the assignment before closing the lesson.

1. *Also, for the next week, I would like you to keep your eyes and ears open for examples of how older people are stereotyped, either on TV, in newspapers and magazines, or in your own experiences. Write these stereotypes of older people down or cut them out—for instance, a TV program that makes fun of aging or an ad in the paper. Next week we'll take a few minutes to discuss your examples of stereotypes.*

    Good luck! See you next week!

P.G.C.'s
"One Life To Live... Ways To Keep It Healthy"

Lesson I.: Introduction

The class will meet every week, same time, same place, for another 3 weeks. It is important to attend every session. At the end of the last class you will have a chance to tell us what you think of the classes and how they have helped you. Then, in one month from the last class, we will return for a review session and distribution of certificates. It is important that you be present at that time. Your cooperation will help us make our program the best it can possibly be!

✓ Stereotypes

A. A STEREOTYPE is what some people think of others because of color, religion, sex, or AGE. It may be incorrect but it's easier for some people to use a stereotype than to get to know the real story.

B. Many people believe that the old are supposed to be sick, needy, or confused so they begin to act that way as they grow older.

But.... It's NOT TRUE !!!

The moral of the story is:

You are not as old as you feel;
YOU ARE AS OLD AS YOU EXPECT TO BE !!!

So LEARN HOW TO EXPECT TO FEEL GOOD AS YOU AGE

UNIT II: THE BODY AND AGING

Time: 40–45 minutes up to suggested break (VI D–7)
      20–25 minutes additional to end of unit

      60–70 minutes total

I   Introduction
      This session discusses cardiovascular changes and arthritis and includes
      a brief reference to digestion. It is designed to emphasize that good
      health is possible in aging, provided that one knows the difference
      between normal and abnormal physical changes. The conditions dis-
      cussed are used as examples of such contrasts, and they are not re-
      viewed in-depth.

      As mentioned later in the outline, it is possible and convenient to
      break this unit into separate sessions. Such a decision should be made
      based on time limitations but could depend also on how attentive
      participants remain after the first half of the session is completed.
      Because of the large number of terms and facts included in the lecture,
      it may be advisable for some groups to stop at the point indicated in the
      outline. Careful pacing is essential to absorb so much factual content.

      Frequent interaction between the leader and the group is recom-
      mended to break up the lecture. This interaction should be based
      strictly on content which the leader may try to elicit from knowledge-
      able group members. Very often, participants have heard the informa-
      tion stated somewhere else, but have never "put it all together" as the
      leader will do.

      It is essential that the leader discourage the bringing up of personal,
      unique, and individual situations. Personal anecdotes, while interest-
      ing, may not only distract from the main content but may also pit the
      leader's lecture content against the individualized advice given to parti-
      cipants by their personal physicians.

      Finally, it should be noted that points to be emphasized by the leader
      during the session have been underlined in the text of the lecture.
      Writing these points on the board or presenting them visually in some
      other way, in addition to including them on the handout, will help
      participants to absorb them.

II   Objectives of lesson
      A. General
          1. Participants will recognize that older people have the power to
              change and prevent illness through adequate health knowledge
              and improved preventive measures.

    B. Specific
       1. In posttest, participants will distinguish between normal and abnormal physical processes of aging.
       2. In discussion, students will indicate changes in the seeking of professional care which reflect a base in knowledge of normal versus abnormal physical processes of aging.

III   References
    A. Dangott, L. R., & Kalish, R. A. *A Time to Enjoy*. Englewood Cliffs, New Jersey: Prentice-Hall, Inc., 1979.
    B. Retirement Living Magazine. *Guide to Health . . . and Your Retirement*. (Retirement Living Magazine, 150 East 58th St., New York, NY 10022 (212 593–2100)
    C. *Osteoarthritis—A Handbook for Patients*. (Available from local Arthritis Foundation chapter, or from The Arthritis Foundation, 3400 Peachtree Road, N.E., Atlanta, Georgia 30326)
    D. National Institute of Arthritis, Metabolism, and Digestive Diseases. *How to Cope with Arthritis*. (U.S. Department of Health, Education, and Welfare, Public Health Service, National Institutes of Health, DHEW Publication No. [NIH] 76–1092.) For sale by the Superintendent of Documents, U.S. Government Printing Office, Washington, DC 20402.
    E. *An Older Person's Guide to Cardiovascular Health*. (American Heart Association's National Center, Communications Division, 7320 Greenville Avenue, Dallas, Texas 75231)
    F. *Quick Quiz on Medical Care for the Aged*. (Isabella Geriatric Center, 515 Audubon Avenue, New York, NY 10040)

IV   Materials and Aids
    A. Blackboard and chalk
    B. Chairs in a semicircle
    C. Handouts (Figures B–2 and B–3)
    D. Pamphlets (optional)
    E. Attendance sheets

V   Methods
    A. Lecture
    B. Large group discussion

VI   Procedure (see pp. 219–228 for special procedure steps)
    A. Introduction of self and group
    B. Review of last session's assignment (no more than 5–10 minutes)
    C. Introduction to session
    D. Lecture—large group discussion with first handout (Figure B–2)
    E. Second handout (Figure B–3)
    F. Assignment

VII Evaluation
A. Ongoing participation in large group discussion
B. Attentiveness
C. Completion of assignment
D. Improvement in results of written text, if given pre- and post-session

Unit II Procedure

Introduction to Session

	1. How many times has a doctor, nurse, family member, or even an older friend said to you, "What do you expect for someone your age?" when you complain about your health? How does that make you feel?
Wait for responses from group.	*a. You may feel angry.*
	b. May decide to give up—you say, "What's the use?"
	2. What is the word we discussed last week which people sometimes use to explain something they don't understand?
	a. STEREOTYPE!!
	3. This week we'll talk about our bodies as we age. We'll discuss what you should expect for someone your age . . . what is normal and what is not normal; what to report to a doctor and what can't be helped. Then you can answer that question of "What do you expect for someone your age?" by saying: "I expect to be treated and to get my health under control."
Emphasize this point.	**With a little know-how, good health is possible at any age!**

Lecture—Large Group Discussion

1. The physical changes we're going to talk about occur differently for each individual. No two people are alike in how aging affects them. What is the same is **the need to know what is normal and what's not.**

Emphasize this point.

2. First, let's think about a baseball player. At what age are many athletes considered past their prime? Thirty to thirty-five years old! That seems young, but there seems to be some loss of muscle strength and functioning at that point, and most athletes retire by the time they're 40.

Wait for responses.

That loss of muscle strength is an expected part of aging, which affects not only how the baseball player swings a bat or how fast he runs, but also affects how the muscles on the inside work.

Write the bold portion of this statement on the board, leaving room below to list several body parts.

3. For instance, in the digestive system your stomach and intestines, which digest your food, are mostly muscle. In the same way as the baseball player slows down, so does your digestion. The food in your stomach and intestines sits around longer, making it easy for you to get an upset stomach and harder for you to get rid of waste through moving your bowels. One way to get those muscles moving is to naturally stimulate them with the right kinds of foods. What helps?

Write "stomach" and "intestines" under previously written statement on board.

a. Fruits, vegetables, high fiber foods, and liquids.

Wait for responses from the group.

b. Laxatives and enemas can be

harmful because they irritate more than naturally stimulate.

Write "heart" at the bottom of the list on the board.
Wait for responses from the group and build a correct definition.

4. *Another part of your body which is mostly muscle is the heart. It loses some strength, too. What is the job of the heart?*

The heart pumps blood through your body every second, every minute, everyday, without rest. That's a lot of work for the muscle to do. So the heart muscle gets a little over-stretched, and it doesn't have quite the same ability to push the blood out through the arteries as it used to. And it is the blood which brings nourishment and air to all the body parts. The result of a weaker heart is that you may get tired a little more quickly than in younger years, but you are still in healthy territory. But if the blood backs up too much, it may clog the lungs and kidneys, and the extra fluid may cause swelling in the ankles and wrists. You may get short of breath. Does anyone know what this is called? It is congestive heart failure, which means that the heart is not pumping as effectively as it did. This requires treatment, and the doctor will probably give you medicines such as Digitalis or Lanoxin to make the heart pump with more strength. The doctor may tell you to get rid of too much fluid in your blood vessels by cutting down on salt, which holds in water, or by prescribing water pills such as Lasix.

Write "blood pressure" on board.

Participants may volunteer the word "stroke."

Have participants contribute steps they know. Write these on the board, erasing other material as necessary.

Erase board. Good time to take break or to stop session and continue another time, if necessary. When stopping here, it is advisable to distribute the first handout (Fig-

5. *Anything you do to give your heart less work will help it. The energy it uses to push the blood through your body is called blood pressure. The harder the heart is pushing, the higher the blood pressure, the more work the heart is doing to get blood to every part of your body. This can damage your heart permanently. If the blood vessels stretch too much from the pressure, they may burst. If these are in the brain, it is called a "stroke." The high pressure can also damage the kidneys.*

6. *Can high blood pressure be treated?*
   Yes!! How?

   a. *Follow the diet your doctor recommends. This will include getting rid of the salt which holds too much fluid in your body.*
   b. *Lose weight with the help of your doctor since every pound is extra work for the heart.*
   c. *Take your medications as the doctor directs, even if you're feeling fine and don't think you need them. Once your blood pressure is under control, it will only stay that way if you keep following the treatment plan.*
   d. *Control stress in your life. Try to avoid getting upset unnecessarily.*

ure B–2) and review it with participants. A suggested assignment for
the next session is to read any pamphlets which are distributed.

7. *Getting back to our baseball
player, if he were the pitcher on
the team and straining joints in
his arm all the time, he would be
likely to have a problem with his
elbow that affects most people to
some degree, sooner or later.*
Wait for response from the group.   *Does anyone know what that is?*
*It is arthritis, and that's what we
will talk about for the next few
minutes.*

8. *There are many kinds of arthritis, and it is extremely important
that the baseball player find out
for sure what he has because the
treatments can be different!*
*One type of arthritis is the
kind that the baseball player
probably does not have. It is
Write "rheumatoid arthritis" on the   called rheumatoid arthritis. This
board.   kind of arthritis causes inflammation of the joints, often
starting with small joints and
then gradually the larger joints.
Rheumatoid arthritis also can
affect the whole body, including
internal organs and causing fatigue, loss of weight and appetite, anemia, and a general feeling of sickness. It can strike at
any age. This type of arthritis
needs attention very quickly and
actively since permanent damage can be prevented if the disease is controlled with special
medications.*

Write "osteoarthritis—degenera-   9. *The baseball player with pain in
tive joint disease" on the board.   his elbow probably has osteoar-*

thritis, sometimes called degenerative joint disease. It is usually due to wear-and-tear of the joints, especially the ones that do the most work. Which joints do the most work? They are usually the ones that bear weight, such as the hips, knees, and the spine. Frequently the fingers are affected. In the baseball player's case, it was his elbow which wore out from being used so much.

Wait for responses from the group. A small stick figure drawn on the board may be helpful to illustrate joints which are affected.

What symptoms will the baseball player feel? Probably pain, muscle weakness and tension, and stiffness. This is not a surprise to anyone. What is a surprise to some people is that there is no need to let osteoarthritis get worse as a part of old age. It can't be cured, but it can be treated. Pain can be relieved, and lost joint movement can be prevented or improved.

Wait for responses from the group.

10. One of the best treatments for osteoarthritis is heat. It relaxes muscles and relieves soreness. The baseball player uses a whirlpool, but a hot bath early in the morning can be just as helpful. Warm packs, heat lamps, or hot water bottles can help too. But take care not to get burned. Heat should be used along with exercises, as prescribed by the doctor, since the muscles are most relaxed after the heat.

The doctor may prescribe aspirin as well, since it is very useful in relieving pain and is safer for many people than *some other drugs. The doctor can advise you about whether you should take any drugs and will tell you which are best for you.*

Get responses from the group and list them on the board.

Other tips are:

a. *Keep moving; staying in bed or a chair causes stiffness.*
b. *Never put a pillow under your knees or cross your legs.*
c. *Get enough rest.*
d. *Wear proper shoes.*
e. *Pay attention to your posture.*

11. *There are many other physical changes that occur as part of the aging process. We have discussed the most common ones as examples of the thought that just as you extend the life of a car or a sewing machine with proper maintenance and care, so you can encourage good health by applying knowledge of how to take care of yourself.*

Second Handout

Distribute second handout (Figure B–3) for session and review briefly. Either the leader or one of the participants can read it out loud to the group. Call for any questions at this time, trying to keep the group focused on the handout and not on personal health problems.

1. *Today's handout contains the major points of today's discussion. Let's take a look at it now.*

2. *I hope that you will use this handout in the next weeks to review today's session.*

Assignment

If pamphlets have been distributed, an assignment could be the reading of those pamphlets for brief discussion at the next session.

An alternative assignment is to have participants look at their own styles of living and list five ways that they could change what they do on a daily basis to stay healthy (using this session's information as a basis), such as getting more

P.G.C.'s
"ONE LIFE TO LIVE ... WAYS TO KEEP IT
HEALTHY"

LESSON 2 : THE BODY AND AGING

✓ With a little know-how, good health is possible at any age. No two people are alike in how aging affects them. What is the same is the need to know what is <u>NORMAL</u> and <u>what's</u> <u>not</u> !

✓For instance, the loss of some muscle strength is an expected part of aging. It can affect **the** <u>digestion</u> since your stomach and intestines are partly muscle. Indigestion and constipation are common problems but can be eliminated by eating the right kinds of foods.

✓ Your heart is also a muscle which can get a little overstretched with age. Anything you can do to give it less work, such as losing extra pounds, getting rid of salt in your diet and taking your medications as directed, will keep your heart at its healthiest level.

✓ <u>Blood</u> <u>pressure</u> is the energy the heart uses to push the blood through your body. Too much pressure can damage the heart and kidneys permanently, or cause the blood vessels to stretch too much. If these blood vessels burst in the brain, it is called a <u>stroke</u>.

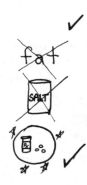

✓ Can high blood pressure be treated ? YES !!! <u>DIET</u> and <u>MEDICATION</u> work ! ◌

P.G.C.'s

ONE LIFE TO LIVE....WAYS TO KEEP IT HEALTHY

LESSON 2: THE BODY AND AGING

THERE ARE <u>MANY</u> <u>KINDS</u> <u>OF</u> <u>ARTHRITIS</u>, which are treated differently. It is very important to see a doctor if you think you have arthritis but haven't told the doctor.

<u>Rheumatoid arthritis</u> involves many joints over a number of years, often starting with small joints and then, gradually, larger joints. It can also affect the <u>whole body</u>, including internal organs. But <u>quick medical attention</u> <u>can prevent permanent damage</u> to the joints and stop the progress of the disease.

<u>Osteoarthritis</u> is the "wearing out" of the joint, due to the strains of work, injury, aging and other factors. It is very common and most people get arthritis in the joints that do the most work – the back, hips, and knees. It comes on slowly and there is <u>no need</u> to let it get worse as part of old age. The doctor treats it with heat, exercise, and medication. Other tips are: KEEP MOVING!!! Wear proper shoes! Never put a pillow under your knees!

exercise by walking to the senior center or the store; taking the salt shaker off the kitchen table; not getting upset when the grandchildren come over.

Of course, these assignments are dependent on which section of content has been covered during that day's session.

UNIT III: THE MIND AND AGING

Time: 60 minutes

I   Introduction

Unit III discusses mental aspects of aging—both normal and abnormal. Its tone is nonthreatening and optimistic. It conveys the point that just as a person has some control over physical health status, preventive measures can be taken to maintain mental health, and treatment is available for many problems.

The subject of "the mind and aging" may be the most threatening aspect of aging to many group members. This should be taken into account during the presentation, and participants should be encouraged to share feelings during discussion, staying within the bounds of the actual lesson content.

II   Objectives

A. General

1. Participants will recognize that older people have the power to change and prevent mental illness through adequate health knowledge and improved preventive measures.

B. Specific

1. In discussion, participants will distinguish between normal and abnormal mental processes of aging.

2. In discussion, students will indicate changes in the seeking of professional care which reflect a base in knowledge of normal versus abnormal mental processes of aging.

III References

A. Books/Articles

1. Dangott, L. R., & Kalish, R. A. *A Time to Enjoy*. Englewood Cliffs, New Jersey: Prentice-Hall, Inc., 1979.

2. Galton, L. *Don't Give Up on an Aging Parent*. New York: Crown Publishers, Inc., 1975.

3. Hooker, S. *Caring for Elderly People*. London: Routledge and Kegan Paul Ltd., 1976.

        4. Kimmel, D. C. *Adulthood and Aging*. New York: John Wiley & Sons, Inc., 1974.
  B. Pamphlets
        1. Stern, E. M. *A Full Life after 65*. Public Affairs Pamphlet No. 347A, The Public Affairs Committee, 381 Park Avenue South, New York, NY 10016.

IV   Materials and aids
  A. Blackboard and chalk
  B. Handouts (Figures B–4 and B–5)
  C. Chairs in a semicircle
  D. Attendance sheet

V   Methods
  A. Lecture
  B. Large group discussion

VI   Procedure (see pp. 229–236 for special procedure steps)
  A. Introduction of self and group
  B. Brief review of any assignments from previous session (5–10 minutes)
  C. Introduction to session
  D. Lecture—discussion
  E. Handouts (Figures B–4 and B–5)
  F. Assignment

VII Evaluation
  A. Ongoing participation in large group discussion
  B. Attentiveness
  C. Completion of assignment
  D. Improvement in results of written tests, if given pre- and post-session

Unit III Procedures

Introduction to Session

Wait for responses from group.

1. *How many times have you heard that if a person lives long enough, senility is inevitable? Is it true? Of course not. Yet here is another stereotype of aging, and very often it is a self-fulfilling*

prophecy. People sometimes act the way they believe they're expected to act. In one experiment, for instance, a group of young college students were treated by their friends as if they were old—they were ignored, belittled, and left out of conversations. Soon the students began to ramble on, talking to no one, and making comments that were out of place. If they had been over 65, they would have been called "senile" immediately.

Write the word "senile" on the board. Then draw an "X" through the word.

Lecture—Discussion

Emphasize this point strongly.

1. *The word "senility" really means nothing. It is convenient to use to describe people whom family, friends, or professionals feel are beyond help.* **But becoming "senile" is not a normal part of aging. Older people who have mental changes which could be called "senile" behavior may be suffering from a condition which could be treated or reversed, especially when the changes have come on quickly.** *Only a small percentage of older people are actually "senile."*

2. *Confusion is usually a temporary condition. It could be brought on by many things such as:*

Get responses from group and write list on board.

   a. *Pain, infection, accidents, stroke, heart failure, tumors, grief, illness.*
   b. *Malnutrition—some studies have shown that some people who were given a balanced diet were cured of what was*

thought to be senility. They were missing the food elements needed to keep their brains working well!

c. *Surgery or hospitalization.*

d. *Moving to a new residence.*

3. *All of these problems can be treated if done quickly, and the person will return to normal. But they are often overlooked by professionals and family members who, expecting the worst about aging, give up too easily. If you or someone you know is experiencing confusion or other mental changes, get professional help immediately!!*

4. *Now that we know that senility is not a normal mental change, let's discuss what is normal. We have wonderful proof that people's mental abilities don't have to go downhill with aging. Think of all the brilliant, talented, and creative people who did or are doing some of their best work while members of the older generation. Can you name any?*

Wait for responses from the group.

Responses may include: Grandma Moses, Arthur Rubenstein, Fred Astaire, Maggie Kuhn, Picasso, Albert Schweitzer, Arthur Fiedler, Golda Meir, Justice William Douglas, etc.

Wait for responses from the group, prompting to elicit appropriate responses. Write list on board and check or underline each when referring to it.

What many people fear most about aging is loss of mental ability. Before we go on, let's decide what kinds of functions come under the category of "mental ability."

a. *Intelligence, learning, creativity, personality, memory, judgment.*

Write this statement on board or
have sign, made up prior to session,
displayed.

5. *First, let's talk about intelligence. It used to be believed
   that people lost intelligence as
   they aged, but there is now clear
   proof that intelligence is pretty
   stable throughout life. It does
   not decline, or if it does, it usually results from a health problem such as high blood pressure
   or heart disease which is not
   treated.*

   *Other people permit them-
   selves to become outdated by
   losing interest in the outside
   world.*

   *The key to maintaining intelli-
   gence is: "What you don't use,
   you lose."*

6. *Learning is possible at any age.
   That business about not teaching
   an old dog new tricks is just not
   true. It has been shown that it
   may take a little longer so give
   yourself extra time to learn
   something. And, if you are feeling sluggish mentally in trying to
   learn something, you should
   check with your doctor since
   there could be a problem with
   your medications or your health,
   in general.*

7. *Creativity is also possible at any
   age, as we have seen from the
   many names we mentioned before as famous for their work.*

8. *Some older persons experience
   some memory loss. For most, it
   is very mild, and only for some is
   it severe. Memory loss should
   not be confused with overall
   mental decline. In fact, most*

Wait for responses from the group, adding these to the list.

people are successful at figuring out a system to remember important things. Do you have any ideas?

a. *Keep a daily calendar handy and turn it every night for the next day.*

b. *Always put things away in the same place.*

c. *Keep a pencil and paper handy, especially by the phone.*

d. *Put all your medicines out for the day, marking them so you know exactly how many you've taken (there are now special containers available in drug stores).*

This may be phrased as a question, such as, "What happens to judgment as we age?"

9. *As you get older, your judgment improves. There may be a slowing down of how you react to a situation, but you probably have a greater ability to understand the situation because of your past experience, and you are more accurate.*

May be phrased as "What happens to personality as we get older?"

10. *Personality does not normally change drastically with aging. People have lifestyles and personalities in old age similar to those they had in young adulthood. And they can continue to grow and change for the better at any age. There is an expression that says "we become more like ourselves as we age." What does that mean?*

Get responses from the group with examples and discuss these.

a. *We maintain some basic personality traits, sometimes exaggerated. If a person has been very careful while younger, he or she may be more cautious when older. An unhappy young person may become a crabby old person, but it was there before the person got old.*

Point to list of mental functions.

11. **Drastic changes in any of these areas are not the result of normal aging. They need to be reported to a doctor.** *Unfortunately, many people feel funny about reporting mental or emotional problems to doctors. Why do you suppose that is?*

Discuss this question thoroughly, prompting personal feelings about seeking care. Use about five minutes to do this. The discussion should lead to the conclusion that just as we have no trouble reporting physical problems, we need to be able to report mental or emotional difficulties.

Responses may include: fear of being considered crazy, people believe they should deal with such problems without help, etc.

Emphasize this point.

12. **Yet, now we know that mental problems can be caused by physical problems or they can themselves be the cause of physical problems.** *The best example of a mental problem that can be the cause of many, many physical problems has been referred to as "the great masquerader" because the people who suffer from it may not be aware of any mental changes, only physical changes. They may experience extreme tiredness, many nights without sleep, headaches, lack of appetite, and constipation. They may think they have some serious disease, especially because they*

(From Galton, p. 68.)

Wait for response briefly.

may be losing weight which is actually from not eating. Can anyone guess the name of this disorder? It is depression, and it may account for more suffering than any other health problem. Even though millions of people have symptoms of depression, very few of those in need get psychiatric treatment. All of us have our "up" days and our days of feeling "down." Everyone has periods of feeling blue, and as we age, we can have many experiences which sadden us—health problems, money problems, family problems, particularly the loss of loved ones. It is normal to be depressed for a period of time. But real depression is a lowering of spirits that is deeper and longer than just feeling blue. It interferes with the ability to function in everyday life. Yet, as mentioned before, many people feel that getting professional help, such as from a psychiatrist, makes them crazy.

We find it easy to go to the doctor when we have physical pain but we have trouble seeing one when we have mental pain.

Emphasize this point.

This is tragic because, in the older generation, depression can be the "great masquerader" in one more respect—sometimes people who are severely depressed act as if they are senile. They act confused, emotionally unstable; they may even urinate at the wrong

*times. And, because the ste-
reotype of aging is that old
people become senile, very
often these depressed people
don't get diagnosed or treated
correctly. They may even be
admitted to institutions by
well-meaning families when
they could, in fact, be treated
by medication and therapy in
any community mental health
center.*

13. *We can sum it all up by remembering that health means
feeling good both physically
and mentally. Our bodies give
us signals when we are not
healthy or feeling bad.*

    *What we've discussed is how
to listen to those signals and
when to get help. Aging can be
a time of feeling good.*

Handouts

Distribute handouts (Figures B–4
and B–5) for session and review.
Either the leader or one of the participants can read it out loud to the
group. Call for any questions at this
time, trying to keep the group focused on the handouts but encouraging personal expression.

1. *Today's handout contains the
basic points of today's discussion. Let's review it now.*

2. *Please look at this again during
the next few days. If you have
any more questions, I'd be glad
to discuss them at our next session.*

Assignment

If pamphlets have been distributed, an assignment could be the reading of
those pamphlets for brief discussion at the next session.

An alternative assignment is to have participants try to find out where they
would go in their particular communities if they had a mental health problem,
for instance, the community mental health center address, the local Area
Agency on Aging, etc.

P.G.C.'s

238

P.G.C.'s

" One Life To Live ... Ways To Keep It Healthy "

Lesson 3 : The Mind And Aging

✔ Becoming "senile" is not a normal part of aging. Older people who have mental changes which could be called "senile" behavior may be suffering from a condition which could be treated or reversed, such as infections, stroke, malnutrition, medication errors, tumors, heart failure, and even depression.

✔ Aging affects the mind in the following ways, according to the latest studies:

* WHAT * you DON'T USE you LOSE so STAY INTERESTED AND KEEP EXERCISING YOUR MIND * . *

1. Intelligence is stable throughout life. It does not decline unless there is a health problem such as high blood pressure which has not been treated.

2. Learning is possible at any age.
3. Creativity is possible at any age.

4. Many people experience some memory loss, but this can be overcome by working out a system to remember important things, such as keeping a pad and pencil handy.

5. Personality does not normally change drastically with aging, although we can continue to grow and change for the better at any age.

6. There may be a slowing down of reaction time or learning something new, so give yourself extra time to achieve your goal.

237

P.G.C.'s

"ONE LIFE TO LIVE ... WAYS TO KEEP IT
HEALTHY"

LESSON 3: THE MIND AND AGING

✓ DEPRESSION in older persons is | often called
"the great masquerader" because | the millions
of people who suffer from it | may not be
aware of any mental changes, only physical
changes such as :
    extreme tiredness   headaches
    inability to fall asleep   loss of appetite
            constipation

✓ All of us have our "ups" and "downs". This is
normal. But real depression is a lowering of
spirits that is deeper and longer than just feeling
blue. It interferes with the ability to function
in everyday life.

✓ Depression requires professional help which
can be provided at your community mental health
center at little or no cost, but many people
feel funny about reporting emotional problems
to doctors. They are afraid they'll be
called "crazy". Many famous people have shown
that it is O.K. to get professional help
for emotional pains, just as it is O.K.
to get professional help for physical pains.

UNIT IV: ORGANIZING FOR BETTER HEALTH CARE

Time: 60 minutes (plus follow-up meeting suggested)

I   Introduction

This session is built on the premise that it is necessary to be a well-prepared patient in order to get quality professional health care. The doctor can function adequately only when given complete information from the patient and vice versa. The focus of the session is a personal health care chart which was designed to provide both professional care provider and patient with an organized picture of the treatment plan. The physician, in helping the patient to complete the form, does a good amount of health teaching at the same time. The patient, in completing the form, has a format for asking important questions. (The professional who refuses to fill out the form or delegates that job to someone else in the office needs to be questioned as to his or her priorities or motives, since these are basic questions relevant to any treatment plan.)

It is highly recommended that when this session has been presented, considerable follow-up be done on an individual or a small group basis, to help participants learn to use the personal health care charts easily. This becomes easier as participants become more familiar with how their own treatment plans relate to their particular health conditions.

This session also contains a great deal of information about drugs and how to take them safely. The handout refers primarily to that information.

II   Objectives of lesson

A.   General

1.   Participants will enhance control of their own treatment situations through the use of a personal health care chart and through appropriate questioning of professionals regarding application of treatment and the safe use of medications.

2.   Participants will be able to organize their own care more efficiently and consistently.

B.   Specific

1.   In discussion, participants will indicate changes in health consumer behavior such as increased questioning of professionals.

2.   In posttest and discussion, participants will indicate changes in their use of prescription and nonprescription medications.

3.   In group discussion and work groups, participants will use personal health care charts for organizing their own treatment plans.

III References

A.   Books/Articles

1.   AARP Pharmacy Service. "How to Help Your Doctor Help

You." *Modern Maturity*, April–May, 1976, p. 62. (Advertising material prepared for AARP by Retired Persons Services.)

2. Gaeta, M. J., & Gaetano, R. J. *The Elderly: Their Health and the Drugs in Their Lives*. Iowa: Kendall/Hunt Publishing Co., 1977.

3. Galton, L. *Don't Give up on an Aging Parent*. New York: Crown Publishers, Inc., 1975.

4. "Physicians' Desk Reference" (33rd ed.). New Jersey: Medical Economics Co., 1979.

B. Pamphlets
   1. National Institute on Drug Abuse. *Elder-Ed: An Education Program for Older Americans*. (U.S. Department of Health Education and Welfare, Public Health Service, Alcohol, Drug Abuse and Mental Health Administration, DHEW Publication No. [ADM] 78–705. G.P.O. Stock No. 017–024–0087–3.)

   2. National Institute on Drug Abuse. *Passport to Good Health Care*. (U.S. Department of Health, Education and Welfare, Public Health Service, Alcohol, Drug Abuse, and Mental Health Administration, DHEW Publication No. [ADM] 78–705 [d] G.P.O., 1979 0–288–828.)

   3. U.S. Department of Health, Education and Welfare. Public Health Service, Food and Drug Administration. *We Want You to Know about Prescription Medicines*. DHEW Publication No. (FDA) 78–3059.

   4. U.S. Department of Health, Education and Welfare. Public Health Service, Food and Drug Administration. *We Want You to Know What We Know about Medicines without Prescriptions*. DHEW Publication No. (FDA) 73–3009. G.P.O., 1973, 0–500–532.

   5. "The What If Book." Roche Laboratories: 21–41–0000–008–088.

   6. "What to Ask Your Doctor." Pennsylvania Department of Health, Division of Community Education, 1400 Spring Garden St., Philadelphia, PA, H302. 135P, 2/78.

IV Materials and aids
   A. Blackboard and chalk
   B. Charts and handout (Figures B–6, B–7, and B–8)
   C. Personal health care charts—two blank copies per participant
   D. If available, in addition to personal health care chart, pamphlet "Passport to Good Health Care" (listed above).
   E. Chairs in a semicircle
   F. Attendance sheet
   G. If available from local pharmacy, library, or physician, the latest possible edition of "Physicians' Desk Reference," as listed above.

V   Methods
    A.   Lecture
    B.   Large group discussion
    C.   Question and answer
    D.   Demonstration and return demonstration
    E.   Small group discussion

VI   Procedure (see pp. 241–248 for special procedure steps)
    A.   Introduction of self and group
    B.   Review of last session's assignment (no more than 5–10 minutes)
    C.   Introduction to session
    D.   Lecture—large group discussion with charts (Figures B–6 and B–7)
    E.   Handout (Figure B–8)
    F.   Assignment

VII Evaluation
    A.   Ongoing participation in large group discussion
    B.   Attentiveness
    C.   Completion of assignment
    D.   Improvement in results of written test, if given pre- and post-sessions

Unit IV Procedures

Introduction to Session

Write on the board before beginning lecture. Be sure to cross out word "can't" and write "can."

1. *What you don't know ca̶n't can hurt you. When it comes to matters of health, that famous expression is not only not true, it is also dangerous. Today we're going to talk about why. We're also going to discuss how to get important information that could even save your life!*

Lecture—Large Group Discussion

1. *You g̶o̶ to the doctor's office and tell him or her your symptoms. After you are examined, the doc-*

Wait for responses from the group, prompting if necessary.

tor writes a prescription for you. At this point, what do you do?

You find out everything you need to know about your condition and your medication so that you can carry out the doctor's instructions properly! You do exactly what you would do before buying anything—you become a smart consumer. You ask questions.

Write "smart consumer" on the board.

2. *So many times we hear complaints that the doctor always seems too busy to talk or to explain things to patients. Have you had that experience? Sometimes you might be afraid to ask anything. Yet, you are doing the doctor a favor by taking such an active part in your own treatment since, with the right information, you are much more likely to make good, safe decisions about your health. You are less likely to wind up in the hospital from doing the wrong thing for your condition or with your medications.*

Wait for responses, limiting them to short anecdotes which emphasize the point.

The questions should be elicited from the group but should be geared to the questions that are actually on the personal health care chart. It is best to approach this discussion by recreating the situation of a doctor's visit in the minds of the participants. Then, write their responses on the board, making an effort to relate the list closely to the personal health care chart (which they have not seen at this time). See personal health care chart for appropriate responses.

3. *What kind of information is the right information to get? Let's see if we can come up with some good questions to ask. Imagine that you're in the doctor's office and the examination has been completed. What do you ask the doctor?*

Pass out empty chart (Figure B–6).

Use personal health care chart which has been filled out already by a knowledgeable health professional (Figure B–7).

4. *We seem to have some pretty important questions here. The next step would be to get them into an organized and convenient form so that you could have the questions ready everytime you talk to the doctor and always available for you to review.*

   Here is a form that could be very helpful to you and to your doctor. It can be filled out by you, as you ask your doctor questions, or it can be filled out by the doctor, the office nurse, or even a family member. If you fill it out, keeping it up-to-date every time you have a change in medications or treatments, it may help you to understand your total health picture better. If you keep it with you at all times, it will help you to remember important facts about your doctor's instructions. It will also provide any new doctor with a record of your health situation.

   Let's go through it and see why each question is important. It is called a personal health chart because it is all about how you take care of yourself. This one is filled in for use as an example.

   a. *Name*
   b. *Date—the last time you updated your chart, changing medications or treatments.*
   c. *The doctor's name and phone is included so that you, or a family member, or a new doctor could call him or her about the chart, if necessary.*

At every step, be sure that **all** participants are at precisely the same point on the chart as the leader and that they can read every word on the chart.

d. *Your next appointment should be filled in so you remember when to check in with your doctor about your conditions and your treatments.*

e. *There is room for you to list six different health conditions. This is the same as the diagnosis that the doctor tells you. This is the name of each condition.*

f. *Next there is room for the doctor to explain what that condition means and how it affects the body.*

g. *Under each condition, there is a section to discuss the medications that go with that condition. You need to know what you are taking for which health problem. You should ask first the name of each medication. If you have trouble remembering which name is which pill, you can also add the color of the pill next to its name. Add to or change this list every time you get a medication change.*

h. *Next, you should find out the correct times to take each pill since if you are taking three different pills they may all be at different hours of the day or night.*

i. *In the next column, you should write how much to take of each medication not just in milligrams but in how many pills or spoonfuls. This column is important because many of the mistakes people* make with medicines are due to taking too much or too little. Some people believe that if a little is good, more must be better. But taking too much can lead to trouble, such as with blood-thinners. Taking too little can allow a problem to get worse, such as with antibiotics or infections. You need to take exactly what your doctor prescribes until you have discussed changes with him or her.

j. The next question to ask the doctor is how long does the medicine take to work? Some medications take minutes, some take hours, some take many days before they start helping. You need to know how soon to expect changes in the way you are feeling.

k. Next, ask the doctor what the medication does. Does it make the pain go away or does it cure the cause of the pain? Does it reduce fever? Does it lower blood pressure? Here you will find out why you are taking the medicine in the first place.

l. The next column contains a question that doctors don't always like to answer because it puts ideas in people's heads if they are overanxious. But it is your right to know how to avoid bad effects from the medicine and, as an alert patient, you will be working in partnership with the doctor toward good health.

Modern medicines are valuable and often lifesaving. But they have risks, just like crossing a street has risks. Just as you would still cross the street if necessary, the risk of the drug should not prevent you from taking it if it helps.

At the same time, you need to know that when you take a drug, the drug affects the whole body, not just the target. If you take aspirin for your headache, it may upset your stomach. If you take cold medicine, it may make you fall asleep.

If you know the bad side effects of the drug, you report them. Then the doctor can change the dosage or switch to something different.

In one study, 75% of patients did not know any symptoms to look out for as side effects from medications. Problems like headaches, nausea and vomiting, weakness, and rashes are not unusual, even from very valuable drugs. In addition, you can go for a very long time without any bad effect and suddenly have a reaction. These need to be reported! Don't change your medicine without the doctor.

m. *Many drugs which are taken with other drugs interact with each other—and often with foods or beverages—to produce a result that your doctor has not intended. It can either reduce or increase the effect of one or both drugs involved.*

For instance, aspirin should never be taken with blood thinners like Coumadin. Some tranquilizers and some cold medicines don't go together. Alcohol can really change the effects of your medicine as can certain foods. Also, you'll want to know if you should avoid driving or other activities on certain medications. The doctor may also tell you to be careful in certain ways, such as getting up from bed slowly while on high blood pressure medication.

n. *Finally, ask the doctor if there are any other special things to do for your condition, such as exercises, hot soaks, diet changes.*

5. *Now that we have gone through a filled-out chart, I'd like to ask you to try it for yourself next time you go to the doctor (give out blanks). Ask the questions and get help in filling it out if necessary. Then, next time we meet, I'll ask you how you did with it and if it helped. We will also form small groups to work on your charts and to make sure you understand how and why you are receiving treatment, and what your responsibilities are in the treatment plan.*

Handout

Distribute handout (Figure B–8) for session and review briefly by reading aloud. Call for any questions, taking care to avoid questions relating to personal medication or treatment problems unless a health professional is present to respond. Also, if available, distribute "Passport to Good Health Care" as a supplement to the personal health care chart and note similarities for the group.

Assignment

See section 5 on page 247.

1. *Today's handout contains a few extra tips on taking medications. Let's go over them now. They are extremely important and I hope you will refer to them frequently!*

WHAT IS MY FOURTH CONDITION CALLED? _____

HOW DOES IT AFFECT MY BODY? _____

WHAT MEDICINES AM I TAKING FOR IT?	AT WHAT TIMES?	HOW MUCH?	HOW LONG DOES IT TAKE TO WORK?	WHAT DOES IT DO?	WHAT SIDE EFFECTS SHOULD I REPORT TO YOU?	WHAT DRUGS, FOODS OR ACTIVITIES SHOULD I AVOID WITH THIS MEDICATION?	WHAT OTHER THINGS SHOULD I DO TO TAKE CARE OF THIS CONDITION?

WHAT IS MY FIFTH CONDITION CALLED? _____

HOW DOES IT AFFECT MY BODY? _____

WHAT MEDICINES AM I TAKING FOR IT?	AT WHAT TIMES?	HOW MUCH?	HOW LONG DOES IT TAKE TO WORK?	WHAT DOES IT DO?	WHAT SIDE EFFECTS SHOULD I REPORT TO YOU?	WHAT DRUGS, FOODS OR ACTIVITIES SHOULD I AVOID WITH THIS MEDICATION?	WHAT OTHER THINGS SHOULD I DO TO TAKE CARE OF THIS CONDITION?

WHAT IS MY SIXTH CONDITION CALLED? _____

HOW DOES IT AFFECT MY BODY? _____

WHAT MEDICINES AM I TAKING FOR IT?	AT WHAT TIMES?	HOW MUCH?	HOW LONG DOES IT TAKE TO WORK?	WHAT DOES IT DO?	WHAT SIDE EFFECTS SHOULD I REPORT TO YOU?	WHAT DRUGS, FOODS OR ACTIVITIES SHOULD I AVOID WITH THIS MEDICATION?	WHAT OTHER THINGS SHOULD I DO TO TAKE CARE OF THIS CONDITION?

NAME **Rose Kaplan** DATE **9/18/79** DOCTOR'S NAME **Smith** DOCTOR'S PHONE # **555-1212** NEXT APP'T. **Oct 10, 10 A.M.**

WHAT IS MY FIRST CONDITION CALLED? **Osteoarthritis Left Hip** HOW DOES IT AFFECT MY BODY? **Joint wears out; becomes stiff, weak, painful; muscle spasms**

WHAT MEDICINES AM I TAKING FOR IT?	AT WHAT TIMES?	HOW MUCH?	HOW LONG DOES IT TAKE TO WORK?	WHAT DOES IT DO?	WHAT SIDE EFFECTS SHOULD I REPORT TO YOU?	WHAT DRUGS, FOODS OR ACTIVITIES SHOULD I AVOID WITH THIS MEDICATION?	WHAT OTHER THINGS SHOULD I DO TO TAKE CARE OF THIS CONDITION?
400mg **Motrin** (orange)	8am 1pm 6 pm (with meals or milk)	1 Tab.	Should work by end of 2 weeks	Reduces Pain, Swelling, & Inflammation	Any Bleeding, Blurred Vision, Rash, Swelling, Stomach Pain	Aspirin	Warm Soaks, Exercise, Stay Warm

---

WHAT IS MY SECOND CONDITION CALLED? **Congestive Heart Failure** HOW DOES IT AFFECT MY BODY? **Heart does not pump blood as effectively as it did. Some blood backs up, causing swelling in ankles.**

WHAT MEDICINES AM I TAKING FOR IT?	AT WHAT TIMES?	HOW MUCH?	HOW LONG DOES IT TAKE TO WORK?	WHAT DOES IT DO?	WHAT SIDE EFFECTS SHOULD I REPORT TO YOU?	WHAT DRUGS, FOODS OR ACTIVITIES SHOULD I AVOID WITH THIS MEDICATION?	WHAT OTHER THINGS SHOULD I DO TO TAKE CARE OF THIS CONDITION?
Lasix 40mg (white)	8 a.m., 2 pm	1 Tablet	Within 1 hour	Causes Body to Lose Water Thru Urine	Weakness, Dizziness, Leg Cramps, Confusion, Vomiting	Salt, Cigarettes, Fatty Foods, Stress	Drink Orange Juice; Eat Bananas; Get Regular Exercise
Lanoxin (yellow) .125 mg.	8 a.m. 8 pm	1 tablet	Must take exactly as ordered to keep working	Strengthens Heartbeat	Headache, Weakness, Yellow Vision, Diarrhea		

WHAT IS MY THIRD CONDITION CALLED? _____ HOW DOES IT AFFECT MY BODY? _____

WHAT MEDICINES AM I TAKING FOR IT?	AT WHAT TIMES?	HOW MUCH?	HOW LONG DOES IT TAKE TO WORK?	WHAT DOES IT DO?	WHAT SIDE EFFECTS SHOULD I REPORT TO YOU?	WHAT DRUGS, FOODS OR ACTIVITIES SHOULD I AVOID WITH THIS MEDICATION?	WHAT OTHER THINGS SHOULD I DO TO TAKE CARE OF THIS CONDITION?

P. G. C.'s

ONE LIFE TO LIVE.... WAYS TO KEEP IT HEALTHY

LESSON 4: ORGANIZING FOR BETTER HEALTH CARE

BE A SMART CONSUMER : ASK QUESTIONS!

Help your doctor by getting information about your conditions and your medications That way you can follow the doctor's instructions safely and properly !!

Use your Personal Health Care Chart

✱ ✱ ✱ ✱ ✱

Some other tips on Medications

1. Always keep an up-to-date list of all the medicines you are taking and show it to any doctor who wants to give you new ones Don't mix new ones without asking the doctor.

2. Follow the doctor's directions on when and how much medicine to take. If you forget a dose, don't try to catch up. ASK the doctor or the druggist.

3. If the drug doesn't seem to be working or if you are having an unexpected symptom such as nausea, dizziness, or others, REPORT it to the doctor right away. Don't stop without asking.

4. Don't share any medicines with relatives or friends. Everybody's problems are different !!

References

Allan, C. and Brotman, H. *Chartbook on Aging in America*. Compiled for the 1981 White House Conference on Aging, 1981.

Antonovsky, A. "A Model to Explain Visits to the Doctor: With Specific Reference to the Case of Israel." *Journal of Health and Social Behavior* 13(1972):446–454.

Atkinson, J. H., Jr., and Schuckit, M. A. "Alcoholism and Over-the-Counter and Prescription Drug Misuse in the Elderly." In *Annual Review of Gerontology and Geriatrics, Vol. 2*, edited by C. Eisdorfer, 255–284. New York: Springer Publishing Company, 1981.

Ball, R. "Rethinking National Policy on Health Care for the Elderly." In *The Geriatric Imperative*, edited by A. R. Somers and D. Fabian. New York: Appleton-Century-Crofts, 1981.

Becker, M. H., Haefner, D. P., Kasl, S. V., Kirscht, J. P., et al. "Selected Psychosocial Models and Correlates of Individual Health-Related Behaviors." *Medical Care* 15(1977):27–46.

Beyer, G. H., and Woods, M. E. *Living and Activity Patterns of the Aged, Research Report #6*. Ithaca, New York: Center for Housing and Environmental Studies, Cornell University, 1963.

Brody, E. M. "The Mentally Impaired Aged Patient: A Socio-Medical Problem." *Geriatrics Digest* 4(1967):25–32.

Brody, E. M. "The Aging of the Family." *The Annals of the American Academy of Political and Social Science* 438(1978):13–27.

Brody, E. M. "The Formal Support Network: Congregate Treatment Settings for Residents with Senescent Brain Dysfunction." In *Clinical Aspects of Alzheimer's Disease and Senile Dementia*, edited by N. E. Miller and G. D. Cohen, 301–331. (Supplement to *Aging*:15). New York: Raven Press, 1981.

Brody, E. M. and Brody, S. J. "New Directions in Health and Social Supports for the Aging." In *The Aging: Medical and Social Supports in the Decade of the 80's*, 35–48. New York: Center on Gerontology, Fordham University, 1981.

Brody, E. M. and Spark, G. "Institutionalization of the Aged: A Family Crisis." *Family Process* 5(1966):76–90.

Brody, S. J. "Comprehensive Health Care of the Elderly: An Analysis." *The Gerontologist* 13(1973):412–418.

Brody, S. J. "The Thirty-to-One Paradox: Health Needs and Medical Solutions." In *Aging: Agenda for the Eighties, National Journal Issues Book*. Washington, DC: The Government Research Corporation, 1979.

Brody, S. J. and Persily, N. A. *The New Old Market: Hospitals and the Aged*. Rockville, MD: Aspen Press, 1983.

Brody, S. J., Poulshock, S. W., and Masciocchi, C. F. "The Family Care Unit: A Major Consideration in the Long-Term Support System." *The Gerontologist* 18(1978):556–561.

253

Brotman, H. B. "Data from Summary Table B based on Middle Series Projections 1982–2050." Washington, DC: U.S. Census Bureau, 1982a.

Brotman, H. B. *Every Ninth American (1982 Edition), An Analysis for the Chairman of the Select Committee on Aging, House of Representatives.* Washington, DC: Government Printing Office, 1982b.

Butler, R. N. "Testimony." In *Medicine and Aging: An Assessment of Opportunities and Neglect,* 12. (Hearing transcript of the U.S. Senate Special Committee on Aging), 1976.

Butler, R. N. Personal communication, 1979.

Butler, R. N. and Gastel, B. "Care of the Aged: Perspectives on Pain and Discomfort." In *Pain, Discomfort and Humanitarian Care,* edited by L. K. Ng and J. J. Bonica, 297–311. New York: Elsevier North Holland, 1980.

Butler, R. N. and Lewis, M. *Aging and Mental Health: Positive Psychosocial Approaches.* St. Louis: C. V. Mosby Company, 1973.

Cantor, M. H. "Neighbors and Friends: An Overlooked Resource in the Informal Support System." Paper presented at 30th Annual Meeting of the Gerontological Society, San Diego, CA, 1977.

Cantor, M. H. "Caring for the Frail Elderly: Impact on Family, Friends and Neighbors." Paper presented at 33rd Annual Meeting of The Gerontological Society of America, San Diego, CA, 1980.

Cohen, G. D. "Approach to the Geriatric Patient." *Medical Clinics of North America* 61(1977):855–866.

Cohen, G. D. "Prospects for Mental Health and Aging." In *Handbook of Mental Health and Aging,* edited by J. E. Birren and R. B. Sloane, 971–994. Englewood Cliffs, NJ: Prentice-Hall, 1980.

Costa, P. T. and MaCrae, R. R. "Somatic Complaints in Males as a Function of Age and Neuroticism: A Longitudinal Analysis." *Journal of Behavioral Medicine* 3(1980):345–357.

Davis, G. C., Buchsbaum, M. S., and Bunney, W. E., Jr. "Pain and Psychiatric Illness." In *Pain, Discomfort and Humanitarian Care,* edited by Lorenz K. Ng and John J. Bonica, 221–231. New York: Elsevier North Holland, 1980.

Davis, K. "Medicaid Payments and Utilization of Medical Services by the Poor." *Inquiry,* 13, 1976. As cited in Ann Kutza, Elizabeth, *The Benefits of Old Aged.* Chicago: The University of Chicago Press, 1981.

Dubos, R. *Man, Medicine, and Environment.* New York: Frederick A. Prayer, 1968.

Dye, C. J. and Sassenrath, D. "Identification of Normal Aging and Disease-Related Processes by Health Care Professionals." *Journal of the American Geriatrics Society* 27(1979).

Eisdorfer, C. "Evaluation of the Quality of Psychiatric Care for the Aged." *American Journal of Psychiatry* 134(1977):315–317.

Eisdorfer, C. and Lawton, M. P. *The Psychology of Adult Development and Aging.* Washington, DC: American Psychological Association, 1973.

English, O. S. and Pearson, G. H. J. *Common Neuroses of Children and Adults.* New York: W. W. Norton and Company, 1937.

Erikson, E. *Childhood and Society,* rev. ed. New York: W. W. Norton and Company, 1963.

Evans, J. G. "Care of the Aging in Great Britain: An Overview." In *The Aging: Medical and Social Supports in the Decade of the '80s,* 13–19. New York: Center on Gerontology, Fordham University, 1981.

Fengler, A. P. and Goodrich, N. "Wives of Elderly Disabled Men: The Hidden Patients." *The Gerontologist* 19(1979):175–183.

Fisher, C. "Age Differences in Health Care Spending." *Health Care Financing Review* 1(1980):81.

Ford, C. V. and Sbordone, R. J. "Attitudes of Psychiatrists Toward Elderly Patients." *American Journal of Psychiatry* 137(1980):571–575.

Francis, V., Korsch, B. J., and Morris, M. J. "Gaps in Doctor-Patient Communication." *New England Journal of Medicine* 280(1969):535–540.

Freidson, E. *Patients' Views of Medical Practice.* New York: Russell Sage Foundation, 1961.

German, P. S., Klein, L. E., McPhee, S. J. and Smith, C. R. "Knowledge of and Compliance with Drug Regimens in the Elderly." *Journal of the American Geriatrics Society* 30(1982):568–571.

Gibson, M. J. An International Update on Family Care of the Ill Elderly. *Ageing International* 9(1982):11–14.

Gibson, R. M. and Waldo, D. R. "National Health Expenditures, 1981." *Health Care Financing Review,* 4(1982):1. (Washington, DC: U.S. Health Care Financing Administration.)

Goldfarb, A. I. "Prevalence of Psychiatric Disorders in Metropolitan Old Age and Nursing Homes." *Journal of American Geriatrics Society* 10(1962):77–84.

Gottesman, L., Moss, M., and Worts, F. "Resources, Needs, and Wishes for Services in Urban Middle Class Older People." Paper presented at 10th International Congress of Gerontology, Jerusalem, Israel, 1975.

Grad, J. and Sainsbury, P. "Evaluating the Community Psychiatric Services in Chichester: Results." *Milbank Memorial Fund Quarterly* 44(1966):246–278(a).

Grad, J. and Sainsbury, P. "Problems of Caring for the Mentally Ill at Home." *Proceedings of the Royal Society of Medicine* 59(1966):20–23(b).

Gruenberg, E. M. "The Failures of Success." *Milbank Memorial Fund Quarterly* (Winter 1977), 3–24.

Gurland, B. "The Epidemiology of Depression in the Elderly." Paper presented at Conference on Depression in the Elderly, Philadelphia Geriatric Center, 1976.

Gurland, B., Dean, L., Gurland, R., and Cook, D. "Personal Time Dependency in the Elderly of New York City: Findings from the U.S.–U.K. Cross-National Geriatric Community Study." In *Dependency in the Elderly of New York City,* edited by the Community Council of Greater New York, 9–45. New York: Community Council of Greater New York, 1978.

Hagebak, J. E. and Hagebak, B. R. "Meeting the Mental Health Needs of the Elderly: Issues and Action Steps." *Aging* (January–February 1983).

Harkins, S. W. and Warner, M. H. "Age and Pain." In *Annual Review of Gerontology and Geriatrics,* edited by Carl Eisdorfer, Vol. 1, 121–131. New York: Springer Publishing Company, 1980.

Harris, L. *Aging in the Eighties: America in Transition.* Washington, DC: National Council on the Aging, 1981.

Haug, M. "Doctor-Patient Relationships and the Older Patient." *Journal of Gerontology* 34(1979):842–860.

Hayflick, L. "The Strategy of Senescence." *The Gerontologist* 13(1974):37.

Hess, B. "Sex Roles, Friendship and the Life Course." *Research on Aging* 1(1979):494–515.

Horl, J. and Rosenmayr, L. "Assistance to the Elderly as a Common Task of the Family and Social Service Organizations." *Archives of Gerontology and Geriatrics* (1982):75–95 (Elsevier Biomedical Press).

Horowitz, A. "Sons and Daughters as Caregivers to Older Parents: Differences in Role Performance and Consequences." Paper presented at 34th Annual Scientific Meeting of The Gerontological Society of America, Toronto, Canada, 1981.

Institute of Gerontology at Wayne State University. *The Safe Use of Medicines*. Information on Aging, no. 21. Wayne, Mich., 1981.

Institute of Medicine. *A Policy Statement: The Elderly and Functional Dependency*. Washington, DC: National Academy of Sciences, 1977.

Institute of Medicine. *Report of a Study—Aging and Medical Education*. Washington, DC: National Academy of Sciences, 1978.

International Classification of Diseases, 9th rev. Clinical Modification, Vol. 1, Tabular List of Symptoms, Signs and Ill-Defined Conditions. Ann Arbor, Mich.: Edwards Brothers, 1978.

Jette, A. M. and Branch, L. G. "The Framingham Disability Study: II. Physical Disability Among the Aging." *American Journal of Public Health* 71(1981):1211–1216.

Kahn, R. L. "The Mental Health System and the Future Aged." *The Gerontologist* 15(1975):24–31.

Kane, R. L., Solomon, D. H., Beck, J. C., Keeler, E., and Kane, R. *Geriatrics in the United States: Manpower Projects and Training Considerations*. Santa Monica, CA, 1980.

Kanner, A. D., Coyne, J. C., Schaefer, C., and Lazarus, R. "Comparison of Two Modes of Stress Measurement: Daily Hassles and Uplifts Versus Major Life Events." *Journal of Behavioral Medicine* 4(1981):1–39.

Kart, C. Experiencing Symptoms: Attribution and Misattribution of Illness Among the Aged." In *Elderly Patients and Their Doctors*, edited by Marie R. Haug, 70–78. New York: Springer Publishing Company, 1981.

Kasl, S. V. and Cobb, S. "Health Behavior, Illness Behavior, and Sick Role Behavior." *Archives of Environmental Health* 12(1966):246–266.

Kay, D. W. K. and Bergmann, K. "Epidemiology of Mental Disorders Among the Aged in the Community." In *Handbook of Mental Health*, edited by James E. Birren and Bruce R. Sloane, 34–56. Englewood Cliffs, NJ: Prentice-Hall, 1980.

Koch-Weser, J. "Psychotropic Drug Use in the Elderly." *New England Journal of Medicine* 308(1983):134–138.

Kosberg, J. I. and Harris, A. P. "Attitudes Toward Elderly Clients." Paper presented at annual meeting of the Gerontological Society, New York, 1976.

Kramer, M., Taube, C. A., and Redick, R. W. "Patterns of Use of Psychiatric Facilities by the Aged: Past, Present, and Future." In *The Psychology of Adult Development and Aging*, edited by C. Eisdorfer and M. P. Lawton, 428–528. Washington, DC: American Psychological Association, 1973.

Lang, A. and Brody, E. M. "Characteristics of Middle-Aged Daughters and Help to Their Elderly Mothers." *Journal of Marriage and the Family* 45(1983):193–202.

Lawton, M. P. "The Functional Assessment of Elderly People." *Journal of the American Geriatrics Society* 19(1971):465–481.

Lawton, M. P. "Assessing the Competence of Older People." In *Research, Planning and Action for the Elderly*, edited by D. P. Kent, R. Kastenbaum, and S. Sherwood, 122–143. New York: Behavioral Publications, 1972.

Lawton, M. P. Activity, Morale and Living Arrangements of the Aged. Funded by the National Institute on Aging (unpublished), 1978.

Lawton, M. P. Time, Space, and Activity. In *Aging and Milieu*, edited by G. Rowles and R. Ohta. New York: Academic Press, in press.

Lawton, M. P. and Cohen, J. "The Generality of Housing Impact in the Well-Being of Older People." *Journal of Gerontology* 29(1974):194–204.

Lawton, M. P., Moss, M., Fulcomer, M. C., and Kleban, M. H. "A Research- and Science-Oriented Multilevel Assessment Instrument." *Journal of Gerontology* 37(1982):91–99.

Levy, M. and Glantz, K. "Drug Misuse Among the Elderly." *Journal of Drug Education* 11(1981):62.

Lipsitt, D. R. "A Medical-Psychological Approach to Dependency in the Aged." In *The Dependencies of Old People*, edited by R. A. Kalish, 17–27. Occasional Papers in Gerontology No. 6, Institute of Gerontology, University of Michigan-Wayne State University, 1969.

Litman, T. J. "Health Care and the Family: A Three-Generational Analysis." *Medical Care* 9(1971):67–81.

Lowenthal, M. F. *Lives in Distress*. New York: Basic Books, 1964.

Luehrs, J. "The State of the States." *Bifocal-Bar Associations in Focus on Aging and the Law* (November-December 1982).

Maddox, G. "Aging, Health and the Organization of Health Resources." In *Handbook of Aging and the Social Sciences*, edited by R. H. Binstock and E. Shanas. New York: Nostrand Reinhold Company, 1976.

McKinlay, J. B. "Some Approaches and Problems in the Study of the Use of Services—An Overview." *Journal of Health and Social Behavior* 13(1972):115–152.

McKinlay, J. B. and Dutton, D. B. "Social-Psychological Factors Affecting Health Service Utilization." In *Consumer Incentive for Health Care*, edited by S. J. Mushkin. New York: Pro-Dist, 1974.

Mechanic, D. *Medical Sociology*, 2nd ed. New York: Free Press, 1978.

Mock, M. B. "Rehabilitation of the Elderly Cardiac Patient Hampered by Bias." *Geriatrics* (December 1977)22–23.

Murnaghan, J. H. "Review of the Conference Proceedings." In *Long-Term Care Data: Report of the Conference on Long-Term Care Data*. (Supplement to Medical Care 14:1–25), 1975.

National Health Survey. USPHS, National Ambulatory Medical Care Survey Questionnaire, Symptom Classification. Washington, DC: U.S. Government Printing Office, 1977.

National Retired Teachers Association-American Association of Retired Persons. National Survey of Older Americans, July, 1981.

Neugarten, B. L. *Personality in Middle and Late Life*. New York: Atherton Press, 1964.

Neugarten, B. L. "Adult Personality: Toward a Psychology of the Life Cycle." In *Middle Aged and Aging*, edited by B. L. Neugarten, 137–147. Chicago: University of Chicago Press, 1968.

Neugarten, B. L. "Personality Changes in Later Life: A Developmental Perspective." In *Psychological Processes in Aging*, edited by C. Eisdorfer and M. P. Lawton, 311–335. Washington, DC: American Psychological Association, 1973.

Neugarten, B. L. "The Future and the Young Old." *The Gerontologist* 15(1975): 4–9.

Neugarten, B. L. "Statement in Section on 'Understanding Psychosocial Man.' " *Psychology Today* 16 (1982):54.

OARS (Older Americans Resources and Services). Multi-Dimensional Functional Assessment Questionnaire. Duke University Center for the Study of Aging and Human Development, 1974.

Oriol, W. *Aging in All Nations: A Special Report on United Nations World Assembly on Aging*. Washington, DC: National Council on the Aging, 1982.

Oyer, H. J., Kapur, Y. P., and Deal, L. V. "Hearing Disorders in the Aging: Effects Upon Communication." In *Aging and Communication*, edited by H. J. Oyer and E. J. Oyer. Baltimore: University Park Press, 1976.

Peck, R. C. "Psychological Developments in the Second Half of Life." In *Middle Age and Aging: A Reader in Social Psychology*, edited by B. L. Neugarten, 88–92. Chicago: University of Chicago Press, 1968.

Pfeiffer, E. "Multidimensional Quantitative Assessment of Three Populations of Elderly." Paper presented at annual meeting of the Gerontological Society, Miami Beach, 1973.

Pincus, A. "Toward a Developmental View of Aging for Social Work." *Social Work* 12(1967):33–41.

Powers, E. A. and Bultena, G. L. "Sex Differences in Intimate Friendships of Old Age." *Journal of Marriage and the Family* 38(1976):739–747.

President's Commission on Mental Health. *Report to the President*, Vol. 1. Washington, DC: U.S. Government Printing Office, 1978.

Raffoul, P. R., Cooper, J. K., and Love, D. W. "Drug Misuse in Older People." *The Gerontologist* 21(1981):147–150.

Riegel, K. R. "Personality Theory and Aging." In *Handbook of Aging and the Individual*, edited by J. E. Birren, 797–851. Chicago: University of Chicago Press, 1959.

Rockstein, M. and Sussman, M. *Biology of Aging*. Belmont, Calif.: Wadsworth Publishing Company, 1979.

Rosow, I. "Coalitions in Geriatric Medicine." In *Elderly Patients and Their Doctors*, edited by M. R. Haug, 137–146. New York: Springer Publishing Company, 1981.

Rowe, J. W. "Clinical Research on Aging: Strategies and Direction." *New England Journal of Medicine* 297(1977):1332–1336.

Schorr, A. L. *Filial Responsibility in the Modern American Family*. U.S. DHEW, Social Security Administration. Washington, DC: Government Printing Office, 1960.

Schorr, A. L. " 'Thy Father and Thy Mother . . .': A Second Look at Filial Responsibility." SSA Publication No. 13–11953. Washington, DC: U.S. DHHS.

Schuckit, M. A. "Unrecognized Psychiatric Illness in Elderly Medical-Surgical Patients." Paper presented at 27th annual meeting of the Gerontological Society, Portland, OR, 1974.

Schwartz, D., Wang, M., Zeitz, L., and Goss, M. E. W. "Medication Errors Made by Elderly, Chronically Ill Patients." *American Journal of Public Health* 52(1962):2018–2029.

Schweiker, R. "Statement to the U.N. World Assembly on Aging." In *Aging in All Nations: A Special Report on the United Nations World Assembly on Aging*, edited by W. E. Oriol, 103. Washington, DC: National Council on Aging, 1982.

Shanas, E. *Family Relationships of Older People*. Health Information Foundation, Research Series 20. Chicago: University of Chicago Press, 1961.

Shanas, E. *The Health of Older People: A Social Survey*. Cambridge, Mass.: Harvard University Press, 1962.

Shanas, E. "Health Status of Older People: Cross-National Implications." *American Journal of Public Health* 64(1974):261–264.

Shanas, E. *Final Report: National Survey of the Aged to the U.S. Administration on Aging*, 1978.

Shanas, E. "Social Myth as Hypothesis: The Case of the Family Relations of Old People." *The Gerontologist* 19(1979):3–9,(a).

Shanas, E. "The Family as a Social Support System in Old Age." *The Gerontologist* 19(1979):169–174,(b).

Shanas, E. "Older People and Their Families: The New Pioneers." *Journal of Marriage and the Family* 42(1980):9–15.

Shanas, E. *National Survey of the Aged*. DHHS Publication No. OHDS83–20425. Washington, DC: Office of Human Development Services, 1982.

Shock, N. W. "Systems Integration." In *Handbook of the Biology of Aging*, edited by C. E. Finch and L. Hayflick, 661. New York: Van Nostrand Reinhold Company, 1977.

Sourcebook on Aging. 2nd ed. Chicago: Marquis Publishing Company, 1979.

Spark, G. and Brody, E. M. "The Aged Are Family Members." *Family Process* 9(1970):195–210.

Steinback, A., Kumpulainen, M. and Vauhkonen, M. L. "Illness and Health Behavior in Septuagenarians." *Journal of Gerontology* 33(1978):57–61.

Suchman, E. A. "Stages of Illness and Medical Care." *Journal of Health and Human Behavior* 6(1965):114–128.

Suchman, E. A. "Health Orientation and Medical Care." *American Journal of Public Health* 56(1966):97–105.

Supplement to the Journal of the American Geriatrics Society. Vol. 30, 1982, No. 11S.

Sussman, M. B. "Relationships of Adult Children with Their Parents in the United States." In *Social Structure and the Family: Generational Relations*, edited by E. Shanas and G. F. Streib, 62–92. Englewood Cliffs, NJ: Prentice-Hall, 1965.

Szasz, T. and Hollander, M. H. "The Basic Models of the Doctor-Patient Relationship." *Archives in Internal Medicine* 97(1956):585–592.

Titmuss, R. M. "Foreword." In *Helping the Aged*, edited by E. M. Goldberg. London: George Allen and Unwin Ltd., 1970.

Tobin, S. and Kulys, R. "The Family and Service." In *Annual Review of Gerontology and Geriatrics*, edited by C. Eisdorfer, Vol. 1, 370–399. New York: Springer Publishing Company, 1980.

Twaddle, A. C. "Health Decisions and Sick Role Variations: An Exploration." *Journal of Health and Social Behavior* 10(1969):105–115.

U.S. Comptroller General of the United States. *The Well-Being of Older People in Cleveland, Ohio*. April 19, 1977, 29. Washington, DC.

U.S. Department of Health, Education, and Welfare (DHEW). Public Health Service. *Home Care for Persons 55 and Over, United States: July 1966–June 1968*. Vital and Health Statistics Series 10, No. 73, 1972.

U.S. DHEW. Public Health Service. National Health Surveys. *Ambulatory Medical Care Survey*. 1977.

U.S. DHEW. *Report of the Secretary's Committee on Mental Health and Illness of the Elderly*, 1977. In *Mental Health and the Elderly, Recommendations for Action*. U.S. Federal Council on the Aging, 1980.

U.S. Department of Health and Human Services (1982). *White House Conference on Aging Final Report* 1(1982):92.

U.S. Department of Labor. Bureau of Labor Statistics. "Labor Force by Sex, Age and Race." *Earning and Employment* 28(1981):167.

U.S. Federal Council on the Aging. *Public Policy and the Frail Elderly, A Staff Report*. Washington, DC, 1978.

U.S. General Accounting Office. *The Well-Being of Older People in Cleveland, Ohio: Reported to the Congress by the Comptroller General of the United States*. Washington, DC, 1978.

U.S. Health Care Financing Administration (HCFA). *The Medicare and Medicaid Data Book, 1981*. Washington, DC, 1982a.

U.S. Health Care Financing Administration (HCFA). National Health Expenditures, 1981. *Health Care Financing Review*. Washington, DC, 1982b.

U.S. Health Resources Administration (HRA). Division of Long-Term Care. *The Future of Long-Term Care in the United States—The Report of the Task Force*. Washington, DC, 1977.

U.S. National Center for Health Statistics. *Health Characteristics of Persons with Chronic Activity Limitation: United States, 1979*. Data from the National Health Survey. Series 10, No. 137. Hyattsville, Maryland, 1981a.

U.S. National Center for Health Statistics. *Current Estimates from the National Health Interview Survey, United States, 1979*. Series 10, No. 136. Hyattsville, Maryland, 1981b.

U.S. National Center for Health Statistics. *Change in Mortality Among the Elderly: United States, 1940–78*. Analytical Studies, Series 3, No. 22. Washington, DC, 1982.

U.S. Senate Committee on Aging. *Developments in Aging: 1959 to 1963*. Washington, DC, 1963.

U.S. Senate Committee on Aging. *Mental Health Care and the Elderly—Shortcomings in Public Policy*. Washington, DC, 1971.

U.S. Senate Committee on Aging. *Developments in Aging: 1981, Vol. 1*. Washington, DC, 1982.

U.S. Senate Special Committee on Aging. *Developments in Aging: 1981*. Washington, DC, 1982.

U.S. White House Conference on Aging. *Chartbook on Aging in America*. Washington, DC, 1981.

University of Michigan-Wayne State University. *Aged Related Vision and Hearing Changes—An Empathic Approach*. Institute of Gerontology, 1975.

Vladeck, B. *Unloving Care—The Nursing Home Tragedy*. New York: Basic Books, 1980.

Wade, O. L. "Compliance Problems." In *Drugs and the Elderly*, edited by J. Crooks and I. H. Stevenson, 287–291. Baltimore, Maryland: University Park Press, 1979.

Weiss, H. J. "Problems in the Care of the Aged." In *Elderly Patients and Their Doctors*, edited by M. R. Haug, 79–90. New York: Springer Publishing Company, 1981.

White House Conference. *Chartbook on Aging in America*, compiled by C. Allan and H. Brotman, 74. Washington, DC, 1981.

Williamson, J. "Adverse Reactions to Prescribed Drugs in the Elderly." In *Drugs and the Elderly*, edited by J. Brooks and I. H. Stevenson, 239–246. Baltimore, Maryland: University Park Press, 1979.

Williamson, J., Stokoe, I. H., Gray, S., et al. "Old People at Home: Their Unreported Needs." *The Lancet* 1(1964):1117–1120.

World Health Organization (WHO). Planning and Organization of Geriatric Services. Technical Report Series 548. Geneva, WHO, 1974.

Zeman, F. D. "Myth and Stereotype in the Classical Medicine of Old Age." *New England Journal of Medicine* 272(1965):1104.

Index

Index